Italy Today

Studies in Modern European History

Frank J. Coppa
General Editor
Vol. 16

PETER LANG
New York • Washington, D.C./Baltimore • San Francisco
Bern • Frankfurt am Main • Berlin • Vienna • Paris

Mario B. Mignone

Italy Today

A Country in Transition

PETER LANG
New York • Washington, D.C./Baltimore • San Francisco
Bern • Frankfurt am Main • Berlin • Vienna • Paris

Library of Congress Cataloging-in-Publication Data

Mignone, Mario B.
    Italy today: a country in transition / Mario B. Mignone.
        p.   cm. — (Studies in modern European history; vol. 16)
    Includes bibliographical references and index.
    1. Italy—Politics and government—1945–   2. Italy—Economic
conditions—1945–   3. Italy—Social conditions—1945–1976.
4. Italy—Social conditions—1976–   I. Title. II. Series.
    JN5451.M53   320.945—dc20   94-5280
    ISBN 0-8204-2659-8
    ISSN 0893-6897

Die Deutsche Bibliothek-CIP-Einheitsaufnahme

Mignone, Mario B.:
Italy today: a country in transition / Mario B. Mignone. - New York;
Washington, D.C./Baltimore; San Francisco; Bern; Frankfurt am Main;
Berlin; Vienna; Paris: Lang.
    (Studies in modern European history; Vol. 16)
    ISBN 0-8204-2659-8
NE: GT

Cover design by James F. Brisson.

The paper in this book meets the guidelines for permanence and durability of
the Committee on Production Guidelines for Book Longevity of the
Council on Library Resources.

© 1995 Peter Lang Publishing, Inc., New York

Printed in the United States of America.

Second Printing, 1995

To Lois,
Pamela, Cristina and Elizabeth

Table of Contents

Table of Contents

Table of Contents

Preface

This book is the result of research and reflections for a course I teach on modern Italy. The success of the course and the growing interest in Italy have led me to believe that there could be a larger audience who might be interested in knowing more about a country as complex and as fascinating as Italy. At present, when Western civilization is being attacked by many, especially in the academic world, it is important to reconsider it. Thus, the book is written with two very different audiences in mind–those who share my fascination with the subtleties of Italian life, and those who do not, but who care to know about the achievements and failures of a democratic Western nation.

The western civilization that produced the failed modern politico-ideological "truth" systems of Marxism-Leninism, mutating into Stalinism, and of Nazism-Fascism, is the same that has most effectively resisted the ideologizing of knowledge. It has defended free thought and created, in the course of its history, the democratic political system. It has done this on a continuing assumption of the possibility of discovering the truth about things through the use of reason.

The values of this civilization, "the West," are now questioned, directly and indirectly, especially in the university controversy, part of which is a debate concerning cultural relativism. People ask why the thought and art of the West should be taught in American schools and universities, rather than the thought and art of China, India, Africa or the pre-literate cultures of the North American Indian. In this debate, Eurocentrism has become an umbrella term for the charge that American culture is hostile to anyone whose ancestors are not European. The political explanation given argues that European or European-descended whites have always controlled western universities and dominated western cultural life, imposing on others what suited them.

This is obviously true but is just as obviously reductionist. Critics of Eurocentrism, playing with the idea of cultural relativism, are influenced by "postmodernism," which says that universal principles and values, and western liberal, rationalist efforts to discover general truths, are no longer credible. This approach attacks the founding assumption of the western university which is based on the fundamental concept that reality is knowable through reason. Postmodern thought holds that reason has become "pluralized," and relativized, and reality is indeterminate. Knowledge exists only as "regimes" of knowledge, which is to say as political systems that dictate that certain things are so and that use power, pain and reward to make this accepted.

A visit to any Italian museum or archeological sight could be a sobering experience for those who believe this. The statues and images that have been rescued from the past, those from the Doric period, before the 5th-century B.C., wearing stylized, idealized half-smiles, seductive but undifferentiated, are faces that become increasingly individual, intelligent, and self-conscious; they become moral persons. They offer the shock of recognizing an individual across 23 centuries. They are part of the classical texts. We still fail to know ourselves, but it seems undeniable that we live in a continuity of intelligence and moral responsibility that began with Greek and Roman rationalism. To cut ourselves off from this, means cutting ourselves off not only from a usable past, but from our essential quality as a society.

Our interest in the West does not imply that we should exclude from our curriculum or interests knowledge of Asian, Chinese, and African history. On the contrary, we have to be inclusive. Besides using Athens, Sparta and Rome as models of ancient civilizations and the first real cities of the world, we have to indicate that in Africa there were civilizations that flourished thousands of years before those Greek and Roman cities; indeed, Mesopotamia was a thriving region with a government and a trade structure that should not be given less importance. The objective of contemporary education must include at least minimal awareness of past multicultural reality. More importantly, we also have to recognize the educational value of contemporary diversity and cultural pluralism. In doing so, we have to reject the "ethnocentric" educators' position of putting race consciousness and group pride at the center of a curriculum to "empower" the "oppressed"; and we have to reject "particularistic" multiculturalism because particularists have no interest in extending or revising American culture; they deny that a common culture exists. Particularists reject any accommodation among groups, any interactions that blur the distinct lines between them.

No scholarship is free of political and cultural biases, but serious scholars resist them. "Knowledge" is constantly revised through a process of peer criticism and review that keeps its distance from both established and revolutionary powers. Western pluralism's evolving truths are imperfect, but the acknowledgment of that imperfection offers footholds to minorities and women. Multiculturalism and feminism do not flourish in the Middle East, Central Africa, India, China or Japan. They have breathing room in the "Eurocentric" West.

Even after the collapse of communism, the West remains the society that, notwithstanding the corruption, incongruities, and "its decline," provides the socio-political structure for a world that can be ameliorated. It would be unhistorical and no less an abuse of the truth to leave out the European tradition, especially the Italian legacy.

This book is an introduction to contemporary Italy, the mother of western civilization and, paradoxically, one of the most stable and chaotic democracies in Europe. It has been written assuming no knowledge of Italy or of Italian politics and history. Of course, the reader who has some acquaintance with the history of fascism or the development of Europe since the war will be at an advantage, as will the reader who has some grounding in economics.

I have been critical of many things in Italy, but much in the way that a progressive minded Italian might be critical. This book tries to look at Italy from within, more from an Italian than an American point of view; and it takes for granted all that is unique, and admirable about Italian civilization. Although I have spent a good part of my adult life in the USA, I was born in Italy and lived there until I was twenty. Since then, I have returned two or three times a year to teach, do research, and see friends and relatives.

A general book such as this has had to rely greatly on other people's research; the list of consulted works gives a good indication of my indebtedness. Those scholars have enabled me, through their writings, to come to some understanding of the complexities of post-war Italy and to substantiate my own assessment. I am also indebted to the *Italian Journal* for valuable updated data and information on many issues. Moreover, I would also like to thank those friends who have read some of the chapters and given me valuable advice; in particular Gianclaudio Macchiarella for his lucid comments, keen suggestions, and broad input; Rocco Rossini who provided me with many newspaper clippings; Prof. Gaetano Iannace whose discussions have always been a source of stimulating insight; Sen. Kenneth P. La Valle for his balanced views on politics, invaluable comments on social issues, and for much support and encouragement; Mr. Fortune Pope of the Pope Foundation for his strong support to Italian Studies; and scores of other generous friends who have aided my efforts, especially the members of the Executive Council of the Center for Italian Studies at the University at Stony Brook: Joseph A. Tursi, Josephine Fusco, Anthony Marano-Ducarne, Lou Parrillo, Paul Ferrotti, Vincent Mannino, Velio Marsocci, Devon Postiglione and Peter Zuzolo. I am also grateful to Ken Gibbons for the scrupulous reading of the manuscript and help to improve it. Much appreciation goes also to Dr. Frank J. Coppa, who as general editor of Studies in Modern European History, provided much assistance and guidance in the last phase of the work.

University at Stony Brook
June 1994

MAP OF ITALY

TRENTINO-
ALTO ADIGE

Bolzano

VALLE
D'AOSTA
Trento

Udine

FRIULI-
VENEZIA GIULIA

Como
Trieste
Aosta
LOMBARDY
Treviso
Novara
Padua
PIEDMONT
Milan
Brescia
Verona
Venice-Mestre
Turin
VENETO

Asti
Parma
Modena
Cuneo
Bologna
Genoa
EMILIA-
Ravenna
LIGURIA
ROMAGNA
La Spezia
Forlì

Pisa
Ancona
Livorno
Florence
LIGURIAN SEA
Arezzo
TUSCANY
MARCHES
Siena

Perugia
ADRIATIC SEA
UMBRIA

Pescara

LAZIO
L'Aquila
ABRUZZI
MOLISE

Rome
Campobasso

Foggia
Bari

CAMPANIA
PUGLIA
Naples
Potenza
Brindisi
Porto Torres
Salerno
Taranto
Sassari
BASILICATA
Nuoro
SARDINIA
TYRRHENIAN SEA
Oristano

Cagliari
Cosenza
Crotone
CALABRIA
Catanzaro

Palermo
Messina
Reggio Calabria
Trapani
SICILY
IONIAN SEA
Agrigento
Catania
Gela
Ragusa
Siracusa

0   km   150

Introduction

When I begin to teach my course on Modern Italy or give a lecture on the topic, I ask those present to tell me with what they associate Italy and the Italians. The spontaneous reactions do not change from situation to situation; people's responses go from excitement to bewilderment. "Italians! They are good singers." "Italy is a good place for a vacation: there is sun, spaghetti and art." "Italians have fine hands: they have a real sense for beauty." Many associate the name of Italy and of the Italians with "Mafia," "pizza," "the Catholic Church," "large, close-knit families," "political chaos," "the Romans," "fine art," "strikes," "high inflation rates," "astronomical deficit," and "gusto for life." Anyone with some acquaintance with Italy and the Italians will admit that these clichés refer to a social, political and economic reality that only partially resembles today's Italy.

Over all, the American view of Italy is still affected by the memories of Italian-Americans who had left crushing poverty for a land of opportunity. And although their sons and daughters are corporate heads, sit in Congress and on the Supreme Court, have risen to the top of many professions, and have been economically successful, their success has not completely erased the memory of their homeland as a peasant, poor and underdeveloped country and other old stereotypes. This negative image has been reinforced by new situations: a country where the government falls constantly to be replaced by another with equally poor prospects, where strikes abound, where the Communists were on the verge of taking power, and where people, in the 1950s and 1960s, were still pouring out of the undeveloped south to seek work in Northern European countries or across the ocean.

The American mass media and the movie industry in particular have created and exacerbated negative stereotypes and the persistent pejorative image of Italy. The American media is more interested in Italian passion and sensational events than in representing the country as a whole. In reporting or portraying the persisting vitality of the Mafia and other forms of corruption within Italian political and social life, the American media necessarily, but unfairly, creates an image of Italians in line with those portrayed by movies like *The Godfather* and *Wise Guys*.

The dominating American attitudes toward Italians have been molded by traditional popular stereotypes and are not uniform. The average American loves Italy's artistic treasures, despises its politics, and envies its gusto for life. Italians are generally perceived to be infatuated with elegant appearance, **bella figura**, rather than the intrinsic (but often dull) qualities admired by the Anglo-Saxons. Thus, Italian cars such as Fiats and Alfa Romeos are admired for their look but are considered suspect in terms of mechanical reliability. In the world of design, the word "Italian" does connote flair, elegance and passion and car makers from Europe, America and Japan do turn to Italian designers such as Pininfarina to design their cars.

The image of Italy has been positive when it is framed in the artistic achievements of its people. Italy has been a champion of the arts throughout the centuries. Through the works of her artists one can witness the whole spectrum of man's creativity in the last 3,000 years. Because of the high achieve ments in the 15th and 16th century, it has been called the cradle of the Renaissance. Franklin D. Roosevelt once said: "If we are children of Western civilization, then Italy is our mother."

The skills and genius of Italian artists and writers, builders and thinkers—and the judgment and generosity of their patrons—were crucial to the cultural development of Western civilization. Dante, Petrarca, and Boccaccio molded an Italian literary language from their native Tuscan dialect, but their words, translated into many languages have become part of the common store of the Western literary heritage. The universal genius of Leonardo da Vinci and Michelangelo sets them beyond the limits of category and chronology. They and Giotto, Donatello, Botticelli, and Raphael—to name just a few of the greatest artists of the Renaissance— shaped a new image of humanity in Western art. Italy has given to Western thought the ideas of the philosopher St. Thomas Aquinas and the political theorist Niccolo Machiavelli, the spiritual fervor of St. Francis of Assisi, the space revelations of Galileo Galilei, the scientific discoveries of Alessandro Volta and Enrico Fermi, and the musical delights of Palestrina, Scarlatti, Monteverdi, Paganini, Vivaldi, Pergolesi, Donizetti, Rossini, Puccini, and Verdi.

For centuries Italy was the Mecca of the cultured. Many foreign writers and poets have sung of Italy's beauty; from Goethe to Stendhal, from Byron to Ruskin to Henry James Italy's natural beauty and her people's creativity inspired their works. However, the foreigner going to Italy today is baffled by many conflicting impressions, for Italy is the land of dualities and paradoxes. For example, although Italy houses two thirds of the world's art—as indicated by a recent UNESCO survey—it is often difficult to appreciate it because most museums and churches are open for limited hours.

"Sunny" Italy is not always all that sunny. Situated on the southern border of Europe and stretching from North to South in the Mediterranean sea for about one thousand miles, the peninsula does not have a uniform climate. Despite its geographical position at the center of the temperate zone (Rome is practically on the same parallel as Boston), Italy has rather variable climatic characteristics, but is warmer than expected. This is due to the presence of the Mediterranean, whose warm waters mitigate thermal extremes, and the Alpine arc, which forms a barrier against the cold north winds. Furthermore, Italy is subject to both wet and moderate atmospheric currents from the Atlantic Ocean and dry and cold ones from eastern Europe. The Apennines chain too, confronting the wet winds from the Tyrrhenian, causes considerable climatic differences between the opposite sides of the peninsula and creates a unique variety of climates for an area that is approximately two-thirds that of California. The Alpine arc has a generally constant rainfall in all seasons, with increased quantities in spring and autumn and much fog in the plain from late fall to the middle of spring. The rest of the peninsula has an irregular rainfall with the most falling in the winter months. In the Southern regions there is a lack of summer rainfall, and in some areas (the Tavoliere in Puglia, Southern Sicily, and the Campidano in Sardinia) the scarce annual rainfall, often produces serious agricultural problems.

Because of its geographical position, with its surrounding islands almost reaching the coast of Africa, Italy has a particular geopolitical function in the Mediterranean as a European country. Italy has direct contact with the main ethnic and cultural areas of the Old World (neo-Latin, Germanic and Slav-Balkan) as well as, through the North Africa countries, with the world of Arab-Islamic civilization.

Consequently, while remaining firmly anchored in the world of Western or European civilization, which was the direct heir of the Greco-Roman culture that developed and flourished on this very peninsula for over a millennium, Italy seems to stretch out naturally towards the opposite shore of the Mediterranean, practically dividing its western and eastern basins. Thus Italy can be considered the most natural link between Europe and the peoples of Africa and Asia, bordering as they do on the same sea and sharing over many centuries both historical events and cultural influences.

It is true that all Italians, from the Alps to Sicily, love espresso coffee, want their *pasta al dente*, watch the same television programs, follow soccer with the same passion, hum the same pop songs, are equally skillful artisans, and have developed an uncommon proclivity for self-criticism. It is hard to tell Northerners from Southerners before they speak and reveal their accent or dialect. There are tall, lanky, blond Sicilians who look like Scandinavians (after all the Normans ruled Sicily in the twelfth century); and there are short, chubby, black-haired and dark-eyed Florentines and Mantuans whose genes may go back to the Etruscans. But there are deep cultural differences which make sociologists question the existence of "one Italy."

One cannot lose sight of the fact that Italy is a relatively young nation. As recent as Metternich's time, Italy was just considered "a geographic expression." Roman law was the widest and strongest historic strand that interlaced the fabric of Italian national identity. However, reminiscences of the Roman Empire and the cultural heritage from the Middle Ages and the

Renaissance have always made educated Italians aware, however dimly, of common bonds and common destiny.

Differences in the social and cultural character of the country persist. During the struggle for liberation from foreign rule and for national unity–the *Risorgimento*–secret societies and uprisings were organized throughout the peninsula. Unfortunately, the Risorgimento was in the main a movement of political and intellectual elites. The masses of the population, particularly the farmers, were apathetic and played almost no role in the Risorgimento. On the other hand, the social class leading the fight for freedom did not have a united political front. Giuseppe Mazzini, the founder of the *Giovine Italia* (Young Italy, 1831), was an idealist and republican, and had a romantic, almost mystical vision, of national unity. For him, Italy's contribution to the family of nations would flow from the resumption of its old role as teacher. His views were opposed by Vincenzo Gioberti who favored a federation of states under the presidency of the Pope. In his book, *On the Moral and Civil Primacy of the Italians,* he attacked the notion of a unitary state and prophesied the difficulties Italy would have under a single statehood. The creation of regions as administrative entities in the 1970s is in a sense the partial realization of Gioberti's plan. Italy was unified according to Cavour's political plan–as the prime minister of the kingdom of Piedmont, he wanted a unified Italy under the house of Savoy. Cavour wanted to unite only northern Italy under a monarchy; and that is what he would have done if Giuseppe Garibaldi, who held democratic principles, had not started his own unification from Sicily and Southern Italy and forced the king of Piedmont to come down from the North and annex the rest of the peninsula.

Contrary to the myths about the *Risorgimento*, this movement for Italy's resurgence was anything but a popular ground swell; it was Italy's failed revolution. Cavour united Italy under a government guided by aristocratic oligarchs who had a great fear of populism and no intention of sharing the national government with the masses.

In 1870, Italy was a nation of approximately 25 million people. Most Italians were poor peasants who could neither read or write. They worked long hours in the fields and lived hard, often miserable lives. Few peasants owned their own land, and the labor contracts for sharecroppers and field workers favored the landowners. None of the 20 million of them could vote. Peasants and politicians lived in two different worlds within the same nation.

The new Italy was a centralized unitary state under a monarchy with a parliamentary government. The king had large-scale powers: he could dissolve parliament, appoint and dismiss the prime minister, appoint senators, and issue proclamations with the force of law. The tradition of local government was retained, but only in appearance; the limited elected local government was presided over by prefects, administrators appointed by the king. Since everything depended upon Rome, the government was inefficient and soon was perceived as an entity far removed from the people. For most the only contacts with government were tax collection and military conscription. Because of the elitist nature of the new state, the condition of the South worsened after unification. A city like Naples, the largest metropolis in Italy and one of the largest in Europe, lost all its political and economical power. From being the capital of the South and a very prosperous city–the Bourbons had developed a strong industrial system and prestigious university centers–Naples gradually became impoverished and lost its luster. Italy had been unified, but only as a political entity. Massimo D'Azeglio, a writer and a senator of that time, said "We made Italy; now we must make the Italians." The task proved difficult.

The new Italian Liberal State, a constitutional monarchy, had a very narrow electoral basis. Only two per cent of the adult population had the right to vote and, of these, less than 60 per cent actually went to the polls. Voting eligibility, based on tax payments, restricted participation in terms of class and of region (fewer in the South because of greater poverty). In many areas, especially in the South, deputies were elected to parliament with only a dozen votes. In the years that followed, the suffrage was extended, but even by the 1909 election only 8.3 per cent of the adult population was entitled to vote. Seventy-five per cent of the population was illiterate and the country suffered from a high mortality rate. The new state was dominated by the Piedmontese and had a system of taxation repressive towards the South. When the South reacted through mass insurrections, or the occasional assassination of prefects and tax collectors, it was repressed by the Piedmontese army. It was clear that the South had been reluctantly accepted into the new state. Italy also suffered because it had not been able to solve the "Roman Question." The Pope had resisted the new state militarily; after he had been pushed into retreat in the Vatican, he condemned the occupation of Rome as an aggression, declared himself prisoner of the Italian state, and threatened to excommunicate any Italian who would take part in the political life of the country.

The separation between the Church and the state did give to the new state the possibility of establishing liberal policies, but it kept the nation divided. Only in 1929, with the Lateran Accords signed between Mussolini and the Pope, was the "Roman Question" resolved. Mussolini, however, did not solve the South-North question. Cultural, economic and social differences between North and South remained. At the end of the nineteenth century and during the first two decades of the twentieth, nationalistic politicians and intellectuals played well on Italian chauvinism rather than focus on the nation's North-South tensions. And Mussolini reinforced that jingoistic spirit.

Mussolini, the leader of the National Fascist Party with around thirty deputies in the Chamber, took power in October, 1922 with the support of the bourgeois and landed interests. The conservative system based on the systematic exclusion of the popular masses from politics was perpetuated. Italy was run by an authoritarian regime of a new type. Although fascist propaganda insisted that the National Fascist Party sought to develop a system that would be neither capitalist nor communist, it did not give any voice to the working class: it kept wages down by destroying trade unions, and it facilitated the rationalization of Italian capitalism. Unlike Marxism, Fascism sought to preserve the capitalist system, neutralizing the internal class struggle by appealing to nationalism as the basis for social harmony. Since the nation was the ultimate good, it was only through the nation that the individual could fulfill his/her potential. By creating the new doctrine "everything within the state, nothing outside the State, nothing against the state," Fascism neutralized class struggle and shifted the struggle elsewhere. The concept of Italy as a "proletarian nation" oppressed by the richer, more developed, capitalist nations was embraced by most Italians.

World War II did not alleviate the split between North and South, indeed, it exacerbated the rift. For about a year and half, the country was literally divided in two. The liberation of the country from the South by the Allies and the occupation of the rest of the peninsula (North and central Italy) by the Nazis had a tremendous impact which affected the evolution of the character of the nation in the democratic era that followed. In that year and half of bloodshed, North and South did not experience the struggle in the same way. The landing of the allies in Sicily on July 10, 1943 quickly triggered strong reaction against Mussolini who had entered the war without much support from either the politicians or the population. In what amounted to a palace coup in Rome, the Fascist Grand Council, including foreign minister Ciano, Mussolini's son-in-law, forced the resignation of Mussolini on the night of July 24-25, 1943 and returned the power of the state to King Victor Emmanuel III. The king had the dictator arrested and appointed Marshal Badoglio prime minister. Badoglio formed an interim government that dissolved the National Fascist Party, granted amnesty to political prisoners, and entered into negotiations with the Allies for an armistice, which was concluded on September 3, 1943, to coincide with the Allies landing on the peninsula at Salerno. Fearing an invasion by Germany, Badoglio quickly (September 8) moved his government to Brindisi, far to the South on the east coast, which was then under the control of the Allies. The Germans, who already had nine divisions in Italy, reacted harshly to the news. On October 13, 1943, the Italian royal government declared war on Germany, but the disintegrating Italian army had been left without a commander. Some Italian troops joined the Germans; some the Allies. Others merged with the partisans who had started the Resistance in the North. Those who resisted the Nazis with no hope of Allied assistance were massacred. In Cefalonia, south of Corfu, the Italians fought for a week. When they finally surrendered, 4,500 soldiers and officers were shot and their bodies were left in the open.

In the meantime, rescued by German commandos, Mussolini had set up a rival government–the *Italian Social Republic*–in Salò on Lake Garda, November, 1943. In the new government there were the most fanatical fascist elements, who were eager to imitate the Nazis. Ciano and others who were held responsible for Mussolini's ouster were executed. The National Racial Code, unpopular in a country where anti-semitism was virtually unknown when the code was enacted in 1938 to impress the Nazis, was now enforced with terrible exactness in the occupied area. Notwithstanding strenuous efforts of many Italians, about 10,000 Italian Jews perished in Nazi concentration camps.

Because of the stiff German resistance to the allied advance, hopes for a quick occupation of Rome were disappointed. A battlefront along the *Gustav Line* during the winter of 1943-44 engaged the allies in a bloody standoff. Rome was finally liberated in June, 1944 after the breakthrough at Cassino in May. A second German defense line in the North, the *Gothic Line*, held until the last weeks of the war. When Mussolini was caught on April 28, 1945, he was shot and his body put on public display.

In that last year and half, an important role was played by the **Partisans** who fought an irregular war against the Germans and Italian Fascists in the North. The **Resistance** movement, started in September 1943 as spontaneous, locally-based popular rising, and by the end of the war had an adherence of 450,000 individuals; 55,000 of them died while about 20,000 remained handicapped from their battle wounds. The *partigiani* excluded no one: rich and poor, professionals and laborers, children, old people, communists, socialists, christian democrats, everyone had a significant role.

An especially important role was played by women. Unlike the Risorgimento, heroines did not simply serve as "mother illustrious" and martyr wives. This time they took to the field, too. The women Gruppi worked in collaboration, not in contention, with men. The Resistance showed that men and women could pursue the same aims, but it also offered women the opportunity to prove that they were the equal of men, just as enduring, strong, brave, resourceful, and implacable.

The activities of the Resistance varied. Besides engaging several German divisions in the fighting, it provided vital information to the allies, helped allied prisoners to escape, engaged in sabotage, disrupted transportation, and organized strikes which slowed down production of war materials. In the last months of fighting the civil war got very brutal. It was a passionate wave of collective hysteria and private vengeance, horrible in its impact but understandable in its context.

Contrary to what happened in France or Yugoslavia, the Italian Resistance was not led by charismatic figures, but was organized by political parties: the Communist Party, the Socialist Party and the Christian Democratic Party. Thus, when the war was over, the only political structures which survived were the political parties. In a popular referendum, June 2, 1946, the first universal suffrage, people not only voted to ban the Fascist Party, but also decided to punish the House of Savoy. The monarchy, discredited because it had given in too easily to Mussolini, was abolished and replaced by the republic. Indeed, the king was forced into exile in Portugal, and never allowed to return. His plea to see his homeland many years later, when he was about to die of cancer, was rejected without much public or political debate.

The result of the elections confirmed the South/North division. Almost all of the northern and central regions voted for the republic; Rome and the South, led by Naples voted for the monarchy (79% for the king). The election of the members of the **Constitutional Assembly** revealed the same split: the South voted more for the Christian Democratic Party and the center-right parties, while the North and central Italy voted more for the Socialist Party and the parties of the left. During this short period, the Communist Party had gained much headway. Palmiro Togliatti played the key role in this transformation. His authority among communist cadres was immense. He was helped in this by the fact that, as the leader of the party, he could enjoy a share of the personality cult which had become established in the communist movement. Undoubtedly the prestige of the USSR played a crucial role in this, but so did the fact that the Communist Party had been the leading force of the Resistance. Togliatti and the Communist Party participated fully in the drafting of Italy's new Constitution. Consequently, next to the principles of liberalism, there were also recognized new "social rights;" freedom of private enterprise was guaranteed but only "as long as it did not conflict with social utility." Since the South did not experience the civil war because it had been quickly liberated by the Allies and had remained under the monarchy, the majority of the people kept their allegiance to the king. The strong emergence of the force of the left which had been organized during the Resistance to fight Nazis and fascists created such strong fear in the South of a possible Communist takeover that Sicily voiced a desire to secede from the peninsula. The political skills of the leader of the Christian Democratic Party, Alcide De Gasperi, and the American political and economic presence in the region prevented both the secession of Sicily and the take over of power by the left. Since no single party was strong enough to capture political power, this had to be jointly managed by the same coalition of parties which had fought in the Resistance: Christian Democratic

Party (***Democrazia Cristiana, D.C.***) 35.1%, Socialist Party (***Partito Socialista Italiano, P.S.I.***) 20.7% and Communist Party (***Partito Comunista Italiano, P.C.I.***) 18.9%.

Although the *D.C.* was the newest party of the young republic, it became the strongest. Its popularity was facilitated by the fact that it was the heir of the Popular Party, the largely peasant-based Catholic party which had been created in 1919 by Luigi Sturzo, a Sicilian priest, and which had already used the vast machine of Catholic social and political organizations. The *D.C.* was able to rely on the support of the Church and the mass lay organizations of the Church itself. The weakness of the old Liberal Party, the nearest equivalent to a clearly pro-capitalist party, made the Christian Democratic Party the only possible choice of industrialists. Because of the kind of base support it had mustered and its ideology, the Christian Democratic Party also became the only party on which the United States came to rely on to take Italy in the North Atlantic Alliance and the Western camp. The *D.C.* dominated the political landscape throughout the post-war period and ensured a remarkable continuity of governments, leading forty-nine out of fifty-two governments. Because it was always in government and because it tended to be a party which actively encouraged the expansion of the public sector, it had at its disposal a vast array of jobs which it could offer to those who were politically reliable. Thus, through professional and trade associations and a clientele system of patronage, the *D.C.* developed a formidable machine, especially in the South where the industrial development lagged far behind that of the North. If the *D.C.* can take most of the merit for the miraculous economic recovery of Italy, it has also to take some of the painful responsibility for the ever-widening economic separation between North and South.

When the country recovered from World War II with surprising speed, foreigners voiced admiration for the **Italian miracle**. The devastating Allied air raids on industrial centers, railroad hubs, seaports, and eventually on Rome itself, were accompanied by the naval bombardment of Genoa, the loss of a major part of the Italian merchant fleet and the disaster of the warships sunk in the harbor of Taranto. Furthermore, battles from Sicily to the Po River, with many civilian casualties and innumerable bridges blown up and buildings destroyed, atrocious Nazi reprisals for acts of sabotage and resistance, and hundreds of thousands of soldiers in prison camps, if not dead, left Italy stripped of much of its manpower and infrastructure. All this plus the restrictions imposed by the peace treaty (Paris, February 1, 1947) forced the new Italian Republic to face many problems of material and moral reconstruction.

Italy was devastated by the 1943 defeat, the agony of the ensuing civil war, and the damage to her physical resources. Paradoxically, however, these setbacks proved less destructive in their effects than the "mutilated" victory of 1918. Indeed, in Italy at the end of 1945 there was an extraordinary sense of real hope. After the many years under Fascism a euphoria of freedom gripped the nation. The great event of 1945 was not so much the disappearance of dictatorship, Fascism, and the monarchy, but rather the affirmation of those principles that animated the Resistance movement: the sudden awakening of the Italians from the long nightmare of war, the rebirth of the nation and its immediate concern with the struggle for survival, the restoration of individual dignity. Many Italians saw the **Resistance** as a new *Risorgimento* because of its struggle against the oppressor and its principles of liberty, justice, and solidarity. It was the Resistance that restored faith in man and his ability to change his own destiny, and it gave rise to the conviction that cultural values could be saved through concrete social and political actions.

At the end of the war, with the installation of the new democratic government and the elimination of the strictest form of censorship, artists and writers also emerged with a reborn sense of civic commitment. Once the strict censorship of the Fascist regime had fallen, they could turn their eyes freely to the observation of reality. The poverty, social disorder, and suffering that fascism had forbidden to be represented, and the humanity ravaged by the war, became their subject matter. The theater, the novel, and the movies became the chief means by which contemporary society was placed under investigation. In the depiction of socio-political situations, it was the search for truth that guided the directors and screen writers in their first **neorealist** works. Filmmakers wanted spectators to be witnesses to the ills of society in order to raise social and political consciousness. Thus, in their masterpieces, De Sica, Visconti, Zavattini, and Rossellini dealt with the themes of real life, expressing them with deep emotional involvement and consuming lyricism with a clear aim: a naturalistic slice of life and a sociopolitical perspective in which antifascism and class consciousness had to bring action. The intensity and fervor of this discovery rendered the artist inseparable from the man.

The neorealist artist generally took an instinctively populist or leftist viewpoint, espousing a more or less explicit faith both in the irresistible power of collective action and in Marxist dialectical conflict and the inevitability of historical progress–all supported by a somewhat mystical notion of Christian brotherhood. However, it did not necessarily share the doctrinaire optimism of socialist realism, with its voluntaristic faith in an ultimate, inescapable positive solution to social problems.

A policy of reconstruction and economic development was pursued by the various governments in power after 1948, the year in which the *D.C.* acquired a large parliamentary majority. Initially this took the form of severe anti-inflation measures and then a lifting of restrictions combined with public intervention through a re-launching of *IRI*, the Institute for the Industrial Reconstruction.

The establishment of the *Cassa per il Mezzogiorno* (Funds for the Development of the South) set in motion a complex series of extraordinary interventions to provide the southern regions with the necessary basic structures (roads, drainage, services, etc.) to assist in economic and, above all, agricultural development. **Agrarian reform** was particularly necessary in combating the centuries-old feudal structure of land estates of the South. However, because of poor planning a new and even greater migration occurred, this time not overseas but toward the countries of Northwestern Europe (Germany, France, Belgium, England, and Switzerland), where the post-war industrial boom required large quantities of manpower. The movement of population was even greater towards the north of Italy (Piedmont, Lombardy, and Liguria) due to the efforts of private initiative in creating an industrialized climate whose rapid and often disorderly growth came to be known as the "economic miracle."

At the beginning of the 1960s, the highest percentage of the working force was employed in the industrial sector, while agriculture continued to diminish and the service industries began their expansion. In the international sphere, with her entry to the United Nations and participation in military alliances and economic agreements with the other western countries (European and North American), Italy began to regain the dignity and prestige due to her geographical position and the richness of her historical cultural traditions. The Italians once again, like the phoenix, had risen from the ashes of the war. Their innate abilities proved to be their best resource. Their multiform tactile skills and their versatility and mastery in shaping, carving, crafting, refining, drawing, styling, painting, and lettering are part of a long tradition. Today's designers of elegant car bodies and casual wear are heirs to a long tradition that embraces the pottery and tomb frescoes of the Etruscans and the anatomical and engineering drawings of Leonardo da Vinci and a host of celebrated and anonymous artists and artisans going back three thousand years.

Gradually the Italian economy changed beyond recognition and has, by and large, caught up with the rest of Europe. In terms of purchasing power and standard of living, the Italian working class has narrowed the gap with Germany and France and is at the same level as the United Kingdom. The 'necessities' of the consumer society, such as remote-control color television, multiprogram dishwashers, freezers, cellular telephones, etc. are as available in Italy as they are in most other Western countries. Its agricultural population has decreased constantly and so has the birth-rate–two other characteristics of major economic powers.

The open market and free enterprise system have played the major role in the diffusion of consumer goods in Italian society. As in the rest of Europe, the state has had to intervene to keep costs of production lower than they would otherwise have been by taking into public ownership some basic production inputs such as energy, and some basic segments of the infrastructure of the nation such as transportation, and subsidizing them out of public funds. Furthermore, the state has also had to ensure that minimum standards of health, housing, education and old age care are maintained. In other words, Italy too became a **Welfare State**. This was achieved and maintained on the assumption that there would be a constant economic growth, which was the case for most of the 1950s and good part of the 1960s. Problems, however, began to surface in the late 1960s and developed in the 1970s, when the economy slowed down and the manufacturing sector decreased. As a consequence of this condition, the public sector was increasingly less able to sustain a high level of employment and large areas of the private sector succumbed and had to be rescued by the State causing high inflation. Italy went through the same phases experienced by the developed West: **development of the Welfare State, State intervention, and crisis of the Welfare State.**

The major socio-economic changes began with Italy's opening to the left, in early 1960, which brought the Socialist Party, previously in electoral alliance with the Communists, into a governing coalition with the Christian Democrats, the Republicans and the Social Democrats. The inclusion of the Socialists in government was the first concrete step in a far-reaching realignment of Italy's political forces aimed at isolating the largest Communist party in the West and forming a stable governmental majority resting on a wider and solid foundation of popular support. The center-left governments of the 1960s may be criticized for excesses in labor legislation and wasteful public expenditures, but they were the only alternative; a center-right coalition with the extremely conservative liberals depending on parliamentary support from the neo-Fascist (*Movimento Sociale Italiano, M.S.I.*), might then have polarized Italian society.

Along with the political and economic changes, the rest of Italian life has changed radically, and most of the changes have been for the better. Compared to 1945, the average Italian is better fed, better housed, better educated, more literate and politically more aware. The enormous gap which existed between Italians and Americans has been practically eliminated. Italians proudly say that "America is here now." That is true on many levels, as we shall see.

After some initial reticence, Italians threw themselves into the consumer society as eagerly as any people in Europe. Some feared that Italy was losing her soul, selling out to an ill-digested Americanization, but most people welcomed this new world of affluence and technology. They were driven by the urge to make money and enjoy the fruits of their labor; like the other losers of the war in Europe, the Germans, they rebuilt and modernized their country through a mixture of technical flair, material ambition and sheer sustained hard work at all levels, from top manager to industrial worker and farmer.

This post-war modernization has been a powerful, heroic process because it was a leap straight from a backward country to a post-industrial nation. Under the momentum of economic advance, society shifted its equilibrium. There was a massive movement of people from agriculture to industry and service, from the country to the towns. With rapid urbanization, many cities tripled in size and many provincial towns became vibrant with new activity.

In private and family life, and in purely social relations, Italy has certainly evolved a great deal in the last thirty years. Women have achieved a striking new emancipation. Sexual permissiveness has developed remarkably in the past two decades. Within the family, paternal authority now weighs less heavily and parent/child relations are more frank and equal. In daily life, the pompous use of titles is waning, and home entertaining has become much more relaxed and casual.

Fewer people go to church on a regular basis, more use contraceptives and more live together without being married. Divorces and abortions are legal while the purchase of pornographic material and the access to risque movies on TV has no equal in the world. The strong presence of the Church and the tradition of puritanical values have not prevented the development of a life style which is, by and large, an adaptation of the many negative aspects of the "American way of life."

Italians have a love-hate relationship with the State: they resent it, yet cling to it and expect it to provide endless benefits. In this, as in many other ways, Italy appears to be a country of paradoxes, especially on the political level. The game of musical chairs that cabinet ministers play, the governmental crises, past acts of terrorism in airports and train stations, high inflation, and mega-scandals which are top news in daily newspapers have led scholars to depict the country as a democracy headed if not to oblivion then certainly toward some mortal crises. The fact that the Italian government has been very fragile and has fallen, on the average, once a year, and that in parliament as many as sixteen political parties were represented, made many political experts, especially Anglo-Saxons, to suggest that the Italian political system was an anomalous democracy that did not deserve to be preserved. On the other hand, Italy has also had one of the most stable democracies in the West; it is the only country in Europe to be ruled by the same party for almost fifty years, and has seen no change in the political élites during that same period. Governing with a multi-party system Italian style was possible only because of the high skills Italian politicians were able to develop in the post-fascist period. Italians were able to make the business of government an art that constantly requires intuition, creativity, tolerance, endurance, and flexibility. The leading party in power, the *D.C.*, dealt with the continuous crisis of the country by constantly changing strategies. Not only the nature of its alliance with the political forces had to change, but the nature of each of the political forces with which it had to deal changed. While the *D.C.* changed by leaning more toward the left, the left changed by leaning toward the center. The *P.S.I.* changed from being junior supporter of the *P.C.I.* in the 1940s and 1950s to becoming a junior partner of the *D.C.* from the 1960s on. Rejecting its traditions of a workers' party and becoming more and more a radical party of the Center, the PSI increasingly espoused the cause of 'modernization.' By being in power with the *D.C.*, it obtained a greater share of political and economic resources, and it abused its power. In so doing, it became another party of patronage and clienteles. The *P.C.I.* increasingly abandoned the doctrine of Marxism-Leninism, opened its ranks to people of varying persuasions including Catholics, accepted with increasing enthusiasm membership in the EEC and NATO, disassociated itself from Soviet foreign policy and supported a *D.C.* government for nearly three years (1976-79). By responding to external political conditions and internal pressure and interest groups, political parties changed. Everyone has changed, but everyone has had to pay a price.

In the present era of transnational corporations, of mass international communication system which penetrate deep into the national culture, and a powerful military system backed by superpower technology, the traditional nation-state is reduced to cosmic insignificance. The shocks of the fall of Communism and the collapse of the Soviet Union certainly affected Italian politics profoundly. The disappearance of a political force seen as a threat to democratic stability allowed political parties to disentangle themselves from old alliances which created a reality that necessitated changes in the political system. As result, in 1993, institutional reforms were enacted and a new form of democracy was instituted. The changes were bold and positive, but their success will require more than official reforms. There will also need to be a change in Italian attitudes, and a new kind of civic spirit.

Especially for the South, the reform of institutions will not bring about automatic changes because the performance of institutions depends on their social, economic and cultural surrounds. We know that if we transplant democratic institutions, they do not grow in the new setting as they did in the old, for the quality of a democracy depends on the quality of its citizens. The difference between South and North has to be attributed by the difference in civic attitudes in the two areas and therefore the way government is regarded; however, the duality of North and South has become greater because there is a lack of serious initiatives to create jobs on the part of Italy's governing national élite. The **Southern Question** is an economic question as well a political one. It is not a matter of simple modernization, or of an increase in state funds. The role of the South cannot even be understood purely in terms of the Italian North; it must be thought of anew in terms of the relations between Italy and the rest of the EC and the Mediterranean. Its problems cannot be tackled independently from the North or the rest of Europe because their economic development is intrinsically connected to the South. The old solutions have done much damage to the South. For the systematic drainage of the South's sole resource, human labor, the South has been compensated by a constant stream of state funds which have underpinned the stability of the *D.C.* regime. This money has not been directed towards "modernization" but has been channelled in a thousand directions under the supervision of all sorts of interest groups including the Mafia. Italy's future depends on its ability to make the South part of the national economic equation.

Despite the Southern question and other difficulties such as high unemployment and some unresolved social injustices, I find Italy today a relatively happy and well-adjusted society, perhaps a little cynical and certainly disillusioned with politics and ideologies, but no longer daydreaming. At the beginning of the 90s, Italians finally became aware that material progress had in itself by no means cured all the basic ills of their society. It is a society still segmented, still beset with barriers and inequalities, still attached to a number of outdated structures of which the most blatant was the over-centralized and too pervasive machine of the State. But there is still much to be done that no government can do, for social change is a matter of habit and psychology more than of politics. As we shall see, the Italians may have changed their life-styles, but their basic character, built around individualism, social mistrust and desire for formalism–the desire to present a *bella figura*–remains.

Part One
POLITICS

I

Political and Social Foundations

Politicization and *Immobilismo*

Italy has always attracted negative attention for the way it conducts political affairs; its government has always been perceived as faulty and unstable. Those who follow the daily press know that Italy has had many governments, much political terrorism and, until the fall of Communism, a large Communist Party. They will know that the government is massive and omnipresent and that the Italian political parties have "colonized" Italian society.

Governments do fall constantly, parliaments are dissolved frequently and, worse, every facet of Italian life is politicized. The mere act of joining a trade union or even a sporting club is inevitably a "political" decision in Italy. Prospective labor union members must choose whether to join the Communist-socialist trade union, *Confederazione Generale Lavoratori Italiani* (**CGIL**), the Catholic union, *Confederazione Italiana dei Sindacati dei Lavoratori* (**CISL**) or the Social-democrat/republican union, *Unione Italiana del Lavoro* (**UIL**). The whole range of cultural and social organizations, associations and clubs is not immune to political penetration. Politics has also led to politicization of economic life, particularly in the public sector: state enterprises, banks, credit institutions, tv networks and newspapers are all politically influenced.

The great majority of Italians complain about a government that does not work, about political leaders who are crooks, but even more about the related problem of *immobilismo*. Contrary to the perception of the foreign press, they usually do not complain about the constant fall of government; in fact, the complaint is that, notwithstanding the numerous governments and parliamentary elections, the same people continue to govern the country and the political system remains *immobile*. That was true until 1993 when radical political changes were instituted.

The Italian form of government may have been similar to that of most parliamentary democracies in structure and constitutional principles, but it functioned in a fundamentally different way. The anomalies that characterize it, although subtle, complex and deeply woven into the fabric of Italian life, are not impenetrable mysteries. If one examines the Italian Constitution in its historical context by acknowledging both the important role that it gave to Parliament and the level of democratic pluralism it had desired, then the postwar Italian political history appears less Byzantine and Italian politicians can be valued for their skills in reaching compromises, and for the preservation of democracy. One will also be able to understand how the real protagonists, the political parties, developed, monopolized power, contributed to corruption, and affected the general life of the country.

One must remember that the post-war period begins with the political parties clearly in charge. They constituted the commanding forces of the Italian Resistance: the Committee of National Liberation was made up of a coalition of six parties–the partisans were organized on the basis of party affiliation.

The Constitution and Popular Sovereignty

When on June 4, 1944 the Allies entered Rome, Italy was already eager to change its form of government: the Committee of National Liberation (**CLN**) demanded a civilian government with clear plans for immediate changes. A six party coalition government representing the political forces of the resistance was formed. The temporary government, initially under Ivanoe Bonomi, had to cope with the disastrous economic legacy of the war and the rehabilitation of the national morale. After moving quickly, by a succession of acts, to suppress the Fascist Party and its dependent organizations and carrying out an extensive shuffling of prefects (state government representatives in the provinces), with a provisional decree on July 25, 1944, Bonomi formalized the Salerno Agreement and established: 1) election by direct universal suffrage of a Constitutional Assembly to draw up a new constitution; 2) obligation of the members of the government not to impede institutional reform, postponed until the liberation of the country; 3) future ministers to swear loyalty to the nation, rather than to the king; and 4) legislative powers to be attributed to the government, by way of decrees approved by the new king who had been given the title of "Luogotenente generale del regno." A provisional decree of March 16, 1946 also established that the "institutional question," the decision to choose between monarchy and republic, had to be resolved directly by the people by referendum.

In the institutional referendum held on June 2, 1946, the electorate voted in favor of the Republic (12,718,641 or 54.26 per cent for the Republic, 10,718,502 or 45.7 per cent for the monarchy). Almost all of the northern and central regions voted for the Republic, Rome and the South (led by Naples, 79 per cent) for the Monarchy. After the results of the referendum were proclaimed, King Umberto, who had inherited the throne on the abdication of his father Victor Emmanuel III, left for permanent exile with the royal family. The elections for the Constitutional Assembly, held the same day, saw the clear dominance of the three popular parties (Christian Democrats with 35 per cent of the votes, the Socialist Party with 20 per cent and the Communist Party with 19 per cent). With this vote two objectives were achieved. First, the Italians had the final word on the institutional question that had divided the country and absorbed considerable attention on the part of the political powers, public opinion and international bodies. Second, they opened the way for the introduction of a constitution which was to signal a new political order with the collapse of the fascist regime and the return to democracy. The new constitution was approved by secret ballot on December 22, 1947 by a vote of 453 to 62, promulgated by the provisional head of State on December 27 and put into effect on January 1, 1948.

By the standards of Italian parliamentary proceedings, or indeed by any standards, the drafting and approval of the Constitution was a speedy affair. Yet the work of the Constitutional Assembly took place in an even more rapidly changing political climate. When the Assembly first met, in June 1946, the Cold War had not yet begun and the Italian Communist Party (*P.C.I.*) was still in the government. By the time the Constitution was approved, the Left had been expelled from the government and Europe was divided into two spheres of influence. Inevitably, the political situation had an influence on the proceedings.

Christian Democrats, Communists, Socialists, Liberals, etc. worked side by side to prepare a governing chart that had to serve the people of the whole nation and that could withstand the weight of time. Since Fascism had violated the fundamental rights of individual and collective liberty and had authoritatively centralized all power, the new Constitution addressed these issues and emphasized the basic rights of private citizens. Heated debates were inescapable as were the inevitable compromises. Some of the most passionate discussions centered on the make-up of parliament: the left preferred one house rather than two. The final approval of the bicameral structure was possible only by giving both houses equal power to legislate as well as to dissolve the government. Another issue that was fiercely debated was the role of the Council of Ministers (the cabinet) and of the President of the Council of Ministers, especially whether the cabinet had to work as a collective body or be divided along internal hierarchical lines with a strong prime minister. Many issues (such as the establishment of regional administration, constitutional court, the referendum, and the freedom to strike) were not resolved and were left to subsequent decisions.

Although the framers of the Constitution had used the American Constitution as a model, they created something unique. In its first part, the Italian Constitution reflects the euphoria of newly acquired freedom and the determination never to lose it again. Consequently, it is rich in rhetoric, exceedingly detailed, extremely thorough, and very progressive.

The democratic character of the Constitution is evident from Article 1 which states that "Italy is a Republic" and reinforced by Article 139 which decrees that the republican form cannot be the object of constitutional change. The choice made by the people through the referendum imposed on the state the character of a republic based on parliamentary democracy. Consequently, political and civil liberties were re-affirmed; the principles of parliamentary government, abandoned under Fascism, were confirmed, as was the division of power established by the eighteenth-century declaration of rights. The Republican Constitution, therefore, founded a political and social order based on a pluralistic democracy.

Of essential importance are the affirmation of the political, economic and social rights and duties of the citizen, the recognition of the role of political parties and trade unions, institutional pluralism, political and administrative decentralization, and protection of minorities. Not only these essential principles of political democracy, but also those of economic and social democracy are considered. The Constitution also provides the mechanism by which plural democracy is achieved through political, economic and social solidarity (Art. 2) and the fundamental equality of citizens (Art. 3).

The very important aspect of the Constitution's treatment of equality and solidarity among citizens has a double significance. On the one hand, it provides legal confirmation of the equality of the Republic's citizens in both their relations among themselves and with the institutions of the State. On the other hand, the removal of obstacles to economic and social equality by public powers is established and regarded as an actual duty. In reaction to the former preservation of social class structure, the members of the Constitutional Assembly wanted to ensure, by constitutional right, that all citizens would have real civil dignity in the social community, at work and in education so as to allow them an active role in society.

The first article of the constitution gives clear evidence of the strong presence of certain political forces in the constitutional assembly. It states: "Italy is a democratic Republic founded on *lavoro*." The use of the word "work/labor" sparked much debate. The recognition of human labor as a fundamental value and right is further reinforced later (Art. 4): "The Republic recognizes the right of all citizens to work and shall promote such conditions as will make this right effective." Unfortunately, however, this strong constitutional right has not prevented Italy's excessively high percentage of unemployment. The Constitution also recognizes that citizens have certain economic rights: to own property; to take economic initiatives within legal limits; to set aside savings and have them protected; and to work. This latter right carries with it considerable implications: representation and trade union protection of professional interests, just compensation, equality of treatment, collaboration in management and social security. In fact, it obliges public powers to stimulate employment and safeguard it at all levels (Art. 35); and it guarantees the fundamental rights of workers concerning equal pay for equal effort, hours of work, weekly and annual paid holidays, equality between the sexes at work, minimum working age, pension and workers' participation in management (Art. 36, 37, 38 and 46). The Constitution also provides social assistance (Art. 38) for those citizens unfit for work and without private means.

Also relevant is the way the Constitution deals with the regulation of private property and wealth: its acquisition, possession, enjoyment and circulation. Private ownership has legally recognized and guaranteed limits so as to ensure general accessibility and accountability (Art. 42). For example, private lands containing energy resources, or firms producing fuel or providing essential services may be transferred into public ownership on the grounds of national interest with the payment of an indemnity (Art. 42 and 43). The law can, in fact, impose limits on ownership and economic initiatives in the name of solidarity and the general social good.

It can, therefore, be said that the economic aspect of the Constitution of Italy is based on the following key elements: a mixed economy for ownership and initiatives, central planning entrusted to public authorities, private enterprise encouraged by a series of guarantees, and extensive protection for workers. All of these aspects are aimed at the creation of equally distributed public wealth.

Another clear and definitive break with Fascism was the recognition and protection of ethnic and religious minorities. Provision was made both for safeguarding linguistic minorities and for the protection of religious worship. Minority rights were then reinforced by way of regional autonomy and the foundation of the first five regions with special status, in particular, the regions of Trentino-Alto Adige with its large German-speaking minority and Valle d'Aosta with its French-speaking minority.

The **government** of the Republic is thus formed by a system of equal constitutional elements: the President of the Republic, the Parliament, the Government (Cabinet of ministers), the Judiciary and the Constitutional Court. The conformity of the law to the Constitution may be subject to verification by the Constitutional Court, which had not been provided for by the *Statuto Albertino*. The base of sovereignty and, therefore, of constitutional power rests on the people. This form of political democracy is confirmed in Art. 1, second clause, of the Constitution. Consequently, the Italian people are the holders of sovereign power, which they exercise both directly through voting in elections and referenda and indirectly through institutional representation. Due to this essential principle of political democracy, the right to vote assumes a decisive constitutional significance. By means of a universal, direct, secret vote the electoral body selects political representatives who intervene directly whenever a referendum is proposed; the latter can be used for the abrogation of a law, for constitutional modification, or even specified regional and local issues which have seen a notable expansion, not always provided by the Constitution. The

Constitution thus makes two essential provisions for the execution of popular sovereignty: first, the exercise of democratic representation in parliament, regional assemblies and local councils; second, participation through referenda (or direct democracy). Democratic voting and elections are the key elements of political representation and the foundation of legitimate power.

Parliamentary Organization and Political Pluralism

In dividing the Italian Parliament into two assemblies, the Senate and the Chamber of Deputies, the Constitutional Assembly was influenced by at least two factors. On the one hand, it considered it appropriate to establish political representation on a balance of power guaranteed by discussion between two assemblies, both of which derived their democratic legitimacy from direct election. On the other hand, it deemed paramount the procedural considerations of the two chambers to allow for a major reflection in the execution of their functions and imposed a need for coordination that would require at least two successive phases of debate.

The structure of the Italian parliament has inherent problems. Constitutionally, the powers of the two chambers are equal and do not represent distinct social or geographic interests. The difference between them is so slight that it is possible to speak of an almost "perfect" double-chamber system. The major difference between them is the functional co-ordination of the two assemblies; in addition, the age of their members and that of their voters as well as the level of proportional representation are also different.

Government *all'italiana* means that the more members the Parliament has, the better the people are served; so, Italy has more than three times as many members as the U. S. Congress, even though the American population is four times that of Italy and has a population make-up that is much more complex. Even worse, to compensate for the high number of parliamentarians, each member has a very small and usually ill-informed staff. Nothing remotely comparable to the numerous aides and well-staffed offices of American senators and congressmen.

Under the Republican Constitution, the Senate is an elected body (unlike under the Monarchy, when the members were appointed by the king). Until 1993, it was elected, every five years, on a regional basis by uninominal colleges or electoral bodies, with the use of regional proportional representation if no candidate succeeded in receiving the necessary 65 percent of valid votes. All citizens 25 years or above may vote, and citizens 40 years or above are eligible for the office of senator. To the number of 315 senators set by the constitution are to be added former presidents of the republic and senators, up to five, nominated by the president in office. These last are chosen among those citizens who have made an outstanding social, scientific, artistic or literary contribution to the country, a very healthy clause in a system that is heavily politicized.

Like the Senate, the Chamber is elected every five years. Until 1993, it was chosen by universal, direct, secret vote according to a proportional system of plurinominal colleges. The number of deputies, fixed at 630, is double of the number of senators and is distributed in 32 electoral constituencies, each one having a number of deputies equal to the division of the entire population (based on the latest general census figures). The seats are assigned in accordance with the population of each constituency based on whole electoral quotients and the highest remainders. All citizens who are 18 or over may vote, and all those who are 25 or older may be elected to the Chamber.

Most of the work of the two assemblies is conducted at committee level in each house, but some is also carried out through a system of interchange and coordination through double-chamber commissions. These are composed of deputies and senators in equal numbers and correspond proportionately to the size of the different parliamentary groups. Double-chamber commissions are used for inquiring into cases of criminal accusation, for directing and controlling the radio and television services, and for intervening in the problem of the *Mezzogiorno* (Southern Italy), as well as for other controls and inquiries specifically set up by parliament.

Where the structure of parliament is concerned, a general observation can be made that each chamber usually has a distinct function. Only in particular cases, specified by the Constitution, do the two chambers unite in common session. The latter occurs for the election and swearing in of the President of the Republic, for the election of the constitutional justices (5 of whom are nominated by parliament), for the election of a third of the members of the Superior Council of the Judiciary, and the President of the Council and his ministers. When it is necessary for the two parliamentary chambers to unite, they sit together in Deputies Chamber at Palazzo Montecitorio, where the Chamber of Deputies is housed, as opposed from Palazzo Madama, the usual home of the Senate. The affinity of the two chambers and their similar functions, in addition to internal political bickering, makes the Italian parliament a very slow-moving body. What made the system Byzantine, as we shall see, is the power that the political parties had acquired in the parliamentary structure.

The relationship between the parliamentary member and the political party from whose electoral lists s/he was elected is complex and attempts at simplification can be misleading. Although the Constitution confirms the classical parliamentary principle that members of the chambers represent the nation and exercise their functions without mandatory restrictions and, therefore, parliamentary members are neither the representatives of their electoral colleges nor the mandataries of the political party to which they are affiliated, political parties do exert a strong control on them.

Parliament has many important functions and immense political power, primarily in its authority to legislate. Each member of parliament can promote a legislative proposal. The right to propose laws, however, is also enjoyed by the government (the executive branch), regional councils, the National Council for Economy and Labor (for matters involving the economy and employment), and a group of 50,000 electors. Parliament controls government (the cabinet of ministers), that is, the executive branch, by its power to approve legislation and through the use of the vote of "confidence."

In the early 90s, various institutional parliamentary reforms were proposed to speed up the flow of the work of parliament, which is often dammed up by procedural obstacles. Proposals were made to introduce a single-chamber system, to drastically reduce the number of members of each assembly, to have uninominal elections, to reduce proportional representation to only parties collecting at least 5 percent of the total votes. Until 1992, every attempt to reform governmental institutions found strong opposition, especially by *D.C.* However, in 1992, by initiative of *D.C.*, an attempt was made to start to correct one of the major absurdities of the Italian political system, that is, the separation between the legislative and the executive branches. In every democracy, that is the norm, not in government *all'italiana.* In that year, *D.C.* established that the offices of Government (the cabinet of ministers) and parliament were incompatible in the same person. Consequently, in accepting a post in government, an *onorevole* would have to give up his/her seat in parliament. Aside from being freed from the potentially serious conflicts that would occur by holding positions in two branches of government, the *onorevole* could not vote in parliament for or against his own government. Most important, the voting down of governments would not be done lightly because members of Government would not automatically return to parliament!

As we shall see, major changes were also approved in the way parliament is elected and political parties get their representation. The changes were so radical that political scientists have characterized them as the beginning of the second republic.

President: Head of State but not of Government

Because the framers of the Constitution were charged with creating a parliamentary republic, they had to avoid giving too much power to one individual (as is the case in the presidential republic where the president is head of state and of government). However, even though the President of the Italian Republic does not enjoy the power held by his counterpart in a presidential republic, he is not a puppet. The last two presidents have given a clear indication of how powerful the president of the republic can be when the executive (government) and legislative (parliament) branches are weak and/or fragmented.

The President of the Italian republic is Head of State but not of Government, and he represents the nation's political unity and "guarantees" the constitutional powers. By the power of his message, the President of the Republic is able to influence political and institutional direction, both from within the institutions and the country at large. The President has an important role as guarantor and political mediator when a government is being formed following a cabinet crisis. When he is convinced of the lack of "governability," the President of the Republic is also able to dissolve the chambers early and call for new elections. The Head of State in the Italian constitutional model is, therefore, charged with ensuring that the constitutional rules for the ordering of political and constitutional relations between the powers of the State are observed, and with intervening to resolve any resulting institutional crises.

The Head of State fulfills functions connected with all the constitutional powers of the Republic. Where parliament and legislative procedures are concerned, the President participates in the formation of laws by 'promulgation' and can send laws back to the chambers for new consideration; he authorizes the presentation of proposed government legislation, and indicates political elections and referenda; he can ask for the extraordinary assembly of the chambers and, in consultation with their president, can order its dissolution; and, he nominates up to five senators. In relation to the government and the executive function, the President of the Republic is responsible for nominating the President of the Council of Ministers (Prime Minister) and, at his proposal, the ministers; he appoints, on the initiative of the government and in those cases provided by the law, the state functionaries; he issues, after government deliberation, decrees having the value of law (legal and legislative), as well as regulations; and he accredits and receives diplomatic representatives.

The Head of State, moreover, commands the armed forces, presides over the Supreme Defense Council and declares the state of war resolved upon by Parliament. Also very important is the formal participation by the President in the exercise of several administrative functions: the recognition of juridical appointments, dissolution of provincial and communal councils, legitimization of natural children, decision on recourse to extraordinary administrations and conferment of honors. In relation to the powers of justice, the Head of State nominates five justices of the Constitutional Court, presides over the Supreme Council of the Judiciary and can grant pardons and clemency.

All the acts of the President, including the exercising of his 'own' powers, must be endorsed by the relevant ministers or by the President of the Council so that they thus assume the political responsibility. Furthermore, the President of the Republic cannot be removed from power on the grounds of political irresponsibility. The only political control to which he is subject is that of public opinion and not being re-elected should he choose to stand again for office. However, the force of political interest and the power of the mass media on the President of the Republic should not be undervalued. The loss of political support, accompanied by unfavorable public opinion, can lead to the President's dismissal from office.

Weak Executive Because of Weak Parliament?

It is the Cabinet of Ministers (Government) that holds the executive function. According to the principles of 'parliamentary government' enshrined in the Italian constitutional model, the government assumes the power of political decision with the consent of Parliament, which is expressed by a vote of 'confidence' in the government by the two chambers. The nomination process usually begins with a government crisis and ends with the swearing in of the **President of Council of Ministers** (Prime Minister) and of the ministers by the President of the Republic. The second stage is that of parliamentary 'confidence.' It opens with the presentation of the government to Parliament, within ten days of nomination, and closes with a formal vote of confidence by Parliament. When a cabinet crisis occurs, the President of the Republic, according to a well-established constitutional practice, engages in political consultations with both individual state figures (former presidents of the republic, the presidents of both chambers and former Prime ministers) and representatives and delegations of political parties. At the end of these soundings, the Head of the State, having judged that the political and institutional conditions exist for forming a government capable of winning parliamentary confidence, will entrust the creation of a cabinet to the designated Prime minister. Usually, the latter accepts provisionally until he has established, through consultations with the various political forces, the concrete possibility of being able to form a government that will be supported by the majority of members of Parliament. The President of the Republic then nominates the President of the Council of Ministers and, on the latter's proposal, the individual ministers who all then take the Oath of Loyalty to the Republic. Within the ten days allowed by the Constitution, the Government must present itself to the chambers who, on hearing the declaration made by the President of the Council, provide a vote of 'confidence.' The President of the Council coordinates the actions of the various ministers and maintains the unity of the general political direction, which is his first responsibility . The Council of Ministers decides on all the general policies of the Government, with specific competence for all the decisions involving the **collective responsibility** of the executive. Individual ministers join in determining the government's political direction, in participating in the sessions of the Council of Ministers and in making the decisions for their respective ministers. Ministers have, above all, a collective political responsibility for all the government's acts and for many of the acts of political consideration that involve the collective responsibility of the government.

The government is in fact the holder of some normative powers: it decides the form in which laws will be proposed to the Head of State, who must then authorize their presentation to the chambers. It also approves laws by decree in cases of emergency and legislative decrees on the delegation of Parliament. These 'materially legislative' acts are then issued by decree of the President of the Republic. Finally, the government is responsible for regulating all the executive activity of the law and the administrative organization. The responsibility can be tested in Parliament through the "no confidence" motion, whose approval obliges the Government to resign.

By creating a governmental body that had collective responsibility and by giving it a leader who potentially could not assume too much power, the framers of the constitution have spared Italy from the abuses of an authoritative government or leader, but they also gave the country the structure for a political system which, as a consequence of the unique kind of proportional representation system, proved to be very unstable and would require skillful maneuvering and compromising in order to survive. As the coalition of various political forces, the Italian government has been increasingly fragmented and fragile. In the approximately first fifty years of Republic, Italy has had about 52 governments; on the average, one government per year, instead of one for every five years, if it coincided with the normal five-term of parliament. Since the great majority of governments were **coalitions** of many parties allied to the Christian Democratic Party (*D.C.*), which was itself fractioned, a spirit of potential conflict and hostility forced a cabinet to fall on the slightest pretext of the leaders of even the smallest parties. The coalition formulas were dictated by possibilities for achieving the required majority in parliament. The Christian Democrats and Socialists, who constituted the core of the coalition, did not form an alliance based on mutual trust, parity or programmatic accord. Their cooperation was driven by suspicion, personal rivalry, and eternal jockeying for position. Overall, the leaders of both parties were more able strategists for their parties than for the country.

The enduring but rather unproductive *D.C./P.S.*I. alliance had blocked the Italian political system in *immobilismo* and corruption. Unfortunately for Italy, until the fall of Communism, there were no credible alternatives.

The Multi-Party System and Proportional Representation

The long morass of the Italian political system was partially due to the overly idealistic aspirations of the fathers of the Italian constitution. In envisioning the role of the political parties in government and society, the framers of the Italian constitution were not only too optimistic, but were also too attached to the theoretical plan.

They rightfully assumed that one of the essential presuppositions to the concept of political democracy was allowing direct political participation to the citizen. To offer a real pluralistic democracy, the juridical channels of consultation, direction and decision should be many and diverse. A real democratic state is, in fact, based on both fundamental juridical guarantees and an efficient interchange between public powers and civil society.

For a country where the specters of Fascism were still very much present and the fear of the advent of Communism was overwhelming–from the very beginning of the Cold War, Italy was at the frontier of the free world–the presence of a strong political party was scary. Proportional representation, without a minimum needed to achieve representation, was intended to foster minority parties and discourage monolithic groups like the communists or the disbanded Fascists to take control.

Both the virtues and the problems on which Italian democracy was founded lay in its proportional representation system, which was one of the most representative in the world: the more an electoral system is proportional the greater the tendency for all political forces to be represented. Thus, from the very beginning a fairly wide array of political forces was represented, and it seems that voters responded enthusiastically to this wide spectrum of political choices. Although voting was not mandatory, there was a high level of electoral participation even in local elections and referenda. In fact, the proportion of eligible voters going to the polls has been the highest in Europe.

However, the system created an unworkable fragmentation of political parliamentary parties: a representation that oscillated between 12 and 16 parties. Moreover, the system did not create among Italians great faith in government. In fact, there is a curious paradox in Italy: a high percentage of voters and a high level of mistrust of government and political institutions. Italy has the lowest index of public satisfaction of any West European industrial state. Surveys taken in the 80s showed the level of trust in the political parties to be only around 10 per cent. In comparison with the turnover rate of members of parliament in other democracies (France, Germany, England, USA), Italy's is constantly higher: each new parliament is approximately made up of one-third of new members.[1]

In politics *all'italiana*, until 1993, although political parties were at the core of the system, personalities did play a role. For the House of Deputies especially, even though many voters simply voted for the party and did not bother to indicate a candidate, voters could express the **preference vote**. They could favor three or more candidates, according to the size of the electoral district. The personal votes were counted and the candidates of each party were ranked accordingly. If a party won, say, six seats in a particular district these would have been given to the six candidates with the most preference votes. A candidate could run for election in more than one district (and many leaders did!) and, if s/he won in more than one, could decide which district to represent. In this case the first of the non-elected obtained the seat that was not filled. The first of the non-elected could also `succeed' a deceased deputy or one who retired during the life of a Parliament.

The **preference vote** system was exploited by the Italian political parties to pull in as many votes as possible. Not only did political parties allow the same very popular individuals to be candidates in more than one district, but they presented lists of candidates that were much larger than seats available. Even though some of the names put on the list did not have any chance of winning, they were given a spot for the simple fact that they could attract a certain number of votes for the party. In preparation for the 1987 parliamentary elections, leaders of the Radical Party had the idea of including Ilona Anna Staller, better known as Cicciolina, a hard-core porno star on their roster of candidates. The intention was to increase interest in the party, which pledged to fight for human rights, including the rights of homosexuals and prostitutes. To show the absurdity of the system, nearly 20,000 voters of the Rome-Viterbo-Latina-Frosinone district chose Cicciolina and she became a legislator. A prostitute became the *onorevole* Cicciolina, member of the house of deputies!

Parties handsomely rewarded those who pulled in votes. There was a constant link between elections, governments and ministerial appointments. The proportional system was, in a sense, applied to the distribution of government positions and these, in turn, depended to a large extent on the preference system. The preference vote, when sufficiently high, opened the door to the continuous holding of ministerial power. Moreover, as the preference vote was the main avenue for political promotion and, given the clientele nature of the system—more votes were translated into more power of patronage, which returned more votes next time around—campaigns for election did acquire a personal flavor. This system created a high degree of stability: a good **preference vote** opened the door to a ministerial position, a ministerial position enabled the holder to exercise patronage, and this in turn increased the size of his personal vote. When sufficiently high, the preference vote opened the door to continuous holding of ministerial power, and the system got locked-up in *immobilismo*.

The method used for the Senate elections was less proportional than the one used for the Chamber of Deputies election and was more favorable to the two largest parties (*D.C.* and *P.C.I.*). For the senate, each party presented only one candidate and the election was carried on regional representation.

Italy's electoral system was geared to a country emerging from Fascism into the cold war. However, even though proportional representation was intended to foster minority parties and discourage monolithic groups like the communists or disbanded Fascists, and provided high level of democratic representation that the system provided, **proportional representation Italian style** produced several problems. It created 52 unstable coalition governments and an unworkable fragmentation of parliamentary parties—with no fewer than 16 being represented in the early 1990s. It made decision making more difficult and did not offer the electorate a clear-cut alternative between potential governments. In that kind of system, the Italian electorate could only influence a possible coalition by strengthening a particular party's parliamentary representation; it did not vote for a future government.

Although political power remained concentrated in the political parties and members of the Italian parliament were elected on the basis of party representation, the latter could act independently of the party because they could use a secret ballot through which they were able to avoid party discipline. And many times it was through such independence that governments fell and political crises became more difficult to solve.

In the eighties and early nineties, proportional representation *all'italiana* encouraged the proliferation of protest movements, local and one-issue groups which, in the 1992 April national elections, fielded more than five hundred slates of candidates. Altogether, a record sixteen parties achieved representation in the national parliament, even though only six of them polled more than five per cent of the total vote. Italian political leaders bickered about reforms for many years with little progress. The small parties were strongly opposed to both the German and French models. In Germany, a party cannot win seats in the national parliament unless it polls at least 5 per cent of the total vote; in France, the major parties benefit heavily from a system keyed to a single constituencies, only partly corrected by recourse to a second round of balloting if no candidate wins out on the first. In Italy, the *D.C.* would have been the main beneficiary under either model, but all, or most of its traditional allies (republicans, liberals, social democrats) would have been wiped out. As we shall see later, because of the fall of communism and the uncovering of political mega-scandals, the will of political leaders was not enough to maintain the status quo.

Partitocracy and Dictatorship in Democracy

However, one of the major problems of the Italian democracy has been the fact that it is a party-dominated system, sometimes referred to as a **partitocracy**, *partitocrazia*. In essence, it means that the formal democratic institutions of government and elections played only secondary roles. Parochial interests of the parties were so strong that they determined the creation and the fall of cabinets. It was the strength or weakness of political parties which determines the nature of the coalitions. However, the size of popular support and political influence were not necessarily correlated. To a large extent, the c-hanges in the governing coalition were primarily the result of party politics rather than popular decisions through elections. This could certainly be illustrated by the fact that the Republican Party, with only a popular support around five percent, shaped many government coalitions, headed many ministries and directed, under its leader, Giovanni Spadolini, the first non-Christian Democratic government.

Americans are well acquainted with the "spoils system" (President Andrew Jackson once said: "to the victor belongs the spoils") that enables a newly elected President (Governor, Mayor, or even County Executive, etc.) to replace the appointees of the previous administration with his own handpicked loyalists. The spoils system, Italian style, is inspired by the same principle, but, by force of circumstances, it is far more complex and has a much wider impact on the country.

Until 1994, political appointments were made in every sector of the Italian economy, from senior diplomatic posts to positions in education, to opera houses, to the sanitation department, to the health service at the local supermarket. In many cases, political appointments started at the top of the management ladder and continued, less officially, to the bottom. For example, most singers at La Scala were connected with the Socialist Party, because that was the leading party in Milan in the 1980s. The party with the most votes got to dish out the most jobs and favors. The patronage system, called *lottizzazione*, worked just like that.

The political parties claimed that their civil servants, managers, bankers, etc. were qualified and efficient. However, we know that such a system, because of its very nature, does not reward quality and easily suffer from excessive abuse. For example, a Milan politician from the Socialist Party who was caught accepting bribes, did not even bother to hide his computer lists of job candidates recommended by his electorate. The lists, which included names of family members, favors granted and political sponsors, was not proof of illegal behavior, as it was not illegal to exchange favors for votes. Regularly, lists of political appointments appeared in local newspapers. At the end of the 1980s, in Milan, a Christian Democrat was named to head the local garbage disposal authority, while a Socialist got the management of the airports and a Social Democrat the city's drugstores. The national health service, the state-owned television networks and banks were among the *lottizzazione* monster's favorite lairs. So, too, was government-controlled industry, grouped under three enormous holding companies. The largest, *Istituto per la Ricostruzione Industriale* (*IRI*), was headed by a member of the Christian Democratic party. The other two, *Ente Nazionale Idrocarburi* (*ENI*)–the state hydrocarbon company–and (*EFIM*)–manufacturing enterprises–were headed by Socialist appointees and had Christian Democratic vice chairmen.

The patronage system is a man-headed monster that won't die easily. The Italian public sector–excluding the massive state holding companies–employs 19 per cent of the work force at the beginning of the 1990s. With unemployment at 11 per cent (about 20 per cent in the South), the monster will always have plenty of breathing space.

To correct the problem, some economists and politicians put pressure on government to reduce the public sector through **privatization.** That is exactly what Italy has been doing in the past few years after much political fighting. It has been a heroic decision because the parties wanted to hang on to their quotas of management jobs, known in Italy as *poltrone*, "armchairs." With public-sector businesses and banks accounting for nearly half of the fifty largest Italian companies in terms of revenue, there were plenty of "armchairs" at stake! To their credit, it must be said that, in spite of the corruption, political parties do not operate in a vacuum. Budgetary problems, the impending union with the rest of Europe and population discontent brought them to the realization that changes were in the best interest of both the nation and the parties.

Indeed, the results of Spring 1992 general elections convinced politicians that the people wanted radical changes. Protest votes hurt the parties most closely associated with the spoils system: the long time ruling coalition of Christian Democrats, Socialists, liberals and Social Democrats. Parties such as the federalist-minded Leagues in the North, *La Lega*, and the anti-Christian Democrat *La Rete* (Network Party) in the South picked up votes from Italians weary of government mismanagement. The biggest changes, however, came as result of the end of the Communist Party.

The Communist Struggle

Italians have not just been weary of government mismanagement, they have also been weary of most traditional political parties. Indeed, they have grown weary of the *classe politica*, the political class. During the long years of Cold War they expressed their disappointment by voting Communist. This means that many Italians voted Communist in those years, not because they firmly believed in Communism, but because they disliked the other parties.

This political behavior had positive, not negative, implications for democratic stability. It gave Italy a political balance and produced profound social reform, most likely unattainable without the presence of a strong Communist Party.

It should be reiterated that the Italian Communist Party was almost unique in its brand of Communist ideology. It was in a position quite different from the East-Bloc Communist Parties ousted from power at the beginning of the 1990s. It had deep, emotional roots in Italy as a workers' and anti-Fascist movement before, during and after WWII, and in the 1970s it was the leader in the Euro-Communist movement, breaking with Moscow on many policy issues and trying to project Marxism as a valid choice within a democratic society.

By rejecting Moscow's direction, Eurocommunism was to be understood as an evolution within Western culture rather than as a revolutionary disruption of it. Resonating in Eurocommunism was Antonio Gramsci's faith that, within Western culture, the Italian branch of Communism was already peculiarly fitted for a humanism of technology and work.

Communists like Antonio Gramsci and Enrico Berlinguer are major historical figures and are even regarded as heroes; many of Italy's top intellectuals, artists, writers and performers have been Communists, and the party generally had the reputation of being more socially active and less corrupt than other major parties.

The Communist Party, too, like other political manifestations, embraced many paradoxes. As the largest, strongest, and in many ways, the most able of Communist parties found among democracies, the party not only refrained from any subversive or revolutionary assaults on democratic institutions and processes, at critical moments it even acted unambiguously to support and reinforce them. Despite the Vatican anti-Communist crusade, the Communist Party was supported by many practicing Catholics and, contrary to all expectations, it was strongest in some of the wealthiest regions of the peninsula and often weakest in the poorest regions.

Though it regularly claimed one-quarter to one-third of the electorate and had considerable power in local governments, the *P.C.I.* was never able to lead a national government. This was due, in part, to an unwritten US veto of a Communist Party rule in a country that was a key NATO member. Without the possibility of being part of a coalition government, the *P.C.I.* remained cut off from Italy's other left-wing parties, such as the Socialists and Social Democrats, both of which were allied with the *D.C.* to form most coalition governments until the early 1990s. However, as we shall see later, the Communist Party was the most important cultural presence in post-war Italian society, even more important than the *D.C.*

The party used a strategy which involved the working-class movement putting itself at the head of an alliance of social forces against monopoly capitalism and the political remnants of Fascism and advancing towards socialism through a combination of legal mass agitations and protests, a full use of the parliamentary and electoral machinery and a constant effort of ideological penetration and struggle. The strategy was designed progressively to disarm the forces of monopoly and reaction and shift the balance of economic and political power democratically towards the working class and its allies.

The party's postwar strategy was also centered on a cultural policy of the masses. Firstly, it sought to manage its own sector of popular culture, to build its own capillary networks of cultural apparatuses (a party press, publishing houses, libraries and sites of popular recreation) and thereby to penetrate "civil society" at all levels right down to the smallest local area. For the post-war Communist Party, popular culture came to mean very largely both autochthonous "folk" or class-based traditions; the "people's culture" was connected with positive notions of popular songs, and so forth, and popular education. It should also be added that in the *P.C.I.* these meanings became distinctively associated with others: "popular culture" was connected with positive notions of popular community, solidarity and tradition; working-class education was connected to a project of popular enlightenment and acculturation which, in turn, was closely linked with the party's long-term political project of working-class hegemony. Second, it sought to win over and mobilize intellectuals, whether "great intellectuals" (leading cultural figures) or middle strata intellectuals engaged in cultural work: teachers, journalists, workers in the theater, film, publishing or broadcasting industries. This meant building a party presence in existing cultural organizations by recruiting new members or attracting fellow travellers. Third, the party sought to project a particular set of cultural values, to promote an aesthetic and a morality which were social and collective rather than individualist or private, progressive rather than decadent, outward-looking rather than introspective, centered upon public civic participation rather than upon private activity and consumption.

While the party created a wide appeal through its cultural programs, it never became convincing enough through its ideology to win over enough voters to become the leading party and take over the government. Certainly, the winds of change that were transforming the Communist states of Eastern Europe into democracies had a determining effect on the fate of the *P.C.I.* In 1992 it changed its name, calling itself the ***Partito Democratico della Sinistra*** (***P.D.S.***), the Democratic Party of the Left, and re-emerged as a new, non-Communist entity that hoped to integrate with Europe's Social Democratic Left and, eventually, come to power. The hammer and sickle that it had held aloft for 69 years was retained, but in a reduced form, submerged beneath the roots of a large, leafy tree that is the dominant emblem. The action was not meant to be a "self-dissolution" of the party, or cutting the roots; rather, it attempted to give the roots new sap, hopefully leading to a new political formation of the Italian Left that would group Communists, left-wing Catholics, Greens, radicals and other reformists and progressive forces.

Old-guard traditionalists, however, felt that Italian Communism was not a worn-out relic but a proud symbol of resistance to Fascism and the construction of a postwar democracy in Italy. Therefore, they claimed, changing the party so radically and ridding it of its Communist identity would dishonor the party's past. Representing about one-third of the party's membership and including key elder statesmen, these people wanted restructuring, but only within a Communist framework. They founded the ***Partito di Rifondazione Comunista*** (Party of Communist Refoundation). They were relics of a political apparatus that had influenced obliquely the course of postwar Italian history and had contributed to the paradoxical "stability within instability" of the Italian political system.

Stability within Instability

Italy's legendary "instability" was an artful illusion in the power game. Despite the air of *opera buffa*, Italian politicians were able, through shrewd maneuverings, to mold one of the most stable democracies in the western world. Foreigners may have talked about instability, but Italians complained of the total immobility, *immobilismo*, of their political system. What Italy did not have was the alternation in power between different political parties common to other western countries. This is perhaps the most peculiar aspect of the Italian system until 1994.

In fact, there was a hidden stability in the Italian political system. Italy actually held two political records. In addition to having had the highest number of governments in the post-war period, Italy is also the only Western democracy in which one political party dominated the government for about fifty years. Italy and Japan were, in fact, the only two industrial democracies in which the same party governed uninterrupted for about fifty years. Alliance and strategies changed, but the Christian Democratic Party remained at the head of 49 of the 52 governments and held the highest number of Cabinet posts in all of them.

Stability also came from a second source. The many changes in governments were rarely due to serious political crises. Much more common in Italy was the "crisis" that was really a disagreement among political leaders or a clash of personalities. This kind of political dispute was fairly easy to solve. The heads of political parties most often patched up their differences and formed a new government, sometimes in a matter of a few days. Occasionally, the "new" government were exact replicas of the earlier ones. The Italians called these "photocopy governments." In fact, the recycling of the same people in government after government was another stabilizing element in Italian democracy.

However, the long longevity in power of many politicians, while provided stability, instituted a kind of dictatorship in a very democratic system. A case in point is the government crisis that occurred in the Spring of 1991. Because of disagreements among the parties in the government coalition, Prime Minister Giulio Andreotti resigned. A few weeks later, he was replaced by none other than Prime Minister Giulio Andreotti, initiating his seventh term as the nation's leader. More than any other politician, Andreotti had become the symbol of Christian Democratic permanent power. Andreotti served in the first post-war cabinet in 1946 and remained at the center of power until 1993. Besides being Prime Minister seven times, he was also Minister of Defense, Minister of the Interior and Minister of Foreign Affairs. Nor is he a unique case; there are several other Christian Democrat notables who have had careers of equal longevity.

How did politicians like Andreotti survive so long? Andreotti belonged to a world of compromise, flexibility, pragmatism, shrewed political maneuverings, and ruthless Realpolitik. As Andreotti himself observed with characteristic wit: "I am typically Italian, typically Roman and therefore untranslatable and unexportable." In the 1960s he was a leader of the Christian Democratic right wing, opposing the entrance of the socialists into the government. Then, in the mid-1970s, he headed the first Italian government supported by the Italian Communist Party. He established his reputation as ardently pro-NATO, but began flirting with the Soviet Union long before Gorbachev arrived on the scene. As Foreign Minister during the "Achille Lauro" hijacking, he allowed the alleged terrorists to slip from Italian custody, presumably because of his design for Italian policy in the Mideast. "In Italy we have the idea that politics is like the tailor's art. If you have to make a suit for a hunch-back, the suit will be crooked," a friend of mine told me.

Compromise and flexibility were almost a necessity in the first decades of the postwar period. Italy was violently split, with threats from the extreme right and left, and the center divided. An American approach of frontal confrontation would have led to civil war in Italy. The *D.C.* deserves credit for lifting Italy out of chronic poverty and for maintaining democracy. However, the *D.C.* should be criticized for its positions after 1980. It continued to maintain itself through the patronage system and allowed a thin line of demarcation between patronage and Mafia in many areas. With the Cold War over, and the Italian Communist Party split and deprived of much of its potency, part of the rationale for the Christian Democratic power system vanished. It was no longer necessary to tolerate corruption and Mafia influence to assure the triumph of light over darkness, so the calls for serious, systemic change had become deafening in 1992. Even the ex-president of the Republic, Francesco Cossiga, a Christian Democrat, sounded the alarm, talking about scrapping the Italian constitution and writing a new one. "The Mafia has taken effective control over the southern third of the country," said the president, "and Italy's system of coalition democracy has become unmanageable." The revelations of political corruption brought to light through "operation clean hands" created such vehemence against the political system by the Italians that political parties could not squabble anymore. Most political leaders had to accept the hard reality that Italy needed to become a "normal" democracy of alternating governments with clear electoral mandates. However, it was not easy to find a credible alternative to the *D.C.*

The Italian political system was unquestionably full of paradoxes when it is compared to other democracies. But comparison of one democracy with another can easily lead to misleading evaluations. In doing that, we would be inclined to believe that American or some other brand of democracy is a "template that can be stenciled onto almost any other country and produce similar effects there. We forget the spectacular failures that followed past efforts to export the American-British constitutional formula to Latin American, Asian and African countries."[2] We all know that no democratic country will look entirely reassuring when measured against some abstract, idealized conception of a democratic state, but the Italian system did need some profound tuning. Nevertheless, in engaging in radical institutional reform to prepare for the "second republic," Italy cannot work in absolute abstraction, even though Italy may pride herself of having always been a great inventor in the field of politics. The experience throughout the centuries— from the days of the Roman Empire to the period of the Renaissance city-states, through unification and finally even during the Fascist dictatorship—as a laboratory for the political experiments of all Western civilization should not be detached from the learning experience that other modern democracies may offer. The most difficult test is the present.

Notes

1. Nothing can be compared to the failings of the American system. Presidents and the large majority of legislators are usually elected with the votes of less than 30 per cent of the people eligible to vote. And that cannot be called a mandate. Moreover, of those who do vote, hundreds of thousands of citizens have no real choice of legislative candidates because they live in one of the dozen of districts where the incumbent runs unopposed or faces an opponent so underfinanced that he has no real chance to bring

candidates because they live in one of the dozen of districts where the incumbent runs unopposed or faces an opponent so underfinanced that he has no real chance to bring his case before the public.

The fairness of the American elections has been compromised by the enormous advantages incumbents have over challengers in terms of campaign fund raising, access to the ballot, legislative mailing privileges, control of the redistricting process and ability to dole out "member-item" funds (given to legislators for pet projects in their districts). The increasing ability of incumbents to use the perquisites of power to underwrite their re-election campaigns explains why the incumbent re-election rate for New York State legislators reached 98 per cent during the 1980s.

Italy not only meets the conditions of poliarchy; it manages to do so under a range of existential factors that, in many other places, would make democratic polyarchy highly improbable, or place it in jeopardy.

2. Joseph La Palombara, *Democracy Italian Style* (New Haven: Yale University Press, 1987), p. 6.

II

Decisive Turning Points and Constitutional Transformation

Ouster of the Communists

As has been stated, the Italian political system can be seen as very chaotic or so stable to be characterized *immobile* or stagnant. Regardless of the perception, we must realize that the Italian democracy has gone through an evolution culminating in some profound constitutional changes. Although the process has been continuous, one can identify five decisive turning points: De Gasperi's ouster of the Communists from government, the "opening to the left," the unrealized "historic compromise," the "fall of Communism," and the "Second Republic."

De Gasperi's expulsion of the Communists from government, with American assistance, was probably the most important turning point in modern Italian history. In 1947 the Left was in a strong position as a result of its role in the anti-Fascist Partisan movement, as we have seen. With this momentum behind it there were striking indications that it could take over Italy in a very few years unless some decisive political actions were taken. Most *P.S.I.* (Socialist Party) leaders, prompted by the myth of "working class unity" and by the expectation that the Soviet army would soon become the dominant force throughout Europe, chose to play secondary role to the *P.C.I.* rather than position their party as a third force between the Christian Democrats and Communists. However, America's intervention and intelligent manuverings by some Italian politicians saved Italy from Communism.

The objective was reached by splitting the socialist party. With encouragement and financial support from US unions and skillful CIA work, many PSI representatives and about one-third of the socialist voters split away to form a Social Democratic Party (*P.S.D.I.*) under the leadership of Giuseppe Saragat.[1] The split, finalized early in 1947, a few days after *D.C.* premier Alcide De Gasperi's return from a visit to Washington, divided the "working class unity" and paved the way to the "unloading" of the Communists from government. The action had also drawn the battle lines for the following general election in the Spring of 1948: Communists and Socialists ran on a joint ticket under the label of "People's Bloc," while the Christian Democrats led a centrist coalition which included Social Democrats, Liberals, and Republicans.

The results of the election went better than expected for the *D.C.* and its alliance. They came close to polling an absolute majority of the votes, scoring an oversized victory. Millions of Italians, who under normal circumstances would have voted either for some rightist party or for some moderate left-of-center faction, cast their ballots for De Gasperi's party as the only available alternative to Communism. The new Social Democratic Party got 7 per cent of the votes. Despite the rather poor performance of the Republicans (*P.R.I.*) and the Liberals (*P.L.I.*) who ran under the label of National Bloc, the centrist governmental coalition won the support of 62 per cent of the electorate, twice as much as the Communist-led Popular Front. The feeling that De Gasperi and the US had saved Italy from Communism was widespread even among the representatives of social groups and economic interests which had not voted for the *D.C.* or had done so with great reluctance.

However, the weakened left still worried the US government because it enjoyed the support of a strong labor union. There was deep conviction that unless workers were snatched away from the leftist labor union through labor issues, the left could have easily regained influence. This led US representatives to press hard for an immediate confluence into a new national union of all workers who were no longer willing to accept the Communist-Socialist leadership of *C.G.I.L.*, the single, all-embracing labor organization revived during the last year of the war. In the summer of 1948 a new national labor union, *C.I.S.L.*, was founded to attract Catholic union members. These political events were a major setback for Communism in Italy from which the party never regained the power to enter government again.

Notwithstanding the changes, the new government, free of the presence of Socialists and Communists, was unable to make the radical changes the new democratic society needed. De Gasperi's task in tackling a full spectrum of reforms was difficult because his centrist coalition included both the non-Communist Left and the moderate Right whose views on social and economic issues are notoriously far apart. The country needed to implement long overdue tax and land reforms as well as a thorough overhauling of the bureaucratic apparatus and of the economic system itself in order to improve the lot of the most destitute and forgotten groups: farm laborers especially in the South, most defenseless before the onslaught of inflation; small industries which had been allowed to wither and die; and labor's stepchildren, the unskilled workers. There was little awareness of the danger that in Italy political stability might turn into stagnation or that the reconstruction drive itself would result in a substantial restoration of old economic and social structures.

For the next decade, labor remained Italy's cheapest commodity—to the fortune of the few who had the money to hire and to the misfortune of the many who had only their labor to offer for hire. For millions of peasants who toiled in the fields, the only hope for change remained emigration. The country continued to be good for the rich, bad for the poor. Economic and political power continued to be vested in few hands: mostly landowners in the South, big business and industrialists in the north. A professional class of politicians, drawn mostly from the swollen ranks of lawyers and university professors, provided a parliamentary veneer. The Catholic Church extended its power in every aspect of life.

Notwithstanding the "economic miracle," by 1961 Italy presented a great discrepancy in the rates of material and civic progress. She unquestionably had all the ingredients for a successful democracy, but neither its social and institutional structure nor its administrative practices had been brought in line by the 1960s with those of the modern Western democracies. The country still lacked an equitable tax system, a farsighted approach to land tenure and agricultural problems, antitrust legislation, efficient regulatory agencies in the fields of power, trade, labor relations, etc., and a modern educational system. Under mounting conservative pressure within the coalition, the progress had been too little. Even the great economic expansion of those years, unattended by adequate social progress and institutional modernization, failed to produce political dividends for the government coalition. The only way to have corrected this situation would have been to strike out on a bold course of social and economic reforms designed to appeal to the bulk of the Communist and Socialist voters.

A transitional government leaning toward a more stable political solution, approved in Parliament with the backing of the neo-Fascists, was greeted by the worst post-war threat to the state and indicated the limitations of political choices in government the Italian people would accept. The danger to Italian democracy posed by this situation became manifest with the bloody riots which swept many parts of the country in July, 1960 taking a toll of 11 dead and more than 1,000 injured. This government, headed by Fernando Tambroni, which survived only two months, remains the sole "attempt" in post-war Italy of a government supported by the neo-Fascist party.

Opening to the Left and the Profound Social Changes
The "**opening to the left**" in the early 1960s, which brought the Socialist Party of Italy (*P.S.I.*), previously in electoral alliance with the Communist Party (*P.C.I.*), into a governing coalition with the Christian Democrats, Republicans, and Social Democrats, offered the opportunity for broadening and consolidating popular support for Italy's democratic institutions as well as for her secure anchorage to the West. By 1962 such an opening appeared possible and desirable to the majority of *D.C.* leaders. Along with an internal evolution, two things happened outside of the party to render the move to the left possible. First, the accession, as we shall see later, of Angelo Roncalli to the papacy in 1958 had boxed-off right-wing clerics in the Vatican. Second, Pietro Nenni's Socialist Party found itself weakened by its de facto alliance with the Communists. Whereas the *P.C.I.* continued steadily to construct its own separate realm, the Socialists, behaving as a traditional party, lost followers to

the *P.C.I.* while winning none from the right. With some new *D.C.* leaders insisting that some of the gains of the economic miracle be applied to such problems as welfare, health, old-age pensions, and education, a reformist majority within the *P.S.I.*, willing to give the *D.C.* a chance to cut its links to political corruption, clerical reaction, and economic injustice, sealed the bargain. Fortunately, John F. Kennedy understood that the US would hurt its own interests if it continued to oppose an opening to the Socialists—it would have also contributed to pushing them back into the arms of the Communists. The "opening" turned out to be the first concrete step in a far-reaching realignment of Italy's political forces aimed at isolating the largest Communist party in the west and forming a stable governmental majority resting on a wider and more solid foundation of popular support.

The center-left government of the sixties may be criticized for many excesses in labor legislation and wasteful public expenditures, but it increased democratization in every area of the life of the country. A center-right coalition with the then extremely conservative liberals, and depending on parliamentary support from the neo-Fascist *M.S.I.*, might have polarized Italian society and blocked needed social and economic reforms. In fact, the "opening to the left" was achieved only after a disastrous attempt to seek support from the right.

American foreign policy, shortsighted most of the times, acted wisely in recognizing these realities and giving the green light to the center-left in 1961-1963, reversing the futile policies of Ambassador Clare Booth Luce, who wanted a Christian Democratic alliance with the Monarchists, and of Deputy Chief of Mission Outerbridge Horsey, who, a few years later, was so hostile to the Socialists (and Republicans) that he considered a government dependent on the support of the neo-Fascists a better means of protecting U.S. interests.

The failings and shortcomings of the center and center-left coalitions helped the Communists not only to keep their role as the main opposition force but to increase their share of the popular vote from just over 20 percent in the late 1940s to almost 35 percent in the mid-1970s.

Teasing with the "Historic Compromise"

The third "turning point" was the failure of the Communist Party's efforts, after its electoral successes of 1972 and 1976, to form a "**historic compromise**" government with the Christian Democrats in 1977-1978.

In the election of 1976, during the last months of the Ford Administration, the Communists achieved their all-time high in an Italian election, 34.4 percent of the vote. They were extending their hegemony in every important area of Italian life—the schools, the press, the judiciary, the trade unions, regional and local governments. It seemed inevitable that they would soon enter the government in a "historic compromise" coalition with the Christian Democrats, possibly compromising both Italian freedom and the country's support of the Western Alliance.

In this atmosphere of crisis, the Carter Administration was pressured with bad advice from two extremes of the US political spectrum. From the right came demands for the US to take a direct role in stopping the Communist threat, through covert operations if necessary. The other bit of bad advice came from the other end of the political spectrum which argued that the *PCI*'s accession to power was both inevitable and desirable. Both groups stood on solid ground in making their argument. Carter gave serious consideration to the counterproductive effects of past covert operations. The Communists were extraordinary experts in giving wide publicity to leaks on covert financing operations by Americans and had been very successful in gaining popular support as the defender of the country's sovereignty against "American domination." Incautious statements made by US officials during this period that appeared to threaten Italy with reprisals if it gave the Communist party a governing role were also detrimental. During the Nixon-Ford years, the P.C.I. had gained in two national elections, raising its vote share from 26.9 percent to 34.4 percent, while steadily extending its influence in key sectors of national life.

The Carter Administration shared with the previous administration the opposition to any formula involving the Communist Party's entry into the government in Italy and the determination to do everything possible to avoid such a development. But there was a clear difference over the strategy to be followed. Ford's and Kissinger's strategy was keyed to the concept of 'trench warfare': hammer away rigidly on American hostility to *P.C.I.*'s participation in the government by means of threatening warnings about its consequences in the international field. Carter's strategy, instead, was built on the concept of `mobile warfare': avoid head-on clashes, resort to a more flexible and indirect method of an outflanking maneuver. This had very positive effects in this critical moment in Italian post-war history. The fundamental result of Prime Minister Andreotti's trip to Washington (July 1977) brought about, through an operation quite typical of Andreotti's, the apparent reconciliation of two opposed purposes. The Premier went back to Rome after having won Washington's green light for a political formula that involved Communist cooperation after having persuaded the Americans that he and his party were intransigently anti-Communist. The Americans bet on Andreotti's consummate skills as a politician and his ability to manage to keep the Communists out of government while governing with their assent.

However, acts of terrorism raised some fears of possible, uncontrollable radical political turns. Even though Italian society had shown itself to be tough and remarkably shock-resistant, the terrorists were trying to demonstrate that it was falling apart. The continued high level of street violence unquestionably carried sinister implications for the future. The wave of riots and terrorism were viewed by the great law-abiding majority of Italians as further evidence of their government's inability to govern and it was making the Communists look increasingly like a party of law and order. The situation was such that the American Administration had to be more explicit on the "Communist issue" in Italy, that is, make greater efforts to underline its 'preference' for political formulas keeping the Communists out of government. Carter, therefore, made public statements that while the US was committed to non-interference in the domestic affairs of any country in Western Europe, it did not want the Communist parties to have an influential or dominant role in the governments of those countries. The best way to help assure that communist parties did not come to power in Western European countries was for democratic parties to meet the aspirations of their people for more effective, more just, and more compassionate government. The Carter Administration used every means available to present its position which was being distorted by the technique of disinformation by a large sector of the Italian mass media. Under the pretext of making a non-political trip to Italy, Joseph Califano, US secretary for Health, Education, and Welfare and the representative of the Italian Americans in the Carter Administration, stated that "the Americans of Italian origin are increasingly aware of the situation in Italy and overwhelmingly want Italy to be free, strong, and non-Communist."

It is hard to gauge the impact the US move had on the future course of events. It was certainly a shot in the arm for many *DC*s, Socialists, Social Democrats, Republicans, and Liberals who looked with dismay at a Communist participation in the national government, and it gave pause to the political factions and individuals in the democratic camp as well as to the economic groups which favored or were ready to underwrite such a participation. The results of this well-planned position, very democratic in nature, were strengthened by the effects of an incident which was part of a revolutionary campaign against the state. As many times before, history may have been changed in its course by events that had the opposite effect from that for which the event was planned. The kidnapping and assassination of Italian Premier Aldo Moro by the Red Brigade was the beginning of the end of any possible "historical compromise" between the Communists and the democratic forces of Italy. The outrage touched the heart and soul of the Italian people, and the elections of that year reflected the outrage.

By the end of 1978, Communist leaders, including Enrico Berlinguer, the top advocate of the "historic compromise," decided to cut their losses by taking the party back into the opposition. This precipitated new general elections which were held in June 1979, two years ahead of schedule. The Communist share of the popular vote dropped from more than 34 percent to just over 30 percent. The myth of the *PCI*'s inexorable, irreversible advance was shattered. In the next several years, the overall Communist performance at the polls showed a marked downtrend: by 1988, the party's vote was cut by almost one-third from its 1976 peak.

The 1979 elections paved the way for a new phase of Italian politics featured by a revival of the center-left coalition. Compared with the government formed after the opening to the *P.S.I.* back in the early 1960s, the reconstituted coalition reflected some significant changes in the political landscape. It included not only a strengthened Republican Party and a Social Democratic Party overshadowed by the newly reorganized *P.S.I.*, but also the Liberals were freed from the conservative approach and leadership which over 20 years earlier had set them on a course of strenuous opposition to the center-left policies. Even more important was the trend toward a more balanced relationship between the *D.C.* and their lay partners, the Socialists first of all. This trend was fueled by the *D.C.* losses at the poll, which, however, was balanced by the growth of the *P.S.I.* vote which powered the party's ambition to win a top role in running national affairs by overtaking the fading Communists, developing a more and more "competitive" collaboration with the weakened Christian Democrats and eventually replacing them as the leading partner in a revamped government coalition. In the 1980s, under Bettino Craxi's leadership, the Socialist Party put an end to the *D.C.* hegemony over the government and to the Communist hegemony over the Italian left. The collapse of the "historic compromise" gave the Socialists a new opportunity to perform as the kingpin of Italian politics. Craxi's *P.S.I.* adopted a pragmatic approach to social and economic affairs, wholly discarding the doctrinaire Marxism which had been a strong and disastrous feature of traditional Italian Socialism. Much before the collapse of the communist block, the *P.S.I.* party symbol was changed from the hammer and sickle to the red carnation. The power in government shared with the communists in local administration gradually came to an end. Italy could enter into a new phase of social and economic changes without the specter of Communism.

The Fall of Communism: Is There a Free Lunch?

The fall of Communism in the countries of Eastern Europe brought about the most radical changes in the Italian political system. Before the fall of Communism Italian elections were as dull and predictable as the turning of the seasons. Despite the country's endless crises and revolving-door governments, every election since 1948 had produced the same result: the Christian Democrats came in first, followed very closely by the Communists. More than any other country in Western Europe, Italy was frozen into political immobility by the Cold War. Politics had become so stable or "stagnant" that shifts of 2 or

3 percentage points were regarded as major electoral changes. The fall of Communism changed all this.

The startling changes in Eastern Europe called into question the core of the traditional politics in Italy too. The fall of the pillars on which Communism had been built over several decades and the shattering of many illusions and myths called for complete reassessment of political behavior and prompted the need for a new set of myths. But the yearning for a distinctively different and better society did not generate quick new recipes, or at least no special recipes.

As in the rest of the democratic West, Italy experienced a "letdown" which made the Italians more aware of the costs than of the benefits of their victory in the confrontation with the Communist East. Mounting frustration and resentment over the apparent failure to reap quick and bountiful "peace dividends" turned into a wholesale indictment of the political and economic groups that had been in control of the nation's affairs in the previous decades.

The end of the "frozen party system," therefore, and the surge of nontraditional political groups, did not come as a consequence of the emergence of a new ideology, rather they are the result of the complete collapse of *an* ideology. Consequently, new political attitudes will have looser political ties to parties and weaker partisan identification. In turn, this means that more Italians are effectively "in the market," shopping around at election time and available to experiment with new alternatives. The consequent broken political system could mean that relatively minor squabbles could provoke the making and remaking of cabinets with minor adjustments and realignments designed mostly to suit factional interests and personal ambitions rather than to reflect policy priorities.

All things considered, the potential for a restructuring of the party system became unavoidable. But the illusion, apparent in many quarters and propagated by the media, that institutional reforms by themselves will cure all the ills of the society is worrisome. If the history of past reform efforts in Italy is a reliable guide, the re-definition of the traits of the political system will be a long drawn out, painstaking process. At the end of the tunnel, it will be discovered that political engineering is no panacea; it can solve some problems but is not a cure-all medicine. All political arrangements have costs. In politics, too, "there is no such thing as a free lunch."

Aged System: Change or Collapse?

It is important to point out that the **erosion** of loyalty to the traditional political parties, which shook up the system in the early 1990s had already been slowly developing with other social and economic changes. The rapid decline of the agricultural sector, the secularization of life and growing liberalism, the occupational and geographical mobility, the higher education level of most of the population which transformed Italian society, had already affected the way society responded to politics as reflected in an increased distrust for the traditional political parties. Although the *D.C.* and the *P.C.I.* had remained the most important parties until 1991, their percentage of votes had been declining. Their combined vote dropped from 73.1 per cent in 1976 to 62.8 per cent in 1983. The party that had been gaining the most was the *P.S.I.*

The fall of Communism may have been the catalyst which coalesced all the distrust that had been increasingly developing through the years. In fact, the political earthquake recorded in the election of Spring, 1992 was mostly the result of pentup anger at the Christian Democrats-led government, long held in check by the fear of Communism.

The Cold War had caused a political immobility. The *D.C.* and the *P.C.I.*, although adversaries, had reinforced one another: fear of the Communists kept the Christian Democrats in power, and intense dissatisfaction with the government kept the Communists strong. There was little room in the middle for the smaller parties, which became satellites of the two big ones. With the collapse of communism, however, the situation became fluid. According to polls, at least 20 per cent of the vote was suddenly up for grabs. Some feared that the new climate of political despair might set the stage for a sharp swing to the authoritarian right. Italy's neo-fascist party, *Movimento Sociale Italiano* (*M.S.I.*) adopted Cossiga's pick-axe as its party symbol and embraced his calls for a presidential republic. There was also an outbreak of neo-Nazi violence with its worst manifestations against illegal immigrants. However, most Italians are more interested in integration with the rest of Europe than in the revival of nationalism. In fact, the new elections did not give stronger political basis to the neo-fascist party, but they also made more chaotic the political landscape. The vacuum of political leadership was filled by a proliferation of special-interest and anti-system parties. There were two different environmental parties, numerous regional parties, even a hunters' party and a pensioners' party. The real novelty was something called the Party of Love, started by porn star Moana Pozzi, who wanted to follow her friend and colleague Cicciolina into parliament. It could have been very possible in an electoral system which gives representation in parliament even to a party collecting only one percent of the votes. Governing Italy was difficult enough with 12 parties represented in parliament; it is unimaginable to think what would happen with a 20 party representation.

The results of Spring 1992 elections provided clear evidence that the old Italian political system could not survive. There were 531 party lists for the chamber of deputies throughout Italy's thirty-two electoral districts, and 9,742 candidates, an increase of about 20 and 13 per cent respectively over the previous elections of 1987. In addition, as David Caputo's analysis showed:[2]

a) The four-party ruling coalition maintained its parliamentary majority, but saw it reduced to a mere sixteen seat majority.

b) Despite retaining its parliamentary majority, the coalition parties captured only 48.8 per cent of the total vote.

c) The Christian Democrats had their worst showing since the war winning only 29.7 per cent of the vote and 206 seats in the Chamber of Deputies.

d) The new Democratic Party of the Left (*P.D.S.*) and the former *P.C.I.* (Communist Refoundation) lost strength when compared with prior results. In 1987, the *P.C.I.* received over 26 per cent of the vote for the Chamber of Deputies while in 1992, the two new parties combined only received around 22 per cent of the total vote cast.

e) The Lombard League improved its standing dramatically, receiving 55 seats in the Chamber of Deputies compared to only one seat in 1987.

It was the "anti-party," the Lombard League, that made the strongest showing. Many voted for the League not to approve a set of doctrines or political program, but to demonstrate deep discontent with the traditional political parties and their continuing tenure. However, it should also be said that perhaps the most serious movement for reform came from within the ranks of the ruling Christian Democrats. Mario Segni, a leader of the party's left wing, championed a national referendum on electoral reform and he built a broad coalition, dubbed "the party that isn't there," that included some Christian Democrats and even former Communists. The pressure on Parliament to approve an electoral reform greatly intensified when the Constitutional Court approved 10 of the 13 referenda proposed by Segni to be allowed to come up for a vote. Since none of the parties had yet made it clear whether it preferred a majority vote based on a British-style single round or the French system of a second-round run-off when a majority has not been obtained the first time, various measures were submitted to referenda. These included one dealing with the majority-type electoral system which would largely dismantle the proportional system and allow voters to elect their mayors and city administrators directly, wrenching local government from the hands of national party bosses. In the Spring of 1993, voters approved by a large margin the eight referenda: this event certainly marked the end of the First Republic and the beginning of the Second.

The Second Republic

The widespread revulsion over the mega-corruption of leading politicians uncovered by Italian magistrates in "Operation Clean Hands" and the broader, mounting resentment over the mismanagement of domestic affairs by the mainstream parties not only rocked the political and economic establishments but forced significant changes in the rules of the political game itself.

In a referendum held on April 18-19, 1993, over 82 percent of the 35 million voters endorsed a shift from proportional representation to a majority system for the election of three quarters of the 315 members of the senate. The switch to a majority system was backed by large margins throughout the country. The only exceptions were registered in Sicily, notably in some districts of Palermo. Several other referenda likewise showed very large majorities supporting curbs on the powers and privileges of politicians. Public financing of parties is now out, for instance; and three government departments must be dismantled, notably the Ministry for State Holdings which represented a larger share of the national economy than elsewhere in the West and have become a major source of patronage, abuses and corruption.

The new government formed after the April referendum embodied several new departures clearly in line with the message from the polls. For the first time since the end of World War II, the Premier was not a politician: Carlo Azeglio Ciampi had been for 14 years Governor of Italy's Central Bank. With full backing from President of the Republic Oscar Luigi Scalfaro, Ciampi chose the members of his Cabinet without going through the customary, lengthy bargaining process with leaders of the parties making up the ruling coalition. One third of the new Ministers had no party affiliation.

Upon taking office, Prime Minister Ciampi stated that if Parliament did not enact an electoral reform along the lines laid down by the April referendum before the summer recess, the government would submit its own bill and ask for a vote of confidence on it. In the summer of 1993 the Parliament approved a new electoral system. The reform reflects an earnest effort to reconcile the main benefits of the majority system with some protection on the minor parties' vital interests. It provides for three quarters of the House members (472 out of a total of 630) to be elected on a "first past the post" basis; i.e., along the British and US models. The other 158 seats will be allotted on a proportional basis among all parties polling at least 4 percent of the nationwide vote. The votes polled by the winners under the majority system will be excluded from the total available to the same parties' candidates to the seats allotted under the proportional system.

It was a courageous act because with that vote members of Parliament not only put on death row some of the small parties that flourished under the old system, but also signed their own death warrant since few of those in office were likely to be re-elected under the new system.

A "democratic revolution" has taken place in Italy even though it is too early to assess its consequences. The aroused public opinion, which acted as the main engine of change and reform and brought about early general elections in spring 1994, completely changed the political landscape. The right wing alliance, led by the media magnate Silvio Berlusconi, won a majority in the lower-house of Parliament and a plurality in the Senate. The election was a three-way contest involving the Freedom Pole, made up of *Forza Italia*, the separatist Northern League and the neo-Fascist National Alliance; the Center Pole, including the *Pact for Italy* and the Popular Party made up of former Christian Democrats; and the left-wing Progressive Pole, composed by the Democratic Party of the Left, the hard-line Communist Refoundation, the Greens, and the anti-Mafia *La Rete*. Official overall election results showed the right-wing coalition with 366 seats (155 to *Forza Italia*, 106 to *Northern League*, 105 to *National Alliance*) in the 630-seat lower house, an absolute majority, leaving its leftist adversaries a poor second with 213 and Italy's formerly all-powerful centrists with only 46. Five seats went to representatives of smaller parties. In the Senate, the right wing fared less well, winning 155 of the 315 seats. The rejection of the old political structure was so strong that *Forza Italia*, whose name is the soccer chant "Go Italy!" and founded only three months before the election, was the biggest vote-getter of the coalition. The neo-Fascists, who for years hovered on the fringes of Italian politics, securing a steady 5 or 6 percent of the vote but no significant representation, emerged with 12 percent of votes and 105 seats in the lower house.

The new political stage has very soft ground because the right wing coalition did not cement together political forces having a lot in common. *Forza Italia* of Mr. Berlusconi favored tax cuts and a push to sell off Italy's bloated state-owned industrial sector; the *Northern League*, led by Umberto Bossi, wanted to distance the affluent North from the central government in Rome; the neo-Fascists, led by Gianfranco Fini, want a strong central authority and have vaguely pressed a claim to territory in the former Yugoslavia.

It should be said that Italian democracy is also experiencing the same situation of many other democracies: established political parties are in deep trouble, their legitimacy suspect and their leader susceptible to attack by populists who preach simple, emotional answers to the complicated questions of the post-cold-war age. With so much cynicism about conventional politics and politicians around, and with the traditional left largely discredited after the collapse of Communism in 1989, it is hardly surprising that outsiders–many of them self-made businessmen with enough money of their own to run campaigns that defy the long-dominant party machine–are popping up. It is going to take some time for the new political forces to clarify their positions.

Politics as a Game and a Show

The causes of political changes at the beginning of the 90s were not only due to the collapse of old ideologies, but also to some basic attitudinal changes among Italians toward politics and the state. For one thing, the welfare state is dead in Italy as is "liberal fundamentalism." There is clearly an anti-traditional party attitude and the emergence of a **new pluralism** which seems to emphasize voluntarism rather than dependency on the state. The rise of a large number of interest groups and self-help associations, new in modern Italian society, indicates that traditional parties are no longer regarded as adequate in defining and satisfying one's needs. Many of these organizations do not have ideological ties or commitments to political institutions and their members wish to make more "privatized" demands on the political system. For example, the aged are interested in pensions irrespective of their individual political affiliation; the same is true of the handicapped, single-parent families, women, alcoholics and drug addicts, consumer advocates, environmentalists, and many others who are strongly interested in issues and problems of their immediate interest.

Although groups have emerged because of the anger and frustration people share over the failure of the state to deal adequately with problems of health, drug addiction, etc, and therefore should signal a greater predisposition toward self-help, as opposed to waiting around for the state to solve problems, the formation of such organizations implies, in the Italian politicized climate, the creation of new political forces. In fact, on closer analysis, what may emerge as the underlying issue may not be an ineffective party system, but rather a populace still too dependent upon government action. It often turns out that most of these groups really want governmental authorities to do more, not less. Notwithstanding the apparent lack of confidence in government, government is still expected to solve for society an astounding variety of problems. Italians' anti-government attitude is very complex: when citizens anger is tested on very important issues, their reaction is always pro-government!

In fact, when Italians have been called to vote in a referendum, a formal mechanism provided to the people by the constitution for expressing their judgement on legislative actions by parliament, they have *always* voted in favor of the actions approved by parliament. Italians have never overturned a law enacted by parliament. It seems that Italians are fundamentally content in the specific sense that they are reluctant to reverse at the polls what their representatives have ironed-out through the law-making process. It should also be pointed out that Italians have demonstrated a remarkable capacity to resist using the referendum for narrow self-interest. No better demonstration of this is offered by the 1985 vote on a law that had modified the *scala mobile* (cost-of-living increases based on inflation) to the disadvantage of wage-rated workers. To the surprise of many political experts, especially the Communists who had campaigned against the measure, and who had anticipated that the electorate would "vote its pocketbook" as opposed to the "general welfare," the Italians demonstrated a high level of civic and political maturity by refusing to annul the new law. It seems that their dissatisfaction with the system had to do more with the natural attitude of people toward the "other," the abstract institutions, than with a deep-seated political lack of confidence.

Italian politics reflects the character of the nation and of the Italian people who prefer the pleasure of *spettacolo*, of show. They allow so much toleration that the unwary observer may be misled to believe that Italians are without standard, or that they do not care whether the political system is working well or not. But the Italian political show always had a script. Even during the most chaotic years, Machiavelli was very much alive; political science has always been practiced with the flavor of an art. Political chaos was avoided because the *spettacolo*, the political show, always had a script with a well established conclusion.

Italian politics becomes more "spectacular" during election time. Public policy often becomes paralyzed, giving way to campaign pontificating and made-for-TV symbolism. Politics *spettacolo* style, fitting very nicely with the Italian character, became more "spectacular" with the advent of television. Indeed, because of TV, political discourse had to become even more than before like a 'show', a spectacle. In the world of television and "sound bite," where political discourse becomes more uniform, it is difficult for politicians to find mechanisms to articulate an ideology to the wider public. TV has created difficulty not only for the parties in power but also for the force of opposition whose entire outlook on communication had been based on the development of "alternative" information.

Yet, in Italy, the language of politics is still very intense because Italians are still passionately intense in conveying their messages. In the process of changing their political structures, Italians should not copy other forms of democracies. Democracies have to be assessed in their own terms, within their particular social, economic, and historical contexts. A people's history and culture, its economic conditions and social norms, its aspirations and its workways, its "national character" will affect the style and structure of its government. Democracy, by its nature, does not have a fixed form; within the same country, it may change. Italian democracy evolved slowly until 1993; that year changes made were more radical and profound.

Labor Unions: Fallen Lions

Even Italy's labor unions, once powerful enough to paralyze the country and make governments fall, have gone through profound changes and are today suffering from lack of public support. A foreign visitor to a major Italian city, seeing streets often filled with demonstrating workers carrying banners with explosive language, might conclude that the unions are still powerful and poised on the brink of insurrection. He would be wrong. These protest marches tend to be little more than remnants of an old ritual, a way of showing the flag and making up for the unions' inability to carry out more effective action. Unions are still strong in public service, but have become quite weak in industry and commerce.

In the political arena and the evolution of Italian democracy, labor unions have played a major role because like the trade unions in most European countries, and unlike those of the US, they have always been deeply politicized. Political motivation and ideological tradition have been more important than economic structure in determining union membership in Italy—[3]as a result, union membership has greater civic significance in Italy than might be elsewhere. Since the early postwar years, the two major labor confederations, *C.G.I.L.* (*Confederazione Generale Italiana Lavoratori*) and *C.I.S.L.* (*Confederazione Italiana Sindacati Lavoratori*), became deeply enmeshed in the struggle between the Communists and the Christian Democrats. In 1950 when the two unions were regarded as not offering enough choice, in the spirit of Italian democratic pluralism some of their leaders and workers left and formed a national union of their own, *U.I.L.* (*Unione Italiana dei Lavoratori*), which made a point of stressing its independence not only from *C.G.I.L.* but from *C.I.S.L.* as well.

By the early 1960s, the three unions had become a very strong political force in the nation and had been able to achieve some important social reforms. Later, in the "hot autumn" of 1968, during a long and bitter confrontation which involved labor, management, and the politicians as well, the unions won sizable wage increases, improvements in working conditions, and promises of concrete progress in availability of decent low cost housing, better schools, hospitals, and public transportation.

By 1969 the unions had forced through the legislature the **Workers' Statute**, one of the most advanced and, as it was interpreted, radical industrial relations policies ever enacted in the West. Even before this piece of legislature was passed, Italy provided exceptional levels of unemployment benefits and highly attractive compensation at the point of work severance. The statute came close to making the worker untouchable inside the work place or, for that matter, outside of it. With the help of politically radicalized judges, laborers could be absent from work with impunity and still claim their pay. Job transfers or reclassification simply could not occur without the consent of the party involved. The slightest infraction on the part of management was an almost certain invitation to a work stoppage. Side by side with these guarantees went improvements in fringe benefits that were as costly to employers as they were instrumental in changing the workers' standard of living. In those years, workers came to believe that a steep upward climb in their condition had become a birthright and that even dismissal from one's job for cause was nothing more than a quaint relic of by gone capitalism.[4] Union demands and ideology of those years were based on the assumption that the institutions of government had to assure the equality of outcome rather than equality of opportunity. As Joseph La Palombara indicated, although Italians tend to doubt that all men are created equal, they tend to believe that the state can go a long way to assure equality of results, regardless of the structure of opportunity.[5]

Much additional bitterness and strife developed when the national labor contracts concluded at the end of 1969 and the new legislature had to be implemented at the local plant level. The major labor organizations found it increasingly difficult to deal with the wildcat strikes and the sabotage of production lines carried out by small numbers of workers inspired by radical leftwing groups.

In the early 1970s, many Italian businessmen thought that the only way to conduct business was to arrange deals with organized labor which had emerged with a vengeance from an all-too-long condition of weakness in a labor market traditionally featured by chronic unemployment and underemployment. Several of those businessmen engaged in dialogues with Communist leaders because the party, which was gaining ground at the polls, maintained a strong hold on the biggest labor confederation, *C.G.I.L.* An accord was negotiated in 1975 by Giovanni Agnelli, president of FIAT and of *Confindustria*, and Luciano Lama, the Communist leader of *C.G.I.L.* A key clause introduced in contracts was the "rigid and pervasive wage indexation system." Big industrialists tolerated runaway inflation as long as the bill for its magnified impact could be passed on to their customers and to the taxpayers in general.

Labor had achieved such supremacy that in the 1975 agreement between organized labor and organized business it was established that the cost of living would be reviewed on a quarterly basis and wages adjusted upward to keep pace with inflation. The technical basis for making these adjustments, however, was such that, whereas the highest wage earners would just barely stay even with inflation, the lowest wage earners would realize wage improvements slightly above the inflation rate. Something very positive came out of the process without fully anticipating such an outcome: the parties to this agreement put in motion a policy that over time brought about an unprecedented redistribution of income.

By 1980, even before Reagan showed how to bust unions in America, Italian national labor unions were suffering from a self-inflicted mortal wound. In early fall of that year, FIAT management decided to dismiss some 14,000 workers as part of its strategy to cope with a crisis that affected the automobile industry all over the world but which had been especially exacerbated by recent developments in the national labor field. The unions called a strike which lasted five weeks and was openly backed by the *P.C.I.* Berlinguer himself (the leader of the Communist Party) addressed the strikers in Turin, FIAT's headquarters, pledging his party's support if they occupied the plants. But the unions' opposition to any compromise collapsed when an estimated 40,000 workers, foremen, and employees marched through Turin shouting "Freedom to work!"

Organized labor had overreached itself and had failed to realize that the tide had turned. Many big and medium-sized industries felt encouraged enough to follow FIAT's example and start restructuring their plants along lines calling for sizable payroll cuts. Absenteeism dropped significantly, while production rose. A major move away from the rigid indexation system was undertaken by the Craxi government in February, 1984. The operation of indexation mechanism was cooled off temporarily by an executive decree. The move was backed by the unions representing Catholic, Social Democratic, and Republican workers as well as by the Socialist wing of *C.G.I.L.* But the *P.C.I.* went on the warpath.

It should be pointed out that union membership is much more common in the more civic regions. In fact, union membership is roughly twice as high in those regions. By contrast, union membership is unrelated to education, age, and urbanization, and the differences by social class are less than one might expect. The civic context is almost as important as socioeconomic status in accounting for union membership in Italy. In the civic regions, solidarity in the workplace is part of a larger syndrome of social solidarity.[6]

Today the trade unions are in decline, the victims of recent transformations in the West that caught labor organizations defenseless. In the space of a decade, the trade union movement went from a condition of unimagined power to one of precipitous decomposition. Like unions in other western countries, those in Italy do not know how to adapt to the economic and social transformations that have occurred during the so-called second industrial revolution. The unions also ran afoul of developments that go beyond recession or economic and social changes. Their earlier, heady successes contributed to their undoing. The conquests in favor of the working class did not produce a sense of gratitude to the labor confederations that engineered them. In addition, the use of robots operated by engineers in white smocks eliminated thousands of blue-collar workers. Moreover, the decline of the steel and shipbuilding industries and the fall in employment in publicly owned industries, also in trouble, are principal reasons for the erosion in labor's strength. Large-scale industry in general has also declined. Today over half of all workers are found in firms of under twenty employees, and such places are notoriously difficult to unionize.

Protests have become fragmented, with sectional interests prevailing. Instead of long strikes, the unions tend to organize one-day token stoppages, which make them appear strong and militant but achieve little; they are a safety-valve for discontent. The old saying "their bark is worse than their bite," well characterizes the labor unions of today. Trade unions have seen their authority increasingly threatened by the rank-and-file organizations of separate categories of workers and the strength of the local groups. The **COBAS**, (*comitati di base*), have mobilized different groups of workers and of the *ceti medi* (middle classes) with notable militancy, but without the ability to achieve, or indeed to seek a unifying strategy. The rise of unemployment in traditional labor-intensive industries that once were union bastions and the anti-system mood of the country that changed the political structure have also affected the once very strong politicized labor unions.

The unions have not been able to suggest acceptable solutions to unemployment, which is one of the most crucial problems of the nation. The claims of some conservatives that the unemployed have little incentive to look for another job quickly because high benefits are breeding laziness, and that many people were earning more on the dole than others in jobs are certainly unfair. Most recognize, however, that the unemployment crisis is not due solely to outside economic factors; it is also structural, linked to changes in technology. The Italians, like others in highly advanced technological nations, will have to learn to live with a high level of unemployment if some social adjustments are not made. The burden can be shared more evenly by a shortened work week so that more jobs are available. As it is now, rising unemployment has led to less job security and elimination of redundancies.

Notes

1. In the fight against a Communist rapidly growing threat in Italy, an important role was played by the Pope Family in the U.S. In the immediate post-war period, mainly through the *Progresso Italo-Americano* (the major American daily in Italian language) and the radio sation *WHOM*, the Pope family carried on a passionate campaign against a Communist take over of Italy. The *Progresso* organized a letter-to Italy campaign among its readers and printed a series of alarming articles about the consequences of a possible Communist take over. This resulted in the dispatch of thousands of letters from Americans of Italian origin to relatives and friends in Italy urging them to reject Russian blandishments.

2. David A. Caputo, "Italy's Parliamentary Elections: New Directions Or Only Minor Deviations From The Past?" *Italian Journal*, Vol. VI, 1992, no. 2 & 3, p. 3.

3. Salvatore Coi, "Sindacati in Italia: iscritti, apparato, finanziamento," *Il Mulino* 28 (179): 201-242, quotation from p. 206.

4. For an overview of the labor union achievements of those years, see: Tiziano Treu, ed., *L'uso politico dello statuto dei lavoratori* (Bologna: Il Mulino, 1975).

5. Op. cit., p. 55.

6. Robert N. Putnam, p. 107.

III

Dangers to the State

Plots and Terrorism

The Italian democratic state has been fragile and continually under a cloud of danger not so much for the kind of democratic system it is governed by, as for the kind of people that have been in government and for the presence of organizations that are corroding its social, political and economic fibers.

Given the fragility of government and the openness of the political system, Italy became fertile ground for terrorist activity and for political forces from extreme sides of the political spectrum. Contrary to the almost exclusive attention given to ultra-left activities by media in the USA, elements of ultra-conservative groups have been no less a threat to the Italian state throughout the modern period.

The political terrorism began with the weakening of the political parties that had been forming the government coalition up to the beginning of the 1960s and the need of broadening the coalition by the inclusion of new political forces. With the admission of the Socialists into government in December, 1963 and the consequent beginning of a new era of social reforms which caused vast sum of capital to leave the country in an artificially created atmosphere of panic, elements of the political forces of the right planned measures to counteract these changes; some were definitively unconstitutional.

Probably the most clamorous publicized attempt by the right to overthrow the government was made by General Giovanni di Lorenzo, Commander of the *Carabinieri* Corps and a former chief of military counter-espionage (*SIFAR*). He had made provision for the arbitrary arrest and deportation of numerous political personalities whose names were given to a select group of Carabinieri officers. These had been told to stand by for the order to proceed and had been given to understand that the general was acting on personal instructions from the President of the Republic and without the knowledge of the Ministers of Defense and the Interior. The plan would have remained a secret if the magazine *L'Espresso* had not published details of the plan. This was somewhat surprising since plots and terroristic acts by the right had enjoyed a high degree of impunity in Italy. In the case of General di Lorenzo, a parliamentary inquiry into the mis-use of *SIFAR* funds and dossiers for political espionage and blackmail was ordered only after a great deal of hedging by the government behind the screen of national security. If the affair had not come to light during the military *coup d'état* in Athens in 1967, it may have remained a secret. Although most Italians discounted the possibility of a similar take-over in Italy, they were shocked to realize that, if the political will for such action were forthcoming, the co-operation of the police and the military would not be hard to obtain.

The military would never have been able to earn any support because the crisis created by the panic of the entrance of the Socialists in government in December, 1963 faded quickly because of their bland and moderate demands. For the duration of the fourth parliament (1963-1968) not a single one of the so-called structural reforms touching regional government, the universities, the magistracy, the penal and civil codes, the health services, pensions and so forth, made any appreciable progress and the program announced by the Center-Left parties in December, 1963 and retained in July, 1964 was still unfinished when the coalition pulled itself together again for a third attempt in December, 1968.

By the late 1960s, domestic order was challenged on several fronts. As long as the Communist Party had a monopoly of Marxist culture, the state had not had any problems in maintaining civil order. But things changed in the late 1960s when that monopoly was seriously challenged and eventually fractured by the student revolt. Extremist groups of the left accused the *P.C.I.* of being revisionist and reformist, authoritarian and bureaucratic in a bourgeois way. The 1968 and 1969 student revolts worsened the situation: anarchist and radical-left terrorist organizations fomented disorder at several universities and openly clashed on the streets with neo-Fascist and far-right groups. This was taking place in a dangerous climate of declining economic conditions and national political stalemate, while various labor unions were engaged in strikes and disorders. The "hot autumn of 1969" occurred at a time when the whole Italian society seemed to be in upheaval. The student movement was not mere anarchy but represented a set of political demands which had to be answered by all Italian political parties. It was not just a protest against the alienating character of the capitalist-consumer society but a specific protest against the authoritarian, paternalistic, hierarchical structure of Italian society and of Italian universities which students took to be mirrors and instruments of the 'system'. The movement became a major political phenomenon and shaped, either directly or indirectly, the crisis of Italian society: from terrorism to the women's movement, from dissent within the Church to the birth of a host of small left-wing parties and to the radicalization of large groups of intellectuals and middle-class radicals.

The student movement had profound influence. The risings in southern Italy, the prison revolts, the demonstrations and strikes in the North all owe something to the new spirit of criticism that came out of the universities and the lycées. The pressures on government were so strong that many of the reforms the students demanded were granted even before the bill itself was passed. Something radical had happened: once so respectful of authority, so anxious to get ahead with the help of protection and recommendations in a society where influence was all, youth was now questioning the structure of that society. Some of the unionists formed anarchist and radical-leftist groups similar to those of the students, and these labor extremist groups also engaged the neo-fascists in street battles.

By the mid-1970s many small revolutionary organizations which had emerged from the youth movement entered into a period of crisis. Organizations such as *Avanguardia Operaia* (The Workers' Vanguard), *Potere Operaio* (Workers' Power) and *Lotta Continua* (The Struggle Goes On) had not been able to establish a significant presence in the labor movement. The crisis of these organizations was in large part due to the fact that they had unsuccessfully tried to subvert the system by using traditional instruments, the political parties. All this was happening while the Communist Party was anticipating an entrance into government. The intended move was a democratic one: to provide the country with a radical reforming government without pushing a large section of middle-class groups and other social forces into positions of overt hostility. In order to achieve a political majority it was necessary to forge an alliance with the Catholic masses and enter into some form of compromise with the *D.C.* The *P.C.I.* realized that a mere electoral or mathematical majority was not sufficient for a national legitimization and that it needed to offer some international guarantee that its presence in government would not signify a shift in the balance of forces between East and West to the disadvantage of the West. The flirtation was working well; in July 1976, for the first time since the break-up of the tripartite coalition of 1947 (the first historic compromise) a *D.C.* prime minister, Giulio Andreotti, appealed to the *P.C.I.* to support his government in Parliament. At the local level, cooperation between Communists and Christian Democrats was becoming commonplace, and by June 1977 a wide-ranging government program had been agreed to between the *D.C.*, the *P.C.I.* and the other parties.

While engaging in a work of compromise with the *D.C.*, the *P.C.I.* had to react to the students' unrest. Although the initial response was hostile to the student movement and although one of its leaders, Giorgio Amendola, asserted that it was necessary to fight on two fronts, i.e. against the government and against the students, the party leader, Luigi Longo, was much more flexible.[1] Longo recognized that it was also the *P.C.I.*'s fault if there was such a wide gulf between the party and the students, that the party had become too sectarian and too bureaucratic and that the importance and political autonomy of the student movement had to be recognized. This strategy implied two objectives: on the one hand, the party was trying to fragment the student movement paradoxically by showing sympathy for the student cause; on the other hand, it was sending the message that the only source of legitimate power in Italy was to be found in political parties.

Though not in government, the *P.C.I.* seemed to have become a party of government and, in the eyes of the extreme left, a **partner** of the established power. For the militant groups, the *P.C.I.* had become a progressive force by betraying its basic revolutionary principles; not only had it sold out by compromising with the *D.C.*, but it had also entered a policy of complete subordination.

For the ultra-left, therefore, the *P.C.I.* had become another enemy of the people, and it was their duty to assume the role of defenders of the oppressed. On the other side of the political aisle it was clear that the *D.C.* had a strategy, not understood by the American government, that is, to transform the *P.C.I.* into a harmless movement for reform which would bring its supporters and the masses it inspired under the political hegemony of a new governing coalition led by the *D.C.*

The radical Left perhaps saw what was happening and acted to prevent it. From December 1969 to the mid-1980s, politically motivated bombings, murders, and kidnappings became a recurring feature of Italian life. Observers estimated that over 14,000 terrorist acts were committed between 1969 and 1985. Hundreds of Italians were kidnapped, "kneecapped," wounded or killed. Most affected were those who represented the establishment: university professors, judges, generals, industrialists, politicians.

All terrorist groups of the ideological left shared the same goal—the overthrow of the bourgeois, capitalist, imperialist state and the establishment of the dictatorship of the proletariat. They also tried to bring the *P.C.I.* back into the fold of revolutionary ideology. This was to be accomplished not only through the dissemination of Marxist-Leninist propaganda but also through attacks on the property of industrialists, as well as kidnapping and assassinations.

The **Red Brigade** (B.R.) was the best known of the left-wing terrorist groups to operate in those years.   To demonstrate their contempt for the democratic state, on March 16, 1978, the *Brigate Rosse* kidnapped Aldo Moro, the party secretary of the *D.C.* and promoter of the "historical compromise" and, therefore, supporter of Communist participation in government. The terrorist groups considered Moro nothing more than a tool of the imperialistic American multinationals. The Red Brigade's act was clearly a declaration of war against the state; the state was under siege. As in other critical moments, Italian politicians, through skillful maneuvering preserved the democracy and defended the state. After intense discussions on how to respond, the government refused to negotiate with the terrorists.

Unfortunately, however, the mass media became deeply involved in this unfortunate event. As in many other instances the mass media played a key role as vehicle for the gathering and diffusion of information, but in this case it also acted as first-person protagonist who managed to instrumentalize the tragedy to its own purpose. The public and the state learned through the mass media, which likes to play on the emotions of people, all the developments of the case. Because of this the Moro case became a memorable example of politics as spectacle. The killing of the five bodyguards in the ambush and the eventual murder of Moro himself, after 40 long days of tension, shook the nation. Certainly, one should not underestimate the cultural dimension: Italians are less prepared than Americans to expect that their president or political leaders may be assassinated.

The explosion of terrorism led the *P.C.I.* to defend the State by refusing to negotiate with the Red Brigade over the Moro kidnapping and by accepting new anti-terrorist legislation. Even though the intention was to uphold the democratic principles of the State and of the Constitution, the *P.C.I.* could not avoid appearing to the extremist groups as the defender of the entire edifice of the Italian State with its corruption, degeneration and bigotry. It was accused by many on the Left of espousing anti-libertarian causes purely in order to become part of the government.

Paradoxically, rather than solidify the *P.C.I.* position, the Moro killing put an end to the historic compromise, for the Red Brigade had destroyed the key man who could have paved the way for the entry of the *P.C.I.* into the government. In the wake of the Moro killing, as well as other *B.R.* murders, 63 members of the *B.R.* were eventually arrested and put on trial. The Moro experience brought together the political, juridical and military forces of the nation in a solid bloc which in skillful cooperation mustered one of the most sophisticated anti-terrorist systems in the world.

The first proof that Italy was able to eliminate terrorism came in December 1981. The kidnapping of General Dozier, then deputy chief of staff for logistics and administration at NATO Allied Land Forces Southern Europe with headquarters in Verona, was foiled when the State Police arrested the captors and freed the general in a counter-terrorism blitz that received praise from the international community, including and above all from the USA. By this time the Italian government had created a special force, "the skin head," to deal with terrorism.

However, other incidents shook up the country before the nation could start to relax. In broad daylight on the campus of the University of Rome, two members of the *R.B.*'s Roman Column gunned down Ezio Tarantelli, a professor of Economics. Tarantelli was an obvious target because he was the author of modifications in the *scala mobile* that the Craxi government eventually adopted as official policy. The "freeze" that Tarantelli's plan placed on wage increases was easily perceived by the RB as an act against the working class. Similarly, Gen. Licio Giorgieri, assassinated in March 1987, was singled out because of his responsibilities in NATO and the space defense program. The victims were individuals who could be associated with the established power structure or its defenders.

The state had also to face the threats posed by neo-fascist right-wing terrorist groups. These groups were more difficult to deal with because they lacked organizational sophistication and murdered indiscriminately. Since their objective was to show the weakness of the state in handling violent political crime and social chaos, and their objective was to create the maximum possible fear, intimidation and panic, they placed bombs in piazzas, on trains or aircraft, or in railroad stations, without making claims for their actions.

Typical of the right-wing terrorist groups was the Armed Revolutionary Nuclei (*Nuclei Armati Rivoluzionari–N.A.R.*), a neo-Fascist organization that authorities have held responsible for major bomb explosions and for the killing of its political opponents. The most terrible tragedy was the carnage caused by a bomb which exploded in Bologna's railroad station on August 2, 1980, killing eighty-five people. This was the peak of the cycle of right-wing terrorism, although not the end to violence. Another neofascist group **New Order/Black Order** (*Ordine Nuovo/Ordine Nero*) claimed responsibility for a bomb attack on the Milan-Naples express train on December 23, 1984 which killed several people.

Because of its strategic position in the Mediterranean, Italy also became the stage for acts of international terrorism. The most heinous act was the attempted assassination of Pope John Paul II on May 13, 1981. Efforts to establish the motivation for the plot were inconclusive, but some evidence suggested an apparent attempt by the Bulgarian secret police, presumably acting on behalf of the KGB to stifle the resurgence of the Roman Catholic Church in Eastern Europe.

Another incident that attracted international attention was the Fall 1985 hijacking of the Italian cruise, **Achille Lauro,** while it was sailing the Mediterranean and the killing of one of its Jewish American passengers. The incident created a major governmental and international crisis because the hijackers, who were a pro-Palestinian group were allowed to escape after having been caught through the United States' role in forcing an Egyptian plane carrying the terrorists to land at a NATO base at Sigonella, Sicily. The incident also sparked a series of government crises. Indeed, for the first time, an Italian government fell largely as the result of an international exigency. The moderately independent stand vis-à-vis the United States adopted by Craxi and the Christian Democratic foreign minister, Andreotti, antagonized the Republican defense minister, Spadolini, who adopted a pro-American and anti-Palestine Liberation Organization (PLO) position during the affair. Spadolini also felt he had not been adequately consulted before a PLO official, Abu Abbas (described by American officials as masterminding the hijacking), had been hastily released from Italian custody.

International terrorism struck again a few months later, in December 1985, when a pro-Palestinian group fired on a crowd of passengers in the Rome Airport terminal, killing thirteen people. More recently, a well-balanced international policy in the Mediterranean, especially towards the Middle-East has helped in establishing a relaxed atmosphere and a cessation of terrorist violence.

Italy has not been immune to planned attempts to overthrow the state by those in charge of protecting it either. In 1981, the existence of a subversive Masonic lodge, the **P2**, which stands for Propaganda Two, was discovered. Its members included prominent figures in the armed forces, in business, and in politics. The precise objectives of the lodge have remained obscure, but there is little doubt that its head, Lucio Gelli, an affable businessman from Tuscany, was seeking to construct an anti-Communist network within the highest echelons of the Italian state. His name remained unknown to the Italian public until the mid-1970s, when the first hints of his role as a power broker appeared in the press. Eventually the media started mentioning him in connection with the sensational insolvency cases of two bankers, Michele Sindona and Roberto Calvi, both of whom died under mysterious circumstances.

To millions of Italians the world of Lodge **P2** was not of as much concern as were the terrorists, even though by 1985 terrorist organizations in Italy could be described as having failed to meet their objective of the radical overthrow of state institutions. Their propaganda and tactics had proved to be ill-suited to bring about any sort of political change. Because of increased popular revulsion and increasingly effective counter-terrorist legislation and activity by the police, terrorist organizations of all ideologies had suffered major setbacks through 1984, and terrorist activity had diminished to barely noticeable levels.

The state won the battle against terrorism. In more ways than Italians themselves may have anticipated, terrorism brutally tested the proposition that Italy's democracy, at the bottom, is a strong, healthy institution. Because the preservation of high level democracy in a pluralistic society may require special security measures, Italians have adapted to a new style of living. Whether stoically enduring long lines outside security entrances to state offices, banks, etc. or voluntarily lavishing money on private security systems, Italians have quickly responded that freedom whatever the price has to be preserved.

Ordinary Crime
While Italians are justifiably proud of this victory over terrorism, they appear to be losing the war against ordinary crime, which has been on the rise since 1969.

Before 1969 kidnapping for ransom and armed robbery tended to occur infrequently except in Sardinia, Sicily and Calabria; but by the mid-1970s it was a serious problem throughout the country and became a major concern for the Italian public. In 1977, for example, over sixty kidnappings occurred, involving members of wealthy families and political figures. In fact, some of the moneyed class people moved away from Italy in fear of kidnappings, while others increased personal security through bodyguards and armored vehicles.

The easy availability of heroin from the Mafia network was viewed as a major reason for the upsurge of crime. The Italian narcotics epidemic had become more virulent than in most other European countries. In Rome, considered also Italy's drug capital, heroin, marijuana, and hashish can be purchased openly in many streets and piazzas all over the city, and any streetwise teenager knows what the going price is for any illegal drug. Used syringes can be found any day in most parks, often jabbed into the trees, and along the banks of the Tiber.

People die every month from overdoses and the authorities seize hundreds of pounds of heroin and other substances. In 1988 no fewer than 758 people in Italy died of drug overdoses, almost three times as many as in 1986. Although precise figures on the total number of addicts are hard to come by, it has been established that as many as two hundred thousand Italians are hooked on heroin and cocaine, while several hundred thousand others frequently smoke hashish and marijuana. Italy, with a population one-fourth that of the United States, has an estimated half as many confirmed drug users; that most of these users are under thirty makes the situation all the more alarming. The situation has become so critical that in January 1993, the government decriminalized the personal use of drugs to cope with the failure of its tough drug law, which filled prisons with addicts and did little to reduce consumption. Instead of prison terms, the new law imposes administrative sanctions–including loss of driver's license, gun permits and passports–for drug users.

Organized Crime

According to police and senior magistrates, in 1984 organized crime in Italy, as embodied in the **Mafia** of Sicily, the *Camorra* of Naples, and the *'Ndrangheta* in Calabria, represented a greater threat to the internal security of Italy than did political violence. These organizations are not inventions of Mario Puzo, Hollywood or the mass media. The title of an article "What Happened to Heroes is a Crime," that appeared in the Book Review of the *New York Times* of October 14, 1990, is significant: for lack of positive heroes, we create bad ones. Mobsters do not need mythification. Organized crime wields economic and social, as well as political power, which has a destructive effect on people and their institutions.

Mussolini had almost eradicated the Mafia by using draconian police methods such as torture and summary execution. However, in a belief that its power could be used in the struggle against the Nazis, it was reinstated in Sicily during WWII by the American Mafia in alliance with the US Armed Forces and regained its influence not only through the collection of "protection money" for guarding property, irrigation systems, and fishing fleets, but also through greater involvement in urban economic affairs. Until the 1970s the Mafia prospered within the DC system of power in the South; and, in turn, it was at the service of politicians. It delivered votes and financed political campaigns. In exchange it obtained local contracts, was allowed to develop protection rackets.[2]

The explosion of the social conflict in the late 1960s and early-1970s had an effect on the Mafia's behavior. Since the state was engaged in the control of these conflicts and showed signs of weakness, the Mafia seized the opportunity to become an independent economic force and its own master. Old techniques were resurrected in order to finance modern economic activities. Using force, it operated as a parasitic middleman between owners and workers, between producers and consumers, between citizens and the state. Not only did the Mafia gain control of the wholesale market for vegetables, meat, and fish and engage in cigarette smuggling as well as real estate speculation, but it also attempted to acquire a share of the vast resources the state was sending to the South for economic development in its attempt to face the social conflicts and the wave of terrorism.

However, the decisive factor in the spread of the Mafia was the drug trade, of which it was the primary operator. By the mid-1970s the Mafia had assumed international dimensions because of its involvement in the world-wide narcotics market. Heroin traffic had become an enterprise of authentic multinational dimensions: it involves the importation of opium from Pakistan, Afghanistan and Iran, its transformation into morphine in the Middle East and into heroin in Sicily, and its eventual transportation to the USA and other advanced industrial countries. Italy itself, especially wealthy Northern cities such as Milan, Turin, Verona, Genoa also became a lucrative end market for hard drugs. The enormous profits in successful drug deals provided the Sicilian mafiosi and their allies with huge funds and tremendous influence. The Mafia drug tycoons used their money to buy flashy cars, build sumptuous villas and enter legal businesses and industries. Many credit institutions in Italy and Switzerland and offshore fiscal havens appeared only too happy to handle all that cash, thereby becoming instrumental in money-laundering schemes. The expansion of the Sicilian banking system was also linked to Mafia involvement in narcotics. According to most estimates, by the late 1980s, the Italian Mafia earned enough money to have covered Italy's 125 billion dollar debt.[3]

The vast sums of money at stake and the greed of the mafiosi brought about a new level of violence. In the old times, a local "honored man" did not very often have to order one of his hitmen to fire the *lupara* at some landowner who would not pay protection money, or to eliminate some traitor who had started carrying out robberies on his own. Until a few decades ago the Mafia could secure compliance with its orders through a simple warning by a go-between or a more tangible form of intimidation. The organization traditionally preferred cooperation with local officials rather than oppose them openly or have them killed. Until the late 1960s attacks on journalists, parliamentarians, police, judges, attorneys, and other representatives of public institutions were unthinkable. In the past rival Mafia clans fought one another, with whole families being wiped out in the process. A kind of Darwinian process regulated their existence. Today's Mafia, however, is different than that of years past.

The change came about with the Mafia's entry into the heroin business, and with streams of billions of liras that the Italian government has been channeling to the Southern regions as financial aid. The attempts to industrialize Southern Italy through large state projects has provided both a gold mine for the Mafia and an opportunity for local officials to get heavy bribes. With the sudden influx of wealth, power structures were reorganized, the rules of the game were revised, and the lifestyles of the mafiosi changed. The Mafia has abandoned its peasant roots. Today the successful Mafia boss has the power of a politician with stable and powerful ties to Rome.

Because of Mafia, drug use has become a bigger problem then terrorism ever was. Solutions are not easy to find because of serious social problems. Increasingly, teenagers become both foot soldiers and casualties in the mafia's battles. At one time, women and children were off-limits to the mafia, but that no longer is the case. Juvenile crime has exploded in recent years, coinciding with organized crime's recruitment of youth from local gangs. Some are as young as age ten. Possibly to blame is a penal code enacted in 1989 which rules out jail for any minor who commits a crime carrying less than a twelve-year sentence. With unemployment at 20 per cent in the South, many teens either move North or turn to crime. Drug couriers are often paid in heroin with the consequence that many become addicts and remain slaves of their new-found "work." It is also impossible for poor teens, once they are recruited and have tasted the glamour and money of organized crime, to free themselves of such servitude.

The Italian court system has had mixed results in responding to the legal challenges posed by the spread of terrorism and organized crime in Italy. On the one hand even though judges and public prosecutors have often been the targets of terrorist and criminal abuse, they have nevertheless managed to help the government withstand and largely defeat the threat that the Red Brigades and other groups have posed to Italian democracy since the 1970s. On the other hand the people who make up the judicial corps have themselves occasionally been tainted because some of them were involved in major scandals, leading to well-publicized resignations and even trials. Many officials of the judiciary were implicated in the "P-2 affair" and had to resign, while connections with organized crime plagued local courts and even the Court of Cassation, equivalent to America's Supreme Court.

Sicilian violence did not cease. A new wave of assassinations started; during a brief two week period in the fall of 1988, eighteen people, including a judge, were murdered by Mafia gunmen. Sicily, Calabria, and Campania now account for 66 per cent of the homicides in Italy although their populations make-up only about 25 per cent of Italy's total. As rival gangs in Sicily, Calabria, and the Naples area started an unending series of murders in their drug-related turf wars, they also killed several magistrates, police officers, and politicians. After each spectacular assassination, high ranking officials of the state government, including the president of the republic and the prime minister flew to Sicily to attend the victim's funeral and use the occasion to deliver the usual political homilies pledging that the fight against the Mafia would be stepped up. Outraged citizens occasionally responded with explosive catcalls and boos. The assassinations of Giovanni Falcone and Paolo Borsellino in 1992, the two leading anti-mafia special prosecutors who were making an impact by jailing hundreds of mafiosi, outraged the nation.

In response to these brutal attacks, in which powerful bombs were used to murder the judges and many of their bodyguards, the Italian government took strong measures, including the dispatch of seven elite battalion of troops to assist Sicilian officials and local law enforcement officers. The troops were assigned to protect officials and vital installations; but they were not expected to participate in investigative procedures conducted by traditional police agencies. Most importantly, the government has at last committed itself to the creation of a national investigative force, along the lines of the United States' Federal Bureau of Investigation, to fight the Mafia. Known by its Italian initials as the DIA, this force will eventually grow to a strength of 3,000 crime agents.

The government has taken other actions as well. Since the members of *Cosa Nostra*, besides being drug traffickers and racketeers, are also legitimate businessmen and farmers, and therefore, are interested in public-works contracts sponsored by local governments, the state has dissolved dozens of these local town councils accused of dealing with the Mafia.

Most Italians are upset with the presence of the Mafia in Italy and are horrified whenever television and the newspapers report the latest savagery in gory detail. They frequently organize massive demonstration to show their outrage. Yet the Mafia continued to flourish until the early 90s. The major problem was that the Mafia lived within the walls of government. Its success had to be attributed to the fact that it infiltrated or actually controlled the nerve center of the regional government. Its collaboration was considered indispensable at election time, and some candidates, the more successful ones, did anything to secure it. In early 1984, officials of the Sicilian regional government were forced to resign and were arrested on charges of corruption. In 1991 twenty-one municipal administrations were dissolved because members were found to be connected with mafia or *camorra*.

Serious attempts have been made by individual citizens to create a civic consciousness of the evil of the Mafia. The two most prominent names are two writers, Danilo Dolci and Leonardo Sciascia. For many years Dolci campaigned in the slums of Palermo and the little Mafia towns of western Sicily. For a long time he seemed to be making no headway at all and though his name was widely known abroad few people inside Italy had heard of him. Again and again, by hunger strikes and other forms of peaceful demonstration, he drew the attention of the outside world to the abuse of the Mafia and the connivance of the Sicilian and the Italian establishment. The task he had set himself was Herculean, nothing less than persuading Italians that things can change simply because enough people—ordinary people without special power and influence—want them to be different. But to do that he had to destroy the ingrained conviction of Italians, Northerners and Southerners alike, that the only way to get things done is by pulling strings.

The biggest hope, however, has to be found in the collective efforts of Southern society which is giving signs of civic maturity. The structure of the Mafia being classically based on vertical relations of authority and dependence, with little or no horizontal solidarity among equals, can be demolished only by establishing a pattern of horizontal trust and the elimination of the vertical exploitation-dependence that has characterized southern culture and social structures for at least a millennium.

The wind of radical political changes, meanwhile, is having effect also on the Mafia. In response to the massive popular outrage, in summer 1992, the Amato government enacted tougher measures against the Mafia and other criminal organizations, notably the *Camorra* and *'Ndrangheta*. Thanks to the new legislation and to better coordination between law enforcing agencies, several hundred mobsters have been arrested (including top leaders of the major criminal organizations). Mafia assets totaling over 2.5 billion dollars have been seized.

White-Collar Crime

Another major problem for which Italy, as a nation, has suffered dearly, is the high level of white-collar crime. Indeed, white-collar crimes and political scandals have been endemic in Italy, and together with organized crime, they represent the major dangers to the nation. For many years, far from joining any campaign to eradicate these problems, many enterprising members of the middle and upper classes invented scams of their own and thereby managed to bilk the state of hundred of millions, even billions, of dollars. A week rarely goes by without learning that an officeholder, politician, banker, industrialist, military officer, television personality or even a magistrate is brought to court and occasionally ends up in jail. Bribery and corruption have infected almost every aspect of Italian life. When a developer, building prisons, was discovered to have handed out millions of dollars in bribes to everyone including the minister of labor, it was called the "golden prisons" scandal. Since then there has been the "golden sheets" scandal, involving lucrative contracts to supply linen for sleeper cars in the Italian railroad. In Rome there is the "golden bedpans" scandal, in which hospital workers hired to empty bedpans were mysteriously promoted into high-paying administrative positions for which they had no qualifications, and finally, the mega-scandal of bribes to political parties. The political scandals reached such proportion as to challenge credulity. Although no party has remained immune, the two parties with the most power, the *D.C.* and the *P.S.I.*, have been shown to be the most corrupt.

Some of these estimates indicate that politicians in Italy routinely steal anywhere from six billion to twelve billion dollars a year. Elections are expensive not because running for office costs much more than in France or Germany but because the candidates pocket a lot of money each time the voters go to the polls. One wonders if the frequent fall of governments and the consequent new elections are not connected to the political scam. This, of course, must be the reason why so few politicians complain about having to campaign so often. It had become a custom that parties paid their general costs with contract kickbacks and "contributions," while candidates paid for their own campaigns with kickbacks from the families that depended directly on them for jobs.

Bribery had been always connected with Southern Italy, and even to some extent with central Italy. The Northern part of the country had always been viewed as immune to such corruption. The Sicilians talked about kickback using the word *pizzo* (an old Sicilian word for a bird's beak, by allusion, when it's being dipped in food or water). The Neapolitans say *mazzetta*, which means a small bundle (of money). In the North, Milanese, Venetians and other cities did not have a word. Not until recently, that is, when the massive bribery scandal which shook Italy to its core started to unfold in Milan in early 1992. It not only demonstrated that the North is not ethically different from the rest of the country, but it also showed that the Italian party-dominated system, that has run the country since WWII, was at the core of the corruption.

Dangers to the State

The investigation, known as *Operazione Mani Pulite* ("Operation Clean Hands"), showed bribe collection to be one of the most efficient and organized arms of the Italian government. Officials had routinely skimmed from 2 to 14 per cent off government contracts made by the industries of the public sector and for every public service, from airports and hospitals to theaters and orphanages. Politicians had immense power because the government controlled, as we shall see later, vast sectors of the economy, from commercial banking, steel, telecommunications, and energy industries all the way down to ice cream plants, grocery stores, and vineyards. For Italian political parties, such activities were giant spoils machines. Much of the private sector too—from Fiat to small construction outfits—had no choice but to come to terms with *partitocrazia*, or rule by the political parties.

By acting as legitimate democratic intermediaries between the individual citizen and the state, and being essentially vote-getting entities, the political parties had spawned an oligarchy of professional politicians, a *classe politica* (political class) to conduct illegal activities in an almost legal way. The political class for years had relied on graft, *tangente* (even in this area the Italians try to use some sophistication; they use a neat geometrical term for a kickback).

The scandal of *tangenti* spread rapidly to dozens of other Northern cities and brought public disgrace and even jail terms to many top politicians. "Operation Clean Hands hit Italian politics like a cyclone," wrote Giuseppe Turato and Cinzia Sasso in a new book (The Looters) on the scandal. "After this, nothing will ever be the same."[4]

It is no accident that the scandal came to light in 1992. As we have seen, during the cold war many Italian voters considered corruption a lesser evil than a government headed by the Communist Party. A majority of Italian voters supported a coalition of parties led by the anti-Communist Christian Democrats and Socialists. But the collapse of communism opened a Pandora's box of pent-up frustration and disgust with the Italian political system; voters started to desert the traditional corruption-ridden parties in droves.

The new political climate and the increased European and global competition in the economic system changed also the relation of the Italian business and industrial system with politics. The system of collusion between government and business which had worked well enough in a relatively closed, protected market, could not continue after 1992 because the onerous tax on businesses made it difficult for business to compete freely with European and other rivals. The clean up that followed was most welcomed. Since most Italians dislike politicians, it was easy for the judges who arrested hundreds of Milanese bureaucrats, businessmen, and politicians, including deputies to the Italian parliament, to become heros. Indeed, the public response was euphoric.

The judge-prosecutor who started the investigation, Antonio Di Pietro, an Abruzzese by birth suddenly became a national hero and his picture appeared on the cover of most major news magazines. Graffiti writers scrawled "Grazie Di Pietro" (Thanks, Di Pietro), across walls in Milan and Di Pietro T-shirts became the most popular items for teenagers.

In the process, over 3,000 people were arrested or notified that they were under investigation for corruption and/or illegal acts connected with the financing of political parties. About half of them were economic operators, including top managers of Italy's biggest private corporations (FIAT, Olivetti, MontEdison) and State Holdings (IRI and ENI). About as many were politicians, including over 150 members of Parliament, four former Premiers and a score of former Cabinet Ministers. By mid-summer 1993, the breakdown by party affiliation showed that every political party was touched: 465 *D.C.*s, 288 Socialists, 71 representatives of the *P.C.I.* (now renamed *P.D.S.*–Democratic Party of the Left), 39 Social-Democrats, 31 Republicans, 20 Liberals, five representatives of *Rifondazione Comunista* (the splinter group of the die-hard leftwingers who refused to join the *P.D.S.* vowing to "remain Communist") and four members of the Neo-fascist *M.S.I.* Estimates put at over 80,000 billion lire (about 53 billion dollars) or one half the budget deficit, the grand total of the payoffs over the last ten years.

What Does it all Mean?

Judging by the mega-scandals and the wide operations of the Mafia over the entire territory of the nation and the power that it exercises on Italian institutions, even governmental ones, are we to conclude that Italy has failed as a democratic nation? Should we conclude that Italians don't know how to behave in a democratic system? Some political experts do think that Italy falls short on many measures we use to gauge the health and stability of democratic societies and governments. It should be pointed out that the very democratic form of government with a very "liberal" judicial system makes it very difficult for the nation to deal with political opponents of the republic and those who threaten the stability of the nation. However, we should examine closely how Italy fares in comparison with other Western countries. On the governmental level, Italy can only draw respect. If the Italians change prime ministers more often than do the British, or than Americans change presidents, this really does not mean that Italian democracy is more unstable than the others. If 85-90 per cent of the Italians vote in national elections, as compared with just over half that number in American presidential elections, is it really the case that the Italian and not the American pattern is pathological? As J. La Palombara has made us reflect, "which is a more serious weakness for democracy: the Italian government's apparent inability to bring the mafia to heel in Sicily, or the failure of other democracies to deal with large-scale crime in their major cities? And which kind of corruption is more insidious: the headline-making scandals that fill Italy's daily newspapers, or the extensive 'white-collar' crime in the United States, that rarely gets any public notice at all."[5]

Despite crime (though Italy is certainly not at the top of the list of crime-plagued nations) and despite unemployment and heavy taxes, it seems that life is still good in Italy. In 1989 polls conducted in the French-speaking Valle d'Aosta and the German-speaking Alto Adige, which was ceded to Italy by Austria after WWI, revealed that although these regions desire greater administrative autonomy, in no way do they wish to secede from Italy. The winds of total autonomy and separatism that are sweeping through Europe are not affecting Italian unity.

Another big challenge that the country will face is the upsurge of regional administrative autonomy that the wealthy Northern regions are going to demand. According to the constitution, regions may have their own administration and chart their own destiny. The Christian Democratic governments, or governments of coalitions dominated by Christian Democrats, had, after 1948, refused to implement regionalism, because they rightly feared that it would lead to Communist regional governments. But it steadily became clear that weak local governments, and excessive centralization, were leading to corruption and incompetence. In the years 1968-70 plans were drawn up for fifteen regions, not only on the periphery of the peninsula—like Sicily, Sardinia, the Alto Adige and the Val d'Aosta, where regional governments already existed—but in the heartlands of the country. The regional councils of these new, large, areas were elected in June 1970. By 1980 the regions were spending 18 percent of the entire national expenditure, and at that time the Communists were in control of three regions: Emilia-Romagna (centered in Bologna), Tuscany and Umbria. Communists and Socialists together ran Piedmont, Liguria (centered in Genoa), and Lazio. The Christian Democrats, on the other hand, controlled only two, both in the South, but shared power in eleven others. The regions exercise wide powers, in fields like welfare and education, and control the expenditure of considerable sums of money. Some of these powers have simply been taken over from the old municipalities, but some, certainly, come from central government. Regionalism has encouraged the growth of grass-roots groups—trade unions and local businesses—but unfortunately in the South has sometimes made life easier for criminal organizations, the Mafia and the Camorra. The Communist-controlled regions in the North have earned a reputation for being efficient and free from corruption. Nor have they found it difficult to work with big business or the multi-nationals. Bologna, under Communist control, had become a symbol of prosperity, efficiency and civility: it was one of the most prosperous cities in Europe, it was immune from political corruption, and escaped the destruction of its ancient beauty.

As the national government continues to be shaken by accusations of corruption, these regional governments, with their inherently closer ties to their constituents, may increase in importance and offer Italy new hope in its quest to combat threats to the nation, and maintain its place in the forefront of western democracies.

Notes

1.G. Amendola, "I comunisti e il movimento studentesco, necessità della lotta su due fronti," *Rinascita*, June 7, 1968; L. Longo, "Il movimento studentesco nella lotta anti-capitalista," *Rinascita*, May 3, 1968.

2.See R. Chinnici, "Magistratura e mafia," *Democrazia e Diritto*, vol 22, no. 4, July-August 1982, p. 81. Rocco Chinnici, an investigative magistrate, was killed by the Mafia in the summer of 1983. Other important anti-Mafia personalities had been murdered the year before. On April 25, 1982, the Sicilian communist leader Pio La Torre, who had been in the forefront of the anti-Mafia campaign, was killed with his driver by the Mafia. Later that year, on September 3, the former counter-terrorism chief and then Prefect of Sicily (with special responsibilities for the fight against the Mafia) Dalla Chiesa, was killed with his wife openly in the streets of Palermo.

3. For a penetrating assessment of the working of Mafia see R. Catanzaro, "Mafia, economia e sistema politico, in U. Ascoli e R. Catanzaro, *La società italiana degli anni ottanta* (Bari: 1987), pp. 255-79.

4. G. Turato and C. Sasso, *I saccheggiatori* (Milan: Sperling & Kupfer, 1992).

5. Op. cit., pp. 6-7.

IV

US-Italian Relations and the American Presence

Italy: Dependent Ally or Independent Partner?

There is no question that America played a major role in the political and cultural post-war evolution of Italy. We have already pointed out that Italian internal political affairs have been deeply affected by the strange relationship between Italy and the USA. The peculiar character of these relations is not based on the existence of any special amicability or feeling of kinship; on the contrary, the American government has usually been indifferent to Italy. The singular nature of the relationship is due to the profound and patent American involvement in Italy's domestic affairs. This meant that for much of the post-war period Italy was a dependent ally of the United States.

US-Italian relations for most of the last forty-five years have been dominated by questions arising from domestic politics rather than international affairs, as is the case with France, Germany and other Western allies. The critical element in American/Italian relations was the existence, up until 1991, of a Communist party potentially strong enough to share power or even lead the Italian government. From Washington's point of view, such an eventuality would have created both a political embarrassment for an American president and a risk that Italy might have left NATO or reduced its alliance commitments. The overriding American aim was always to forestall any form or degree of Communist participation in the Italian government.

When president Carter was elected in November 1976, Italy was considered the greatest potential political problem the US had in Europe. In the final months of the Ford administration, the Communists had achieved their all-time high in an Italian election, 34.4 percent of the vote. They were extending their control in every important area of Italian life–schools, press, judiciary, trade unions, regional and local governments. It seemed almost inevitable that they would enter the government in a "historic compromise" coalition with the Christian Democrats, eventually hindering the country's support of the Western Alliance.

The American right was putting pressure on the President to stop the threat of communism through covert operations if necessary. But Carter wisely rejected that option and decided against the financing of Italian political parties, the manipulation of Italian political events, and the attempt to tell the Italians how they should vote. In making such a decision, the President was influenced by the counterproductive effect of such efforts in the past. As Richard N. Gardner, Carter's ambassador to Italy, pointed out, "early in the Nixon years...large sums of money were given by the U.S. Embassy in Rome to the right-wing general who subsequently ran for parliament on the neo-Fascist ticket. Wide publicity was also given in Italy to reports that another covert financing operation was discussed and then aborted in the Ford Administration. Both of these episodes helped the Communist Party to gain support as defender of the country's sovereignty against `American domination'."[1]

Italy's political moves had been closely monitored by the USA since the war's end because the strong Communist Party had always been regarded by American governments as a danger to the security of the West. During the first months of 1948, Italy was already seen as the hottest battleground of the cold war against Communism. In their conflict with the Soviets, American governments felt free to intervene at every level of Italian domestic affairs.

Much of the intervention went on behind the scenes through covert operations. In the early postwar period the American government had provided encouragement and funding for the establishment of a political party–the Social Democrats–and two trade unions–the UIL and the *C.I.S.L.* Subsequently it dispensed funds to a variety of individuals, groups, and parties most especially the *D.C.* and a Catholic national labor union (*C.I.S.L.*). The American policy did not consider the danger that such moves could turn political stability into stagnation or that the reconstruction drive itself would result in a substantial restoration of old economic and social structures. In seeking their own self-centered aims the Americans missed an opportunity to broaden the foundations of Italy's democratic institution. Economic and political power had always been in the hands of the few: mostly landowners in the South, big business and industrialists in the North. The predictable results of American intervention were to further strengthen the trend toward stalemate and "immobilismo," a term that became fashionable in those years to describe the performance or lack of performance by the De Gasperi governments.

In the 1950s America saw Italy as "an ally in distress" and even wondered whether she was about to become a "lost ally." During the Eisenhower years, the American ambassador to Rome, Clare Boothe Luce, based her assessment on the danger that the *P.C.I.* might "take over" in the near future or at least gain enough additional votes to "overtake" the *D.C.* and become the number one political force in the nation. The fear was such that US officials in Rome announced that aid might be discontinued if the leftist and/or rightist opposition parties gained ground in the 1954 election. In later statements America let it be known that contracts would be denied to factories where communist-dominated unions continued to poll a majority of the workers' votes. The whole program of economic assistance in Italy became controversial, especially when the spotlight fell on the US intention to use economic aid not only to strengthen Italy's international commitments but to condition domestic developments. Top representatives of the US administration felt that the Italian government did not display all the desirable vigor in the battle against Italian Communism. They suggested, for instance, that the municipal Council of Bologna (the biggest Red stronghold in Italy) be disbanded.

Unfortunately, America was not concerned with the fact that, in 1954, despite a remarkable post-war recovery, Italy was a country where 50 million people were governed by 5,000 in the interest of 500. Mrs. Luce was still toying with the idea that the right could make a useful and possibly decisive contribution to solving Italian problems. She was terribly worried about Gronchi's ascendancy to the Presidency and his reported inclinations toward neutralism in foreign affairs and "socialistic openings" in domestic politics, even though he had clearly voiced his support for the Atlantic Alliance and for Western cooperation and solidarity. Gronchi let it be known that he was not happy with the way Italy was being treated in the Atlantic Alliance; he felt that his country was entitled to a more equal standing in an alliance that was practically run by the US, Great Britain and France.[2]

This US slight towards Italy was not caused simply by fear of a possible Communist takeover, but also by certain international economic policies with which Italians were having significant success. At this time, the US also had a bitter aversion to Enrico Mattei's initiatives in a cooperation on an equal footing with the oil rich countries of the Third World and to Italy's sharing in the economic development of the underdeveloped countries. With the coming to power of a Republican administration in America, many key positions were entrusted to people close to the big oil corporations. Traditional ties with powerful private groups and strong hostility to public intervention in economic affairs prompted large sectors of the US media to sharply attack Mattei and the Italian state oil and gas agency, *ENI*. Mattei was smeared as pro-Communist, a typical charge brought against anyone with whom one disagreed in the fifties. The situation was exacerbated by his ability to achieve significant success in Egypt and other Third World countries, including Iran, thanks to an approach keyed to partnership with local governments. In October 1957, president Gronchi protested to the American ambassador in Rome:

> quite often the actions of your oil concerns are backed by American diplomatic representatives. We feel that the behavior of these corporations does a great disservice to the United States. Just when the British and French 'imperialism' has come to an end in this sector, the `imperialism' of the North American corporations is getting under way.[3]

During the same time the Italian government was trying not to be subservient to the US in foreign policy and was complaining to the US about its failure to consult with Italy in European and, especially, Mediterranean policy. The US conferred almost exclusively with France and Great Britain, even in the Mediterranean where the two former colonial powers had lost their clout. Italy, on the other hand, had left a good bridge with her ex-colonies and enjoyed a good relationship with most of the Arab world; she felt that the US should have supported her pursuit of political prestige and economic expansion in that part of the world. The Italian government was telling Washington that there was nothing wrong, or that it was perfectly possible for a Mediterranean country like Italy to pursue a policy of friendship toward the Arab world while continuing to cooperate with her partners in the Atlantic Alliance. In 1957, during the Eisenhower Administration, the US started to reassess its relationship with Italy. Vice President Nixon, on his trip to Italy in the Spring of 1957, stated that it would be useful if in the Middle East, the US could act in closer cooperation with Italy and with other major countries more directly concerned. However, it was not easy to change American government attitudes toward Italian internal politics. Arthur Schlesinger Jr., who was to become a high-ranking adviser to President Kennedy, wrote that US policies toward Italy required a thorough updating. In subsequent years, he became more and more convinced that the US would greatly benefit, directly and indirectly, from the coming to power in Italy of a coalition based on collaboration between Christian Democrats and Socialists. However, many key posts, notably in the State Department, continued to be held or controlled by officials whose ideas about Italy were cemented in the early post war years. When the shortcomings of the center governments became unsolvable, they tended to look to the right rather than to the moderate left.

The US was loath to allow the socialists in government because their leader, Pietro Nenni–even though he had criticized Stalinism and the Soviet behavior in Hungary and had stated that the US, having been called upon twice to save European liberties, first from German militarism and then from Nazi-Fascism, had acquired a historical title and vested interest in European freedom and security, and had spoken against the Italian Communist Party–had not dropped his requests for the withdrawal of US forces from Europe and for a neutralist Italian position. Despite America's opposition, Aldo Moro spared no efforts to make sure that the dialogue between the *D.C.* and the PSI would make progress. But the center-left coalition was only possible after a short-lived government had been formed with the support of the neo-fascists which brought the nation to the brink of a civil war and also after the change of administration in Washington. Public opinion polls supported the view that the opening to the left would not have brought about a pro-Soviet government.

USA Gives the OK to the Socialists

At the end of the 50s and early 60s the leader of the Socialist Party, Pietro Nenni, was constantly trying to clarify the position of his party for an eventual participation in government. He emphasized that Italy's links with NATO represented an irreversible position and that Italy's approach to European integration had to be closer to that of President Kennedy which was founded on democratic and supernational principles rather than on a confederation of nationalistic countries as advocated by the regime of French Premier Charles de Gaulle. Nenni repeatedly stated that his party's objectives were to bring Italy's social and institutional framework in line with the high rate of industrialization and increase in production.

The possible participation of Socialists in government was not opposed by the Vatican, even though some Italian cardinals did express reservations. Ever since the election of Pope John XXIII, the Vatican had adopted a policy of less direct involvement in Italian politics and viewed with benevolent neutrality the flirtation of the DC with the PSI; the Church's position was in line with its new emphasis on social aspects of its traditional doctrines, as reflected in such papal pronouncements as the encyclical *Mater et Magistra* (*Mother and Teacher*).

 The gap between Italian political reality and its perception by the US diplomatic corps was narrowed during the first year of the Kennedy Administration. As pointed out by Arthur Schlesinger in his book, *A Thousand Days*, Secretary of State Averill Harriman played a key role in turning around US diplomacy and persuading those US officials who had opposed Socialist participation in the Italian government.[4] Schlesinger felt that the opening to the Socialists provided a good opportunity for both Italian and US interests and therefore deserved to be strongly supported by Washington; Italy had to proceed with its plan of social and economic reforms. The American administration's support for the center-left paid dividends during the crisis over the deployment of Soviet missiles in Cuba. Nenni did not share the pro-Soviet and anti-American views expressed by the Communist Party and the pro-Communist wing of his own. The course followed by the center-left coalition in international affairs became even more of an asset for the Kennedy administration because of the sharpening differences with Gaullist France over its opposition to the entrance of Great Britain to EEC and its concept of a European unity on a federalistic basis. The American support for the center-left strengthened the resolve of the Italian government to oppose the Italian conservative forces, in which many US diplomats had long put their faith.

The position taken by the American administration was not followed by most of the American media which kept repeating old charges and prejudices. Editorials and articles published in Spring 1962 were a clear reminder of how ill-informed and biased was the American press. The slanted reporting of some sectors of the US news media and their inability to understand Italy and Italian politics emerged most flagrantly when the conflicts within the Socialist camp led to the failure of Moro's first attempt to form a new center-left government. The gains scored by the Communists at the general elections in Spring 1963 were quickly interpreted as a rejection of the coalition political forces by the electorate. The American press did not realize that the Communist gains at the polls had to be interpreted in the context of spreading protests fed by practical rather than by ideological factors and circumstances. Echoing Italian conservative fears as seen in rightist papers, the American press prophesied Italy's near abandonment of solidarity with the West, of a free economy and of an open democratic society.

This biased coverage of the Italian political scene has been criticized by politicians from the full spectrum of Italian political life. Except for occasional references, the American media did not make real efforts in those years (and most of the times) to address the political and economic life and assess Italy's presence as a modern industrial society. Very rarely did American journalistic reports include some sort of insight or analysis of Italy's political, economic, or social conditions and prospects.

Many in the US media, for instance, also failed to understand or badly underrated the significance of the student movement which in early 1968 was already surfacing as a new and important component of Italian society. A challenge to the entire Italian establishment was naively presented as a simple resentment of an antiquated university system. The *New York Times* (February 12 and March 12), for instance, stated that the groups involved did not represent any significant percentage of the electorate.

As there was a complete American media panic on the outcome of the Italian election of May 19-20, 1968 when the Communists scored a big gain, so there was an over-reaction in the positive when the *P.C.I.* criticized the Soviet invasion of Czechoslovakia in the same year. The gains scored by the *M.S.I.* in the local elections held in mid-June 1971 unleashed another wave of alarm in the US media. *Newsweek* (June 28) went so far as establishing a parallel between the social conditions that spurred Mussolini's rise to power and the chaotic state of present-day Italy! Predictions of civil war, impending Communist takeover and/or rightist coups were often bandied about in the headlines. When *P.C.I.* leaders bid for a deal with the Christian Democrats and probed US reactions in the mid-70s, the American media reached its most reactionary paranoia. Unusual attention was devoted to Italy by the major US media in 1975-1976 which reflected their fears for the *P.C.I.*'s growing electoral strength and prospects.

American interference in Italian domestic politics was used by the *D.C.* to justify their politics. The Christian Democratic Party attributed its policy of slow modernization of the country to the fact that the party did not have complete freedom. The tendency to use the USA as a justification for a whole range of internal political decisions was useful to the *D.C.* but it conveyed the perception that Italy was an American satellite.

Writers and other artists criticized the USA. A leftist actor-playwright, Dario Fo, staged a play, *The Lady is Fit to be Thrown Away*, in which the 'lady' America becomes the metaphor for a monstrous machination organized for the glorification of a system dominated by an obsession for money and by the overwhelming power of capital. Like much of the intelligentsia of the left as well as radical and leftist journalists, Fo sought to make real the idea that Italy has been, and still is, a "province," a most compliant and exploited province, of the "American empire."

The covert funding of many activities certainly did not help the American image in Italy. For instance in 1972 the US provided ten million dollars to certain political parties to help them in the national election that year. Ambassador Graham Martin gave 800 thousand dollars to General Vito Miceli, the extreme-rightist head of Italian military intelligence, without conditions on the money's use. He later became a candidate in the neo-Fascist party. A 1976 report of the House of Representatives stated that the CIA had disbursed over 75 million dollars to Italian parties and candidates during the preceding three decades.

All this should not suggest that most Italians, or even a majority of them, have become anti-American. Most Italian officials and the majority of the Italian public have tolerated such interference with remarkably little resentment. However, respect and admiration for America, which is still more prevalent in Italy than in any other European nation, has dwindled; scars due to past mistreatment remain deep.

All in all, therefore, the relationship between the two countries is not based on mutual trust and respect. Americans do not take Italy seriously, and Italians respect the US for its power, not for any wisdom in its handling of international affairs.

The American Cultural Domination
Even more than in political and military circles, America has come to be a dominant force on the Italian cultural scene, especially through film.

The presence of American film on the Italian peninsula has always been strong. By 1925 some four-fifths of the market was held by American films. Why? The causes were predominantly economic (Hollywood's search for export markets in Europe; Italian exhibitors' demand for popular films), attitudinal (a change in public taste in Italy), political (inadequate import controls by the Italian government and the American government's drive to promote a certain set of values through the medium of film). The Fascist government did very little to combat American domination, either culturally or commercially, presumably because Hollywood was not sending out movies that could be interpreted as critical of the Fascist ideology. But the American film popularity has to be found also in the wealth and organizational maturity of the American film industry–vertically integrated, geared to making exportable films. The United States was a vast country with many movie houses. A successful American film would recoup its production costs on its first run at home before being exported. This meant that it could be offered to distributors and exhibitors abroad at a lower price than films produced in their own countries, which still had to make up their costs.

There was a significant contradiction in the Fascist period between official attempts to construct a national culture, and the fact that much cultural consumption—both of high culture and popular culture–was of non-national products. The massive preponderance of American films in Italian cinemas continued until 1939, when more effective protectionist measures were introduced and for the first time during the Fascist rule the number of Italian films in circulation exceeded that of American films. The "Americanization" of the cinema in the 20s and 30s in turn influenced Italian production, because it imposed a commercially popular style which Italian filmmakers were pressured into adopting if they wanted to have a chance of competing at the box office. Effective restrictions to limit the amount of foreign material only came during the last years of the Fascist regime.

How should the presence under Fascism of a large quantity of light entertainment material, much of it foreign, be interpreted? It served a political purpose; it provided a form of escapism. The regime promoted it, or was happy to let it circulate, because it fit into a "bread and circuses" policy of keeping the masses happy.

After 1945, the movement known as neo-realism attempted to redefine the function of Italian cinema, to introduce to popular audiences a different sort of engagement with reality. All the stress in neo-realism was on the hidden underside–poverty, unemployment, illiteracy, the legacy of Fascist neglect and the difficulties of postwar reconstruction. But American films continued to be overwhelmingly popular. In the late forties and early fifties, a strong marketing push by American film distributors was abetted by a hostile attitude towards neo-realist films by the center-right government, by much of the press, and by Italian promoters eager to get their hands on commercially viable films and make a lot of money. These situations made it very difficult indeed for native filmmakers to get their work financed and shown.

The American supremacy also was a result of advantageous terms the Americans were able to negotiate during the time of Rome's liberation. Italy was inundated by a huge quantity not just of new productions but also of old films and re-runs because the wall of protectionism came down as a result of assiduous work by the United States government and film industry to help its commercial interests. Ellis Arnall, president of the Society of Independent Motion Picture Producers, reported on a visit to president Truman in 1949:

> The president readily agreed that our government has a responsibility to see to it that American-produced motion pictures be utilized to the fullest in carrying the message of Americanism and Democracy to the rest of the world. He expressed these views to the Secretary of State, Mr. Acheson, and requested Mr. Acheson to take such steps as feasible to the end that foreign countries would not discriminate against American-produced pictures and would maintain no unreasonable quotas or unfair restrictions against them.[5]

There was a period in the early 1960s when it looked as if the tide had turned. RAI, the Italian state-run radio and television network was protectionist, while in the cinema the share of Italian box office obtained by American films plummeted to less than a third. Italian national production, supported by that of other EEC countries, seemed sufficient to satisfy public demand. It looked as if European culture could counterbalance the avalanche of American culture. This proved to be an illusion, for while European co-production made economic sense in the cinema, the cultural character of the co-produced films could rarely be described as 'distinctively' European. From the 1970s on Hollywood dominated on Italian screens, especially TV. The shows are for the most part cheap to acquire and undemanding to watch.

The American Myth in Literature
The success of American films in Italy is also due to a general Italian fascination for America. The average Italian always had a fascination for America, even more so when the only way to reach America was through fantasy. The Italians perceived America from the time of its first discovery, as a New Eden, a recovery of innocence. The Europeans had to believe that somewhere there was a land free from the plagues and famines, the dynasties and social classes, the hypocrisies and cynicism of the Old World.

Most Italians, unable to visit or emigrate to the US, had to be content with an imaginary journey made possible through the accounts and letters of relative and friends. For them, America was a strange, mythical land, whose extraordinary wealth and generosity were often the subject of animated conversation. America was the great land of opportunity (fictionalized in the short story *"Aunt Bess, In Memoriam"* by Giuseppe Berto (1914-1972) and thus an alluring haven for the hundreds of thousands of immigrants who, during the latter part of the nineteenth century, began leaving en masse for the United States, in search of a better life.

The literary experience of the Italians illustrates poignantly the position America enjoyed in the aspirations of those who emigrated to America. Indeed, the Italians, like many other groups who immigrated into this hemisphere, built a kind of mythology that remains alive even today; the more ignorant, illiterate and poor they were, the more they were likely to maintain this dream. The peasant, especially from the South, dreamed of America not because he necessarily hoped to be here, but precisely because America represented something fabulous, and, for that reason consoling. In Italy the myth of America was also nourished by the lack of work and land to sustain its population. The land that does not have products to export, exports its own children, or makes their minds fantasize about other lands; the people who do not find in their own country their fulfillment will search for it across the ocean among other peoples. Poverty, or relative deprivation, does not by itself create a sufficient or even necessary "push" to go elsewhere. If poverty is combined with personal goals and expectations that are perceived as not attainable at home, and if a place to relocate becomes available where such hopes appear to have a great chance of realization, the desire to emigrate may become irresistible.

The myth of America in Italian literature is strongly founded in the rich popular fantasy. Probably, *Fontamara* (1930), by Ignazio Silone (1900-1978) provides one of the best stereotypes of America–as the Eden of the poor. The central characters are a group of peasants in the Abruzzi mountains whose water rights are stolen by the local Fascist landowners in league with the local capitalists. To these peasants, among the most poverty-stricken and exploited in Italy, the word "America" has the power of a fetish: it stands simply for the opposite of hunger and deprivation. It is part of their private vocabulary of values and has nothing to do with the real United States. Some of the Fontamaresi, the luckier ones, have made the voyage across the Atlantic, and after years of dogged work in America come back with a little money which they soon lose cultivating the dry and sterile earth. Their only mistake was to come back. After a while, they fall back into the old lethargy, "holding like a memory of lost paradise the image of life glimpsed across the sea." This novel gives the sense of desperation that pushed many southern Italians to emigrate.

Cristo si è fermato ad Eboli, (*Christ Stopped at Eboli*, 1945) by Carlo Levi (1902-1975) gives a more balanced view of America. On the one hand, it portrays the positive views of America held by Southern Italian villagers; on the other hand, it suggests the high price of emigration. Influenced by his own experience as an exiled in Gagliano in the 1930s, Levi gives a compassionate view of peasants' desire to emigrate, and even a sympathetic view of America as a symbol of prosperity and material progress. A journalist, he records without rancor and almost with a kind of ironic sympathy the fact that Gagliano, in the Basilicata region, had become a cultural colony of America; when he went there in 1935, it had 1,200 inhabitants, and there were 2,000 emigrants from Gagliano in America. However, he treats his material, which is factual, in a novelistic style and he has a novelist's insight and flair for character. He thus manages to be both objective and personally involved in his material at the same time. He concludes that emigration is not a permanent answer to any problem, either personal or social. Life in America is good, but the price—to be uprooted from your native soil and to lose the source of strength one drew from the earth—is high.

A work by Mario Soldati (1906-) gave the first real confrontation between Italian and American culture for he was among the first to combine his intellectual interest with an actual visit to the United States. For Soldati, America was a barbaric country without culture, a fact he particularly noticed in daily American life. His *America primo amore* (*America First Love*, 1935), the first detailed account of daily life in America, adds new and strikingly different images and interpretations of the New World. It is a novelist's kind of travel book: impressionistic, vivid, and highly personal. The title makes clear from the outset that the author offered the book not as a sociological or political study, but simply as a story of a personal encounter. First loves are an ecstatic experience, but they are also emotional and unrealistic and they frequently end in disenchantment. Throughout the book Soldati's emotional relation to America is obvious; he writes about America the way any sensitive novelist would write about the girl he was in love with when he was twenty and with whom he then became disenchanted. The mood is disillusioned, often ironic, but rigidly honest and never totally hostile.

An interesting dimension can be found in Livia De Stefani's *Passione di Rosa* (*Passion of Rosa*, 1958) because as a woman writer who spent two years in the US, she addresses directly the theme of dislocation to another culture. Her novel communicates the experience of being a Sicilian and a woman in an America free of the male-oriented norms which dominate Sicily. Her book captures the flavor of America as it seems to an Italian, in a way few other books do. In addition to her feminist point of view, the other pole of the novel is her birthplace, Sicily. Part of the interest of *Passione di Rosa* relates to the geographical resemblance of Sicily and California; the two regions are physically alike, and yet their people and customs are totally different. This difference in the two societies and the effect it has on a young Sicilian emigrant is the focus of the novel. America is presented as in a dream, and as a dream it lasts only as long as it remains a dream; at the first contact with reality it dies. For many immigrants America became a shattered dream because it had been too much idealized.

Part of the fantasy, and also because of intellectual curiosity, is the continuing desire on the part of Italians to encounter America and Americans through writings. This phenomenon happened almost accidentally. The vogue of American literature in the thirties was assisted by a quite incidental fact: that the younger generation of Italian writers, their own creativity discouraged by the Fascist regime, turned to reviewing and translation for economic support. A high proportion of these young translators went on to become important novelists and critics. One was Cesare Pavese (1908-1950) who translated Melville, Lewis, Sherwood Anderson, Dos Pasos and Faulkner. His successful translation of *Moby Dick* became for the young Italians of Pavese's generation, more than any book, what America stood for.

Although Pavese never came to America and never even seems to have entertained the idea, in many ways emigration would have been the logical solution to his personal problems. He felt alienated and restless in Italian culture, and from the time of his first poems portrayed America as representing a new start, a return to the primitive and genuine. But even if he never considered it as a personal possibility, the idea of emigration always lies just beneath the surface of his writings. Indeed, his first poem of *Lavorare stanca* (*Working is Tiring*, 1931) is about the myth of emigration. The protagonist emigrant, who really existed, is metamorphosed into myth; upon his return, after twenty years of wandering over the world, he tells stories to match those in the *Odyssey*. The emigration theme is further developed in Pavese's *La luna e i falò* (*The Moon and the Bonfires*, 1949), considered one of the best post-war Italian novels, in which the emigrant, a peasant, returns with two different contradictory images of America: the traditional emigrant legend of a land of opportunity and easy riches; and the other, of an America he had discovered in his books—the America of the *Pensive Barbarians*, the mythic soil of Whitman, Sherwood Anderson and *Spoon River Anthology*. It was the example of these writers that led Pavese to search his own native soil for meaning to life. The protagonist comes to the realization that Americans, like Italians, did not know each other and suffered from private loneliness.

Nevertheless, the desire to encounter America is not always felt with the same intensity. Because of changes in the economic condition of the country, of political propaganda of America as a world political and military power, and the perception that America puts money ahead of moral values, Italian interpretations of America have not been uniformly positive.

Therefore, the image of America as the home of the violent and the land of the gun has also become a popular and enduring one in the minds of the

average Italian. For years moviegoers have watched massacres of white settlers by vicious savages and the slaughter of unarmed Indians by blood-crazed
cavalrymen. They have seen shootouts at the OK CORRAL and gang warfare
on the streets of Chicago. And most prominently they have witnessed American fighting men from John Wayne to Rambo as they mowed down hundreds
of Nazis or Japanese or Vietnamese or some other "enemy." The glittering
image of America is also tarnished by American images that reflect profound
social differences in the American society. In fact, aside from the images of
mass mayhem, Italians have also watched visions of skyscrapers, the landing
on the moon, the manicured and well equipped American college campuses,
mansions of billionaires as well as the poverty of the South Bronx, Harlem,
and Watts, the kind of images that reflect the worlds of both the very rich and
the very poor.

American Cultural Penetrations: Language and Consumerism

The strong presence of the American film on Italian screens has not only
colored the Italian image of America, it has had a profound impact on Italian
life. In fact, the fifties saw the introduction in Italy of American supermarkets,
frozen food, electric appliances, jukeboxes, pinball machines, pony tails and
pleated shirts. The American presence was so strong that some film directors
felt it as a real cultural colonization and conveyed their message in some of
their movies (Federico Fellini in his *Vitelloni*, 1953 and *The White Sheik*,
1952). A number of films of the fifties with the comic actor Alberto Sordi
(e.g., *An American in Rome*, 1955) simultaneously encapsulated and parodied
some of these cultural transitions. By the 1960s the model of social behavior
and the consumption habits described in American situation comedies was
something which was no longer seen as the image of a distant society characterized by great wealth, but as one which could be attained by many Italians
through the expansion of their market.

In fact, the American way of living penetrated especially the Italian
working-class house. During the years of the 'Economic Miracle'–1958-
1963–Italy turned into a consumer society along American lines. Italians
sought consumer durables–cars, refrigerators, washing machines, dishwashers,
etc.–first as luxuries or providers of social status, but then quickly as necessities. The 1950s saw the expansion in Italy of those industries which could
supply these goods, while mass market, American-style "women's" and
"home" magazines extolled the virtues of the custom-built kitchen and the
labor-saving advantage of the electrical appliances, which the Italians called
elettrodomestici. The ideal home of these years contained a version of the
American 'dream kitchen' as seen in Hollywood films and American television soap-operas.

America served as a model of behavior for the younger generation, through a specific youth market based on cultural forms such as clothing and music. The profound influence that America had in this area cannot be underestimated. Exports by the US to the rest of the world included not only the technical infrastructure for the construction of a youth culture but also the main cultural forms themselves—cheap records, cheap clothes and the know-how to produce them including the system to transmit via radio and television the new music and the new modes of speech. The formation of this youth culture occurred in the 1960s as television became universal in Italy and as small transistor radios became available at a low price to virtually everyone. In the course of the 1960s in Italy, more than anywhere else, the US cultural form of the youth generation, music, clothes, etc., was partly integrated by highly politicized forms of protest. This remarkable politization was more deep-rooted and had a longer lasting effect than the French 1968 movement, the only other comparable phenomenon in the rest of Europe.

America also had a strong influence on the use of media by politicians. Since the late 60s, politicians have adapted to package their political discourse through the media techniques.[6] Italian politics was already delivered with a high dose of theatricality; television and American influence made the political discourse even more like a show, a spectacle. By becoming more "Americanized" the political discourse became more uniform: all politicians were subject to the same rule.

English has become the *lingua franca* all over the world; in Italy it is practically the second language. From the schools to the business office, in both scientific and social worlds, Italians are becoming anglo-phone. This new passion is not so much due to a new love, as much as to the necessities imposed by new economic and industrial world realities. The passion has spilled over and has affected the Italian language. English linguistic penetration or "intimate borrowing" abounds. There has been a more permanent incursion of English terms into the everyday vocabulary of Italian business and technology, where words like marketing, cash-flow, pipeline, design, fast food have become common currency simply because no one has invented adequate Italian equivalents. The Italian government did not become alarmed at this trend, as did the Giscard Government in France which in 1977 adopted a bill which made virtually illegal the use of foreign words where French alternatives can be found in advertisements, official documents, and even on radio and television.

The two languages, as it is well known, have a resemblance in a base vocabulary. Words containing a Latin or, more generally, a Romance Language base, abound in the technical, intellectual, and philosophical discourse in English. Such words most often give rise to loans. Aside from the remarkable number of phonographs (idea, trombone, opera, propaganda, piano, zero, piccolo, chiaroscuro, panorama, etc.) and the quasi-phonographs (umbrella, volcano, tobacco, pantaloons, etc.) to ancient Latinisms and Italianisms, there are also a number of word pairs which differ only in their respective endings (letter-*lettera*, animal-*animale*, second-*secondo*, stories-*storie*, horoscope-*oroscopo*, allergy-*allergia,* solidarity-*solidarietà*, problem-*problema*, govern-*governo*, state-*stato*, comic-*comico*, television-*televisione*, list-*lista*, infinite-*infinito*, deposit-*deposito*, violent-*violento*, brutal-*brutale*, concert-concerto) or in the suffix (-ion and *-ione*, -ty and *-tà*, -ent and *-ente*) which are responsible for the phenomenon of the so called "false friends."[7] Expressions such as (public relations, *relazioni pubbliche*; new frontier, *nuova frontiera*; the rest is silence, *il resto è silenzio*) can be translated almost automatically and are directly responsible for the formation of loan shift. In other cases the "transparency" is such as to make translation unnecessary. For instance, the reference to palm+olive oil in the American noun palmolive works in such a way that palmolive is rarely felt to be a foreign word. In fact, even well educated Italians think of palmolive as an Italian word and palmolive soap an indigenous product. Such lexical likeness points to the fact that the influence of English in Italian takes place between two languages that have a large common base to begin with.

English words by the hundreds have entered in common speech. It is not unusual to hear in daily conversation words such as: OK, babysitter, picnic, bar-be-que, hamburger, popcorn, fun, rock, tester, shopping, basket, management, manager, business, leader, bus, taxi, shock, show, wham, wow, yippie, week-end. Business, Marketing and Advertising, Sports, Tourism, Fashion and Cosmetics, and News are the fields in which the use of English abounds. In the business world, the presence of English is so strong that quick reference dictionaries have been created specifically for greater understanding of English terminology widely used in companies ("The Influence of the English Language in Italian Companies, in Finance, in Marketing"). The prevailing reasoning in this area seems to be: why not make the means your own if it is indispensable for your survival.

This ability of the Italian business world to adopt to changing trends highlights the fact that this aspect of life probably represents the best of Italy. No society seems better attuned to the free-enterprise system than that of the Italians; private initiative in many fields has been indeed the secret of the "Italian miracle." Italian cabinet ministers must attend conferences around the world trailed by a score of interpreters because Italian politicians notoriously speak no language other than their own. Italian businessmen on the contrary are proud of their versatility in international communication. Not only do they attempt to minimize the linguistic barriers, but they also try to maximize their understanding of others by getting to know their culture.

Notes

1. In "Foreword" to Leo J. Wollemborg, *Stars, Stripes, and Italian Tricolor* (New York: Praeger, 1990), p. xv.

2. L. J. Wollemborg, p. 23.

3. Ibid., p.40.

4. A. Schlesinger, *A Thousand Days* (Boston: Houghton Mifflin, 1965), p. 879.

5. Quoted in Thomas Guback, 'Shaping the film business in postwar Germany: the role of the US film industry and the US state,' in Paul Kerr, ed., *The Hollywood Film Industry: A reader* (London and New York: Routledge and Kegan Paul, 1986), p. 250.

6. Giovanni Cesareo, 'Il "politico" nell'alba del quaternario,' *Problemi del Socialismo*, vol. 22, no. 22, (1981), pp. 28-29.

7. For a comprehensive study see M. Cortellazo and V. Cardinale, *Dizionario di parole nuove: 1964-1984* (Turin: 1985).

Part Two

E C O N O M Y

V

The Economic Recovery

From Ashes to World Economic Power

There is no other country in Europe that has changed so enormously and rapidly in the post-war period. In fact, Italy has changed more in the last forty years than during the previous two thousand. Compared to 1950 the average Italian is much better fed, housed, educated and receives better health care. The enormous gap which once existed between Italians and Americans has been considerably reduced. Indeed, many Italians are proud to openly claim that "America is here now."

The British have viewed all this with a mixture of envy and admiration. How have those damned Italians managed it? If it is not wealth in natural resources, it must be the result of some deep renewal of national ambition and the will to work hard, allied to the dynamism of a new breed of entrepreneurs for whom the state bureaucracy is less a help than a hindrance. Of course, Italy was starting from a much lower level than Britain and France, and the late industrialization partly explains the high growth rate. But the so-called "economic miracle," in its Italian context, was one of the most remarkable in the world, for it was achieved in the face of Italy's fundamental shortcomings.

The economic development in the postwar era has been extraordinary, exceeded only by that of Germany and Japan. As in the case of those two countries, the very scale of the destruction suffered in the war was a blessing in disguise: it brought a chance to make a new start on modern lines. The British who had the "misfortune" never to be defeated, lacked the same impetus.

In 1945 Italy, or a large portion of it, was one of the poorest countries in the West. A land bereft of natural resources, with only a quarter of its land suitable for farming, the country had suffered more from the war than any other Western nation but Germany. In 1947, as a loser of the war, Italy was obliged to pay within seven years $100 million to the Soviet Union, $125 million to Yugoslavia, and $105 million to Albania, besides having to mourn the loss of half a million of its citizens, care for several million wounded, face the destruction of many factories, the annihilation of the merchant marine, the loss of one quarter of its railways, 35 percent of its roads, and thousands of bridges. At the end of hostilities, destitution was widespread, with the population suffering the classic earmarks of poverty: high illiteracy and infant mortality, poor diet, and limited education. Most housing lacked baths and much of it even running water. Unemployment and underemployment were high; inflation was rampant and taxation regressive. Banditry and black-marketeering had flourished. At Tombolo deserters from the US army had set up a robbers' republic. Panic seized the middle classes, and class hatred or class fear begat hostility to the national environment. A late industrial developer, Italy had only a modest manufacturing sector, which was centered in a narrow area of the Northwest and depended heavily on tariffs and state assistance. Merely a third of the labor force was employed in industry; more than half was engaged in small-scale agriculture. In 1945 industrial production was only about 25 per cent of what it had been in 1938, and agricultural production was reduced by about 40 per cent. Per capita income was lower than at any time since unification and half what it had been in 1938.

However, by 1962 Italy was experiencing one of the fastest growing economies in the world. Economists labelled this progress as the "economic miracle." It was a miracle because of the pace with which Italy recovered from a destructive war while lacking natural resources and having a topography which does not favor productive agriculture. By 1970 Italy had become the world's seventh-ranking industrial state, was a leading international exporter, and held some of the most substantial gold and foreign-exchange reserves in Europe. In the 1980s she had passed England and contended with France for the fourth-ranking world industrial position. Whole new industries, such as steel, chemical, and oil refining, had been established with the most advanced technology and were able to compete with the best in Europe. Old private firms, like FIAT, Pirelli and Olivetti, had revived to become European leaders in their fields. Unemployment had dropped from over 10 per cent to half that figure. In about thirty years, more than 5 million agricultural workers had moved into industry, and the farm population had been reduced to about 11 per cent of the total working force. Italy had passed from an essentially peasant society to a largely urban one.

For some time now Italy has been numbered among the top five industrialized countries in the world. Leaving behind the troubled 1970s, where economic mismanagement and social disorder jeopardized its future, Italy was also named the economic miracle of the 1980s. Today, measured by almost every index of well-being, Italians are better off than most of them ever imagined possible. Fewer of their babies die in infancy, most adults live longer, and everyone eats better. In the crasser terms of consumer goods–telephones, cars, washing machines, television sets–Italian ownership matches and on certain goods even exceeds the Western European average. True, the well-being is not evenly distributed–for the South still lags far behind the north–but things have improved everywhere beyond all recognition.

The progress made has been achieved through an economy which is dualistic in character: rich North vs. poor South, private vs. public enterprise, multinational companies vs. small family owned firms. A study of the relation and change in these sets of areas gives a clear view of how Italy changed in the last thirty years.

The amazing growth can best be appreciated when it is related to the low level of available natural resources in the country.

Poor in Natural Resources

For a country of 57.7 million people Italy is only modestly provided with agricultural resources and is considerably worse off with respect to other kinds of natural resources. With a few exceptions the geological characteristics of Italian territory do not comprise high deposits of industrially useful mineral resources, and only four regions (Sardinia, Tuscany, Sicily and Trentino-Alto Adige) have a mineral content of any interest. A considerable part of the world's mercury is mined just north of Siena; quantities of sulfur are found in Sicily and near Naples. The only fuel found in any quantity particularly in the Po Valley, is natural gas (methane) though there is consistent exploitation of geothermal resources. Small quantities of crude oil were discovered at Maloss, near Milan, and some oil was found near Gela, Sicily. There is widespread extraction of lithoid and incohesive sediments (clay, gravel and sand) from alluvional plains; numerous quarries are scattered throughout the country, frequently responsible for ruining the landscape and disturbing the stability of sloping ground.

The lack of fossil coal had already forced the country to build a number of hydroelectric power stations in the last century, mainly in the Alpine valleys, though also in several sites in the Apennines.

After the war, however, industrial expansion had to utilize power generated by coal or hydrocarbon power stations. At present a quarter of the electricity produced is obtained from water resources and three quarters from thermal sources. Italy has to import 82 per cent of the sources of energy supply.

In spite of the variety of topographical conditions and the extent of mountainous terrain (80 per cent of the country's area is mountainous or hilly), only 12 per cent of Italian territory (buildings, roads, wasteland, waters, etc.) is actually unproductive. Apart from forests (about 21%), abandoned and rough ground and service areas (about 9%), the surface effectively destined for annual or stable permanent cultivation amounts to little more than 58 per cent of the entire national territory.

Referring to the organization of **agriculture**, the last general census of agriculture also indicates that of a total relative surface cultivated by more than 3 million farmers (about 78% of national territory), little more than half (about 53%) was effectively utilized. Most of this land is owner-farmed (94%) and less than 2 % is under the sharecropping system, once common throughout most of the country (especially in Veneto and the central regions).

Peasants' conservatism has also been a hindrance to solving the problem of land parcellization. Fly over many parts of Italy and you will see a crazy quilt of thin strips; quite a modest farmer may have several tiny fields, not next to each other but scattered over miles. This is mostly the result of the equal inheritance laws, as farms were split up between sons with each new inheritance. Sentimental values remain very strong: how can a farmer give up a field where his father taught him to plough or leave the cherry orchard his grandfather planted? In a nation with so strong a rural tradition, *la terra* can still rouse powerful emotions.

The land continues to be split up among a very large number of small farmers and many of the farms are not big enough to support a family. Three-quarters of the farm holdings are less than 5 hectares and almost one-third less than one hectare. Italy has the smallest average (7.2 hectares) in the E.C. with the exception of Greece. Since 35% of arable land belongs to large farms (over 100 hectares), which in themselves fail to account for 1.1% of the total number of farms, Italian agriculture presumably consists of medium-sized farms (5-100 hectares, 23.5%) covering practically half (48%) of all arable land. However, the situation is changing. The period between the last two agricultural censuses (1970-1982) showed the drop in numbers of small farms and the increase of medium to large holdings (20 hectares and more). This trend has been accompanied by fairly limited changes in land ownership and, in the case of smallholders, by abandonment of the land for the town in order to emigrate or, in any case, take non-agricultural employment.

Between 1970 and 1982 the total number of farms dropped by 10% and the cultivated area by 6%. The drop in the number of farms of all kinds and in the land area they cover may be attributed to a number of socio-economic phenomena acting in different degrees on soil usage according to the country's various regions. A part of the cause is to be found in the persistent decrease in the population of the mountain areas, with a consequent increase in building construction; other causes are tied to the structural changes going on now in the farm sector. For example: the massive exodus of labor from farming, which has encouraged the formation of farms of greater land area; the changes that have taken place in the legal nature of farm contracts (especially as regards sharecropping and colony forms of farming); the different usage being made of land now, and, finally, the improved configuration of farms now, especially in areas that were formerly highly fragmented.

Certainly, the variety of climatic and geomorphological conditions together with the heterogeneous nature of the soil are factors which have contributed, together with the force of tradition, to influence or determine the yield and kind of **crops** the country produces. Wheat and maize are the major cereal crops with barley now increasingly grown, while rice is a specialized crop exported in large quantities. Olive, citrus, and other fruit trees are the commonest and best known which, together with vineyards, make the country a leader in the Mediterranean and in Europe, though international competition is now strong. Italy is the largest producer of wine and the second largest olive-producing country in the world. The region with the highest production of olives is Puglia, followed by Calabria, Sicily, Latium and Tuscany. Fruit is also important, particularly apples and peaches. Important also is the production of vegetables (tomatoes, lettuce, beans, cauliflower and others that are deservedly well known throughout the world) which are grown especially in Southern Italy—Campania, Calabria, Sicily and Sardinia. The fine agricultural products combined with refined cooking skills have brought about the recent resurgent interest in Italian agricultural products and cuisine. The "Mediterranean diet"—lots of pasta, olive oil, little meat, and plenty of vegetables and fruits—has been touted by nutritionists in most economically advanced countries.

Floriculture is now expanding rapidly, favored by the mild climate and widespread greenhouse cultivation. Now replacing floriculture designed for local needs only is an industrial type floriculture, aimed at meeting the demands of a huge national and international market. Flowers are grown for commercial purposes mainly in Liguria, along the coastal arc reaching from the western Riviera between Ventimiglia and Albenga, and, to some extent, along the eastern Riviera. The crops are cut flowers (carnations and roses especially), bouquet flowers (bulbs, gladioli, chrysanthemums), ornamental plants, and flowers and leaves for perfume manufacture.

Of localized importance is certain tree-type crop production such as chestnut and hazelnut, utilized principally by the confectionery and bakery industries. Among other industrial-crops are sugar beets and tobacco. Relatively unknown until WWII, sugar beets have become one of the important Italian agricultural products for industrial utilization. The production of tobacco is also important; the richest plantations are to be found in the Puglia, Veneto, Abruzzi, Campania and Umbria regions.

Livestock breeding, a traditional agricultural activity, has also suffered the effects of the crisis in this sector, as is apparent from underdevelopment in the last few decades. Methods are somewhat backward except in the Po Valley, and consequently inadequate to the national demand for meat. Certain old customs, such as transhumance in the Apennines, are now dying out; however in the North, high altitude Alpine pastures are still grazed in the summer. One livestock sector of considerable importance to the Italian farm economy is bee raising , which has made unprecedented progress over the past few years.

Agricultural Reconstruction

In the 60s and 70s Italian farming went through a real "revolution." In no other aspect of Italian life was change so dramatic, or the conflict between old and new so sharp. Farm mechanization changed the landscape of the countryside at every level. The process was not easy: imagine those poor farmers, accustomed to an instinctive rapport with oxen or horses, when they were suddenly confronted with a tractor.

Since the end of the war, the state has taken several measures to transform the very primitive agriculture that existed. A series of laws approved in 1950, to respond to the peasants' revolts of the late 1940s, provided that large, uncultivated, or badly cultivated, estates in huge areas of Sicily, Sardinia, and mainland South were to be expropriated by state agencies. These agencies improved the land and then sold it to landless peasants, at low cost and on long term mortgages. The state also provided, through the *Cassa per il Mezzogiorno*, essential services (irrigation, electricity, houses, roads, livestock) at public expense. Similar kinds of state intervention in agriculture had been done also during Fascism (e.g., the reclamation of the Pontine Marshes); but in the 1950s land was actually expropriated and given to the people.

The land reform had major political consequences. It ended the "latifundium" after more than 2,000 years and, therefore, it broke the political power of the big landowners, who, however , remained economically powerful because they invested in the booming building industry the capital they received from the sale of their land. It also created a "client class" dependent on the agencies. The new peasant-owners grew what the agency told them to grow, lived where the agency told them to live (often in houses built by the agency), and sold their produce through agency-run cooperatives. They also voted for the party that ran the agency, usually the *D.C.* Altogether, about 70,000 families acquired land, but that was only one per cent of the rural population.

This program had some shortcomings. Most of the new owners had been landless peasants, inexperienced in farming techniques. Their holdings were normally on poor land and were usually too small to support a family. These failings became more evident in later years with the increasing use of tractors and specialized machinery which are difficult to use on small farms, and with increased competition from the North and Common Market farming. The land reform, far from solving the "land question," simply increased the number of poor peasants who quickly became even more dependent from state subsidy.

In 1970 half the peasant landowners of Italy were not full-time farmers; they were forced to derive much of their income from other sources: industry, commerce or welfare. Net welfare payments to small landowners rose from 50 billion lire in 1954 to 245 billion lire in 1960 to 909 billion in 1968 and to 1,412 billion lire in 1971. By this time, about one-third of the value of all agricultural production was going in welfare payments, a system that was producing votes for the Christian Democratic Party.

Still, Italian agriculture has improved considerably because of direct government intervention. At the end of WWII production was only 40 per cent of what it had been in 1938, but by 1950 it had surpassed the 1938 figure and by 1960 was 40 per cent above it. The increase continued steadily through the 60s and 70s. Food production doubled between 1950 and 1970. Yields per hectare increased sharply because of better seeds, mechanization, more fertilizers, irrigation, and technical assistance. Because of government policies and financial assistance, Italy has become the world's leading exporter of durum semolina and pasta products and the leading rice producer in Western Europe.

The agricultural successes and the overall affluence in Italy contributed to some rather surprising changes that could not have been foreseen. The "problem of wheat," so central to Fascist policy, became one of overproduction and under-consumption. People ate less bread and less pasta, but consumed more dairy produce. In 1958 imports of cheese exceeded exports for first time ever! The people also ate twice as much meat. Not only was there an increased caloric intake, but also a rising standard of dietary demands that emphasized meat and other protein products. However, the gap between meat production and consumption makes meat the most significant food-deficit item and makes Italy the world's third largest importer of meat and meat products. Italy has to import half the beef and veal it consumes. For many years, the Italian economy showed another paradox: Italy was at the same time an importer and an exporter of meat; it had to export the second cuts of imported meat, because Italians ate only first cuts. Since the arrival of the American fast food restaurants (MacDonald in Rome grosses the highest amount of any restaurant in the chain), Italy does not export any more meat!

The introduction of the American system of chicken raising, Perdue style, has also helped to meet the increased national consumption of chickens. At the beginning of the 1960s Italy imported chickens from the US; sacrificing quantity for quality, today Italy has become the second largest producer of poultry meat in the EC.

Italy is the EC's leading producer of fruits and vegetables which significantly contributes to export earnings. By 1960 Italy was the world's largest producer of wine; it bottled about a quarter of all wine in the world and had improved its quality by putting on the market some of the most renowned wines in the world. By introducing an effective quality control, first by creating the **DOC** (Denomination of Origin Controlled) wines, later the **DOCG** (Denomination of Origin Controlled and Guaranteed) for very few exclusive wines, exports increased considerably. Not only did the wines from the more traditional areas of wine country (Chianti and Brunello da Montalcino in

Tuscany; Barolo and Amarone in Piedmont; Soave and Bardolino in the Veneto), consolidated their position on the world market, but wines from the South (Taurasi and Aglianico, in Campania; Corvo from Sicily) conquered a good slice of the market reserved to prestigious wines.

However, over-production of wine has created serious problems in the EC. French farmers resorted to riots in the 70s to stop the competition presented by some of the more cheaply produced and often more robust Italian wines. The issue was solved when the two nations banned all planting of new vineyards and granted new subsidies for uprooting poor vines. Many producers have now pulled up their vines and changed to other crops, with the help of special grants from Rome and the EC.

Through acts of legislature, the government has also been trying to consolidate farm holdings: anytime a farmer puts property on sale, by law, the adjacent owners must be informed and must be given preference, if interested, in the sale.

Overall, the government has succeeded in substantially improving the social conditions and status of the farmers. In the 1950s the peasants still fell into the lowest income bracket; they had the least access to modern conveniences (running water and indoor plumbing) and owned the fewest consumer items (appliances and automobiles). They had the lowest level of education, and their occupation (working the land) was accorded the lowest social prestige. Much of the peasantry's apparent resignation had in fact been a result of its long history under a static and feudal system. In the Italian tradition, culture resides in the city, in the *civitas*; life outside of the city lacked any refinement or spiritual fulfillment. Ignazio Silone, in his well-known novel, *Fontamara* (1934) represented with somber intensity the life of poverty and sacrifice endured by Southern farmers and the scorn to which they were subjected. Farmers used to be a social class apart, afraid of progress. In the 60s the situation started to change and there has been a radical change in the self-image of the peasants and their attitude toward the social system. Improvement in their living conditions, advances in communication (local roads, transport, availability of telephone, special TV programs dealing with agriculture issues and farm life) and awareness of the world beyond the boundaries of their own community have made farmers accepted citizens of the wider community.

Traditional peasant society, once such a strong and picturesque feature of Italy, is passing away, and the new-style farmer is more like a small businessman; he often has a beautiful car and a modernized home, and his children are scarcely different from town children. Thus, although the old-style peasant, semi-illiterate, living little better than his animals, still exists in some areas, especially in certain areas of the South, a new generation of modern-minded young farmers, with a totally different outlook from their parents, has arisen.

They have promoted a new creed, entirely novel in this individualistic milieu, a creed of technical advance, producer groups and marketing cooperatives. Finally, the old class of *contadini* or *cafoni* (pejorative terms for farmers) has largely become integrated into society.

Unfortunately, as old problems were solved, new ones emerged. The Italian government has had to face an aging farm population and an alarming shortage of skilled agricultural workers. Many small farms are in the hands of people who are recorded as employed in manufacturing or service or as unemployed, and who use family farm plots to supplement their food supplies and their incomes. Worse yet, Italian farming is still plagued by a high degree of traditional individualism. Thus, the country has to solve major dilemmas: the old one of how to reconcile the nation's economic needs with the human demands of the **family** farm; and the new one, shared with the rest of the EC, of how to reduce costly food surpluses without hitting farmers' incomes.

The Changing Face of the Industrial Sector

The most significant improvement in the Italian economy and society came through a very innovative and largely expanded industrial sector. Today, Italy has a large industrial-based economy with heavy dependence on imported energy. Manufacturing is the largest sector of the economy, comprising 35 per cent of GDP and employing 30 per cent of the labor force.

The structure of industrial production and service industries is characterized by the prevalence of small and medium-sized companies (94% and 5.6% respectively), employing 70% of the work force, 30% being monopolized by large companies (more than 100 workers) though these comprise only 0.45% of the total. This means that companies are widely dispersed over the whole country, obviously with significant location and concentration of industry, and more than half the industrial companies operate at little more than workshop level, as is seen by the small work force in each production unit.

There are only a limited number of cooperative companies (food sector and the transformation of agricultural products), while large companies tend to become multinational. The presence of companies with foreign capital monopolizing specific commodity sectors (pharmaceutical, photographic materials, electronics, cosmetics, etc.) is far from rare.

One particular kind of development may be seen in medium-sized companies. Frequently these have expanded from small family-run businesses and with a specialized production, and through management flexibility and technological innovations, they have succeeded in reconverting production and increased competitivity. They have penetrated international markets and have contributed to the consolidation of the Italian image and presence throughout the world. It was due to the high productivity of this sector of the industry that in the mid 80s Italy experienced the second so called "economic miracle."

In addressing the specific industrial sectors, the country's economic revival in the immediate postwar period was essentially sustained by development and expansion of the basic industries, particularly the steel industry, itself conditioned by the importation of raw materials such as ores, scrap iron and coal.

Membership in **ECSC** (European Community for Steel and Coal) enabled the Italian steel industry, which had installed the integral processing cycle, to attain extremely high levels of production, thus satisfying increasingly greater domestic demand, such as that of the engineering industry, as well as the export market. Although this sector is now stagnating due to the international economic situation dominated by strong competition from Japanese industries and plastics, leading to overproduction in the principal European countries, it gave a strong impetus to the Italian industrial structure in those years of industrial recovery.

Mechanical engineering production became extremely varied and included companies such as shipbuilding, aerospace, car building etc. with complex work cycles, together with manufacturers of simple tools. Component manufacturing also became well developed and closely allied to companies producing durable goods not easily classified in any one sector (for example, non-metallic materials used in the car industry: rubber, glass, plastics, etc.)

In practice, mechanical engineering with its diversification and multiple relationships with other industries is still today considered the mainstay of the national productive system in terms of the large work force employed (over 2.2 million according to the 1993 census). Apart from cars and other vehicles, the most highly developed industries are tools, household appliances, electronic equipment, precision instruments, etc. The industrial machinery sector is particularly active with extensive overseas markets, and includes components for complete process cycles.

Another very important change in the industrial sector of the Italian economy was the surge of the **chemical and energy industry.** The chemical industry is closely linked to mining and quarrying and uses mostly liquid (oil) and gaseous hydrocarbons (methane) from which a high range of materials is produced (rubber, plastics, synthetic resins, synthetic fibers, fertilizers, etc.) in addition to the traditional utilization of heating fuel, engine fuel, etc.

Like the steel industry, the chemical industry went through a critical period due to over-production and problems related to plant modernization. One serious additional shortcoming is the need to resort to large-scale importation of raw materials for transformation, and the consequent submission to fluctuating conditions on the international market.

In any discussion of industrial sectors that greatly spurred the Italian economy, it is important to mention the **textiles industry**. Textiles are, in fact, the oldest Italian industry. Although widespread throughout the peninsula, they are chiefly concentrated in four regions (Lombardy, Veneto, Tuscany and Marche) and are frequently linked to the rural community which provides plentiful low cost labor. In the postwar period, this sector faced a period of crisis caused primarily by the use of antiquated machinery and inefficient working methods, though also by competition by foreign producers, particularly in developing countries which were already raw material suppliers (cotton, wool, jute, etc.). The crisis in the textile industry has deeper roots in the progressive decay of some traditional related activities, such as silkworm breeding and the cultivation of hemp and flax. The utilization of artificial fibers derived from cellulose, and later on synthetics derived from hydrocarbons, together with renewal of production plant (mainly automated) and job reorganization, has enabled far higher levels of productivity to be reached, offset by a considerable decrease in the work force and concentration of companies in a few areas.

For its raw material supplies (synthetic fibers) and the utilization of the fabrics produced, the textile sector is closely allied (also by vertical merging of companies) to the chemical and garment manufacturing industries. The latter, in particular, is still scattered over the country, in the form of small firms.

Another sector that must be mentioned is the **food industry**. Development of this industry is a direct consequence of the expansion of large urban centers and progressive industrialization. Strictly allied to the primary sector (agriculture and livestock), it makes considerable use nevertheless of imports, the result of insufficient national agricultural and livestock production. A scattering of small artisan-type firms generally oriented towards meeting local demand has now been joined by numbers of medium-sized companies operating at a national level, using advanced systems of processing, conservation and packaging, themselves flanking the pasta, wine and oil producers, and other traditional companies. The food conservation industry is in special position connected with agriculture, livestock and fisheries.

The diversification of Italian industry has reached the point where it becomes difficult to classify producers in specific sectors. Certain industries, some traditional, have made a highly important contribution locally or in a specific context to the country's development. One example is the building industry in general (constructions, roads, etc.), particularly the housing sector which after the depression affecting the whole country between 1975-85, appears to be in a new phase of development. Satellite activities include cement production, with Italian raw materials (lime, marl, etc.), other building materials (ceramics, bricks) and glass manufacture. The woodworking industry, a solid, generally localized industry, uses mainly imported raw materials specifically in the production of household goods and furniture. The manufacture of paper and allied materials has been traditional for centuries and is linked to the production of packaging and particularly to printing and publishing.

Industrialization and State Industries

Lacking basic natural resources to become an industrial nation, Italy had to create a transformational economy much as Japan has done. This implied major changes and gambles because Italy became a nation dependent on raw material and a target nation for the export of manufactured goods and, therefore, vulnerable to changes in the international economy. But Italy accepted the challenge and quickly fostered a policy of open economy to stimulate international trade. The major event was the establishment of a **European Common Market** (Treaty of Rome, March 1957) which opened a larger market for Italian products.

The Italian industrial sector is part of a dualistic economy: private enterprise with a large public sector. Except for agriculture, there are few sectors of the economy in which the state does not operate and several in which it dominates. Not only do many companies have mixed public and private ownership, but all firms, both public and private, are subject to many legal and financial restraints and carry heavy burdens of social welfare responsibility.

Until the early 90s, in no other country with a free economy, was the government asked to play such an important role in the economy as in Italy. The Italian government was asked to restructure industry, to improve exports, to make Italy more competitive in world markets, to win it more prestige and respect in international politics, to close the amenities gap between the north and the south, to protect the lira and keep inflation within bounds, to reduce inequality, to provide cheaper energy and curb nuclear power, to guarantee everyone work, adequate housing and health care, and to take care of every special interest group.

Today, as we shall see, governments bend to allow more freedom to free enterprise, for the view has gained credence that too much State control puts a damper on private firms' initiative, especially in a competitive free market. This may well be so now. But it does not invalidate the policy of state economic intervention or participation in the earlier post-war decades which was largely a source of strength, at a time when private industry was backward or non-existent and needed a strong lead. In fact, there seems to be no doubt that during that period dynamic State leadership was able to do much for economic development. Governments were able to plan bold new ventures and build up certain key industries.

At the beginning of the 1990s, the government's involvement in the economy was still extensive especially through state-owned industries. Indeed, the basis for public intervention in the economy was the system of state holdings—regulated by the Ministry bearing that name, established in 1956—which represented a necessary tool by means of which the state could exercise control over, and act directly in, the country's development, causing it to attain those results dictated by state economic policy.

Initially concentrated in the vicinity of large cities, busy ports or sources of energy and raw materials, with the declining importance of agriculture, industry moved nearer smaller centers with adequate infrastructures, before spreading right into the countryside competing with agriculture for land and changing the face of the country. Nevertheless in both the North and South the most highly industrialized and urbanized areas are mainly in the densely populated regions.

The traditional industrial triangle (Lombardy-Liguria-Piedmont) has now widened to include practically the whole Po Valley, with the highest concentrations along the foot of the Pre-Alps, Pre-Apennines and the Adriatic coast as well as the large Alpine valleys. Industry in Tuscany and Umbria is concentrated on the plains and in hollows near the Arno and Tiber river basins; in the Marches it spreads over the whole region, scattered throughout the network of valleys. Industry in Latium and Abruzzo is concentrated in the intermontane hollows and along the coasts as well as around the larger cities.

The distribution of industry in Southern Italy, however, follows an irregular pattern, with excessive concentration in certain coastal zones (such as the Caserta-Naples-Salerno belt) or in a number of geographically favorable positions (the Bari-Taranto-Brindisi triangle). Industrial areas on the islands are generally peripheral to port cities.

Three state holdings played a very important role in the Italian economic recovery: *IRI* (Institute for Industrial Reconstruction), *ENI* (National Hydrocarbons Agency), and *EFIM* (Agency for Holdings in and Financing of the Manufacturing Industry). Until the beginning of the 1990s, they covered every sector of the economy, including banking.

IRI had seven sectorial holding companies: STET (Telephone Holding Company) whose task was to manage IRI holdings in the telecommunications and electronics fields; *FINMARE*, for shipping company holdings; *FINSIDER*, for steel industry holdings; *FINMECCANICA*, for machine and mechanical holdings; *FINCANTIERI*, for ship-construction company holdings; *ITALSTAT*, for the urban infrastructures and urban planning sector; and *SME*, the Southern Holding Company, for the food, paper, and automobile sectors in the South of Italy, and for the commercial distribution and promotion of various activities there.

Before the privatization in the early 90s, in the banking sector *IRI* had a large majority of the share capital of such banks as the *Banca Commerciale*

Italiana, the *Credito Italiano*, the *Banca di Roma*, and the *Banco di Santo Spirito*, all of these being banks that carry on their activities in the field of short-term credit. Approximately 90% of the banking activity was in the hands of public sector banks.

Besides the companies headed up by the holding companies and the banks, the Group also included a number of firms that were directly controlled by *IRI*. Among these, the most important were the firms operating in the air transport sector (*Alitalia*), in the toll-expressway sector (*Autostrade*) and in the radio-television sector (RAI).

To give a broad idea of the level of its presence in the Italian economy, it suffices to say that in the services sector the telephone company *SIP* (a company belonging to *STET Group*) covers 82% of the Italian *TLC* traffic; *ALITALIA* 91% of air transportation; *FINMARE* 21% of maritime transportation; *Autostrade* (a company belonging to the *ITALSTAT* Group) 45% of highways. In manufacturing, *FINSIDER* has 55% of total national production of steel, *FINCANTIERI* 70% of shipbuilding; *Ansaldo* 60% of power supply components, *Selenia* and *Aeritalia* 55% of aerospace; *Italtel* 50% of *TLC* switching; *SGS* 98% of micro-electronics.

In 1982, one year before the start of the "recovery schedule" recorded in 1983, *IRI* had over 535,000 employees (ranked second in the world, after General Motors, in number of employees). That year it had a turnover of 32.9 trillion lire ($26 billion) and grew to an estimated 47.6 trillion lire in 1989, ranking it 14th in the world and third outside the US. The privatization that took place in the early 90s reduced considerably the size of *IRI*.

ENI, the National Hydrocarbons Agency (1953), is a public holding company whose purpose is to promote and carry out initiatives in the nation's interest in the hydrocarbons and natural steam fields. The group's organizational structure breaks down into four main sectors: hydrocarbons (coal, oil), chemical and nuclear, engineering and services, manufacturing. Operating in the **hydrocarbons** sector is *AGIP*, which oversees various activities from prospecting for coal and petroleum and uranium ores, to mining, and to the distribution of petroleum products. *SNAM*, too, operates in the hydrocarbons sector, carrying on the transport of hydrocarbons and the importing and distribution of natural gas. Another is the Italian Petroleum Products Industry, which operates in the refining and distribution sector. In the **chemical and nuclear** sector is *ANIC*, which works in the chemicals and refining industry, and *AGIP Nuclear*, heading up all activities concerned with the nuclear industry. In the **engineering and services** sector is *SNAM Progetti*, which oversees the study, design, and construction of gas and oil pipelines and of petroleum facilities and petrochemical plants; it also oversees scientific research activities. *SAIPEM* carries on drilling activities and the assembly and construction of pipelines and industrial plants. *TECNECO* sees to both general and detailed development planning for water resources and for developing the territory in general. In the **manufacturing** sector textile weaving activities are headed up by the *TESCON* holding company, incorporated to give the management policies of the companies it holds greater coherence, and to give them more strength on the financing level. The main companies under *TESCON* are *Lanerossi*, *Lebole*, *Monti*, and *MCM*. With privatization taking place, it is difficult to predict what *ENI* will look like by the end of the 90s.

EFIM, the Agency for Holdings and Financing of Manufacturing Industry, privatized in 1992, had as its purpose intervention in the industrial sector to aid further development. Its activities were carried on through firms controlled and coordinated by means of sectorial holding companies. The most important were: the *Ernesto Breda Holding Company*, chiefly concerned in the mechanical sector, instrumentation in particular; the *Breda Railway Company*, operating mainly in the means of transport and motor sector; *SOPAL* (Food Holding Company) which carries on a large scale activity in sectors running from procuring raw materials for the food industry to their conversion, and to the distribution of food products in Italy and abroad. *INSUD* is a holding company that specializes in projects in the South, promoting and carrying out initiatives there in the tourism and manufacturing-industry sectors, in combination with Italian and foreign partners. *EFIM* supported, monitored and coordinated the leader holding companies and operating companies subject to it. This job was carried out not just through financing but through the performance of services and functions as well, which make it possible for even average-sized firms to get into foreign markets and to make use of more efficient computer system and management systems, and more effective applied research.

In the 80s, these state industries became too inefficient and were even considered a liability. Under the new world trade conditions of open frontiers and multinational groupings, the Italian economy can prosper only if it becomes more market-oriented and firms cease to rely so much on the State with its political considerations. Even more detrimental to the national economy was the fact that the big state projects have too often been directed with an eye to political kudos rather than economic usefulness. The public sector has been ruled more by political needs than market demands, and this situation has to change if Italy is to compete in the open markets of the future.

The Economic Phoenix

Italy's economic development has evolved in several phases and followed a tortuous road. Economists are in broad agreement that the basis of the launching pad for the economic growth was provided in the immediate post war period by Luigi Einaudi's harsh deflation policy, with its tight credit and cuts in government spending which brought inflation under control, stabilized the lira, and won international confidence. The internal policy was supported with aid from the Marshall Plan which provided a massive infusion of funds to finance vital imports; the discovery of natural gas in the Po Valley which gave Italy its first indigenous energy source; and a great reservoir of cheap and highly mobile labor. The continuing high level of unemployment was largely due to the massive shift of population from the South to the North, from rural areas to the cities, from agriculture into manufacturing and services. Between 1958 and 1963 the number of workers in agriculture had declined by 50 per cent. The resulting low labor costs also helped to make Italian goods highly competitive in world markets. In this situation profits were high and, reinvested in capital stock, produced rapid industrial growth.

The years between 1958 and 1963 were a time of economic growth so remarkable that it has appropriately been called an "economic miracle." During that period the gross national product rose at an annual rate of 6.6 per cent, against a European average of 4.5 per cent. In 1960 alone industrial production went up by 20 per cent.

With the Italian entry into the European Economic Community in 1957, the country not only gained an expanded market but also was forced into free-market competition in which its products surprised everyone by selling extremely well. In fact it was exports that led the economic miracle to its heights between 1958 and 1962.

In the early 1960s, many US and other Western observers suddenly discovered the Italian "miracle." They extolled the unexpected developments which seemed to enable Italy to join the leading group of the major industrial nations of the West. Improvements were given additional luster and appeal by a happy season of Italian creativity in such disparate fields as interior decoration, movies, shoes, architecture, and office equipment. To label miracle Italy's performance represented not only a dangerously superficial reading of events but was grossly unfair to many Italians. The economic "boom," as it was also labeled, happened thanks to the politicians who had fought successfully to replace the protectionism traditionally prevailing in Italy with a wide-ranging liberalization of the country's foreign trade. The "boom" took also place because of the industrialists, technicians, and businessmen who had risen to the challenge by making many Italian products competitive on the international markets. It also took place because of the millions of hard working and often poorly paid Italians who had played a decisive part in the `quality jump' of the "Made in Italy" label.

The growth was due mainly to low wage rates which were possible because of high unemployment in the South, weak trade unions, mobility of population, and international monetary stability. The exodus from the farms, which gave factories a steady supply of new recruits, with a peasant's readiness to work hard for low wages helped to keep down the price of Italian goods and make them competitive on the international market. Another factor that affected the growth in those years was the fact that export prices rose 3.8 per cent per year while the cost of imported raw materials fell on the average 2 per cent per year. The resulting profits provided substantial capital for investments.

The rapid economic expansion soon brought problems, however, because it ameliorated some of the basic conditions which had helped to spark it—notably the low level of wages and mass consumption that reflected in turn a large and chronic unemployment and underemployment. Too many Italians did not foresee that any sudden speedup in economic growth involves and sharpens tensions, imbalances and frustrations. In the case of Italy, the costs could be very high because the benefits of the 'forward jump' were mostly concentrated in the industrial sector (and did not affect all of it, either) and because the country's administrative, economic, and financial structures were far from adequate to the requirements of a modern democracy.

In 1963, when the unemployment rate reached a record low of 3.6 percent, unions started to press for concessions especially in wages. Gradually these increases went above productivity growth, squeezing profit margins and reducing investments. With more money available, private consumption increased and demands became greater which resulted in high inflation. The industrial system reacted in its traditional conservative way: lower investments and more utilization of existing labor. As one may expect, the economic crisis brought about a social crisis which then exploded in the "hot fall" of 1969.

It is clear in retrospect that economically Italy was a puzzle. The country may have had all the trappings of a modern democracy, but neither its social and institutional structure nor its administrative practices had been brought in line with those of the other Western democracies. The country still lacked the facilities to deal with its problems: an equitable and effective tax system; a foresighted approach to land tenure and agricultural problems; antitrust legislation; efficient regulatory agencies in the fields of power, trade, labor relations, and a modern educational system. At the same time, the tremendous development of television and other communications, although state controlled, was bringing home to more and more Italians the great gap between the formal ideology which was supposed to guide the country's affairs and their daily experience of the way those affairs actually were conducted.

The Communist Party did not miss the opportunity to exploit this situation and increasingly strengthened its position as champion of social and economic reforms and fighter against arbitrary authority, public graft and mismanagement, and against attempts to hush up scandals and abuses.

The 60s were years of workers' struggles and political changes. During the recession in 1964, the Socialist Party joined the Christian Democrats in order to form a government based on a program of economic development. This coalition attempted to make the economic system more dynamic by **nationalizing** certain corporations in the electrical and chemical sectors, including many public services, and started a program for far-reaching reforms and modernization of Italian administrative, fiscal and financial structures. This economic program was supposed to contain the tools necessary to carry out the reforms required to do away with the chronic geographic and social imbalances and to insure, at the same time, a steady growth. This program was also supposed to render the Communist opposition, already weakened by its decision to engage only in parliamentary struggle, completely ineffective.

Social Transformation

By early 1967, it was clear that very little progress had been made in implementing the center-left's program agreed upon in 1962-1963. The paramount need to avoid an economic slump, following the disorderly boom of the early years, led to the delaying or watering down of the other social reforms originally pledged by the alliance. This had suited most Christian Democrats, who sought to gain votes from the fading parties of the Right. But most socialists, fearful of losing ground on their left, were pressing again for more vigorous action.

The Italian people, for the most part, had become restless. Unprecedented protests and rebellion by university students represented the most significant challenge to the political establishment and were the most evident symptom of the problems besetting a country which had become one of the seven leading industrial and trading nations but still retained many institutions and administrative practices which had changed little since the turn of the century (this topic will be treated in greater depth in chapter IX). The student population, which was less than 60,000 in 1935, had now reached almost 450,000. Despite some progress, physical facilities had expanded at a much slower pace and the number of professors had risen to only 8,000 against 2,700 in 1935. Many, moreover, were too busy in politics or business to show up for classes, let alone to devote sufficient attention to their students. University power was (and still is) concentrated in a small and self-perpetuating group of deans and full professors. Students demanded a complete revision of the system and wanted their own representatives, as well as those professors of junior rank, to have a voice in running university affairs. Under the leadership of a small group of activists, sometimes self-labeled as 'Maoists,' 'Castroites,' or 'anarchists,' students turned into a vague but loud and even violent revolt against society. Such a development was taking place just when the center-left governmental coalition had finally presented a reform bill intended to correct at least the most outdated features of the university system.

Similar dissatisfaction was behind industrial and civil servants' strikes and recurrent unrest over such issues as reorganization of the bureaucratic apparatus, modernization of the social security system and hospital reforms. In those and other fields, the center-left coalition had achieved more than previous governments, but less than it had pledged or had been possible.

A turning point came in the Fall of 1969, when workers set in motion a revolution in industrial relations. The delayed effects of the prolonged series of strikes in the industrial sector during the "hot autumn of 1969"—which continued well into early 1970 and resulted in sharply higher labor costs and lower productivity—were eventually felt throughout the economy beginning in the late 70s.

In 1969 the trade unions changed tactics. They became more militant; not only were they asking for better wages and job protection, but they also demanded better working and living conditions. The newly urbanized migrants from the rural South were increasingly dissatisfied with living conditions in the fast growing cities in the North and demanded better housing, schools, shops, transportation, and health care. The demands were accompanied by frequent strikes and violent demonstrations.

Italian society wanted to change and demanded legislative action. One truly startling shift had taken place in the Italians' views on such issues as divorce and birth control. In a 1967 public opinion survey, 58.6 percent of 12,645 Italians interviewed were in favor of introducing divorce and three out of four favored birth control. Two out of three said their views or behavior on the subject were not affected by Pope Paul's pronouncement reaffirming the Catholic Church's rigid ban on contraception. Just five years earlier, a similar survey, conducted in 1962, had shown that almost seven Italians out of ten were against the introduction of divorce.

The outcome of the Italian election of May 19-20, 1968 sent a message of concern to the government. Although the center-left coalition had slightly increased its share of the popular vote and parliamentary representation, the Communists and the extreme left Socialist splinter group scored sizable gains, jolting the governing coalition.

As a consequence of all these manifestations, the Italian government started to plan for radical changes. The early 70s went down in history as the years when Italy enacted some of the world's most advanced social legislation.

Unfortunately, at the same time the quadrupling of oil prices beginning in 1973 dealt the Italian economy a tremendous blow. Having to import 85 percent of its energy needs, Italy was hit harder than any other Western country and had to work feverishly to avoid a complete economic collapse. The combination of wage and oil price increases badly hurt industrial profits and drastically reduced the competitiveness of many public and large private enterprises. Consequently, in 1975 Italy experienced the worst postwar recession. In the first half of the 70s there was a significant deterioration in economic performance. In 1975, for the first time in post WWII, the economy contracted. Real gross domestic product (GDP) dropped by 3.5 per cent, industrial production fell by 9.5 per cent, and inflation topped 17 per cent, the highest in Europe. Most of these losses were regained in 1976 with a 5.6 per cent increase in GDP and a 12.4 per cent jump in industrial production, but inflation, caused mainly by the demands of militant labor unions, and unemployment remained at high levels. The Andreotti government took steps to restore the economy to steady growth without high inflation. A series of measures to check the growth of government budget deficits and labor costs was adopted, paving the way for a $250 million standby loan from the International Monetary Fund in April 1977 and another $500 million from the European Community. By 1978, these measures, plus favorable exchange rates, had given Italian exports a tremendous boost and moved Italy's current account and even its trade balance firmly into the black, despite the skyrocketing prices of imported oil.

In addition to the increasing energy costs, there were many blunders and actions which hindered company productivity more than was necessary, or possible, in order to reach the desired level of social justice. Many economists link the beginning of Italy's chronic economic troubles of the 70s to the wage settlements that resulted from the labor unrest that characterized the Autumn of 1969. Industrial wage increases averaged 25.5 per cent in 1973 and 24.3 per cent in 1974, while increases in the consumer price index in those years were 10.8 and 19.1 per cent respectively. During the first five years of the 1970s the consumer price index rose to 171 while on the same scale wages rose to 249. These developments virtually wiped out the low labor cost advantage enjoyed by Italian industries in the late 1950s and early 1960s which was, as previously mentioned, a major contributor to the economic boom of that period. More damaging to trade performance were the strikes, absenteeism, and high labor costs that rose continuously throughout the seventies—accounting for a 40 per cent increase in the price of Italian manufacturers between 1977 and 1979 alone.

However, employers were able to regain the upper hand. The FIAT strike of 1980, which ended in a large number of redundancies, was a major test of strength and a turning point. At Olivetti Carlo De Benedetti took over an ailing firm and restored it to profitability with aggressive anti-trade unionist stance (by the late eighties he would be setting his sights on a takeover of Mondadori).

From the end of the seventies, a prolonged economic crisis and the rise in unemployment had weakened the bargaining power of the unions and pushed them onto the defensive. In 1983-84 the Craxi government was able to exploit the new divisions in the union movement to push through anti-inflationary measures. Another factor was the emergence of a self-confident, new-look political center, based around Craxi and Christian Democrat party leader Ciriaco De Mita. The latter had taken the helm as part of a move to refurbish the party's image after the damaging scandals of the mid-seventies, culminating in the resignation in 1978 of President of the Republic Giovanni Leone, named in a scandal that involved Lockheed Aircraft.

After 1980, strikes and absenteeism dropped, productivity and capital inflows improved, and profits in many industries soared. Unemployment went from 6.4 percent in 1977 to 14.2 percent in 1985, with some three-quarters of the unemployed estimated to be persons under the age of thirty.

In the mid-eighties the Italian economy presented, in short, a bewildering spectacle. It continued to be plagued by high unemployment, high interest rates, high labor costs, high inflation, vast public expenditures, and a staggering public deficit. At the same time exports were back at an all-time record, some state industry was being restructured and modernized, large private firms were once again European leaders in their fields, the performance of small and medium-sized companies bedazzled observers, and a general sense of prosperity pervaded the country.

Nevertheless, in the early 90s, the state enterprises still held a dominant position. The purely private-sector economy was still proportionately the smallest of major Western industrial countries, accounting for 35 to 40 per cent of Italy's industrial production. This private sector is remarkable for its large number of small producers and its small number of large producers. At least 90 percent of Italy's industries employ fewer than a hundred workers. The major industries at the top of the pyramidal structure of the private sector are, and have traditionally been, concentrated in remarkably few hands—a narrow cartel of northern entrepreneurs.[1]

The Agnelli family, which owns 40 per cent of FIAT, Italy's biggest private-sector company, remains at the center of power. The purchase of Alfa Romeo has given FIAT a virtual monopoly on the production of cars in Italy; it also owns Lancia, Ferrari and Autobianchi. FIAT has 60 per cent of domestic car sales—a bigger share than any other European carmaker has in its home market. FIAT remains Italy's forte today for it produces a very popular range of smaller family cars with relatively low gasoline consumption, maintaining its competitiveness in an oil-anxious age. But FIAT is going to have a difficult time when the Japanese are allowed more access to the Italian market. Italy is much less well placed than Germany to meet the Japanese challenge in other countries, for she does not produce the same kind of luxury high-performance cars such as BMW, Mercedes and Porsche which have no Japanese equivalent—the Ferrari is completely in a league of its own. The Italian price range is too similar to the Japanese.

Not limited to just automobile, FIAT dominates many parts of the Italian economy. Cars accounted for only half of the group's turnover of 38 trillion lire (4% of GDP); the rest includes components, commercial vehicles, factory automation (robots), aviation, telecoms and financial services. The subsidiaries of IFI, the family holding company, include Rinascente, a department-store chain, Prime, Italy's second biggest mutual fund, and stakes in banking, publishing and television. The Agnelli family interests account for a quarter of the Milan stock market. The group also controls 24 per cent of Italy's national daily newspaper sales: it owns *La Stampa,* a Turin-based daily, and effectively controls Italy's biggest publishing group, Rizzoli, which owns *Corriere della Sera*, Italy's most popular newspaper.

The other industrial superstars are Carlo De Benedetti, who took over *Olivetti* in 1978, Raul Gardini, head of the *Ferruzzi-Montedison* agribusiness and chemicals group which include an empire that spans publishing, insurance and retailing. The Agnelli family, De Benedetti, Leopoldo Pirelli, Carlo Bonomi, and Attilio Monti all control large holding companies with a wide array of interests.

Recently, the major firms have changed their character considerably; for one thing they have become increasingly multinational while giving the appearance of shrinking in size. Through merger, association with large foreign companies and restructuring, they have increased international competition, improved productivity and become financially more solid. In the process, the most striking change was the decentralization of production through subcontracting to small specialized factories and cottage firms. FIAT, for example, reduced its working force by 24 percent from 1981 to 1985 while increasing productivity by 24 percent.

Italian business has long been dominated by a few families. In the past the power of private business was balanced by a large public sector and strong unions. Today the trade unions, as we saw earlier, are weak and the public sector is slowly being dismantled through privatization; there is, therefore, a greater danger that the power of private business will go unchecked. Italy is the only EC country that does not have any antitrust laws, and demands for such legislation have been mounting.

Notes

1. Six Italians were listed among *Forbes Magazine*'s annual survey (1992) of the world's richest people. The family names of Agnelli, Benetton, Ferrero, and Ferruzzi, and those of Silvio Berlusconi and Salvatore Licresti, once again made the list of 291 billionaires. The Agnellis are first among the Italians, with an estimated fortune of three billion dollars.

VI

The Changing Face of Industry and Social Transformation

The Economic Boom of the 80s

By the end of the 1980s, Italy had become one of Europe's great success stories. Suddenly, it had become a land of upward mobility, of vital computerized industry, of bustling young business managers and slick middle-aged tycoons who had abjured their sixties ideals in the sacred cause of profit.

Even the English, long critical of Italy, at the end of the 1980s were saying that the Italians must have been doing something right, and doing it despite a political and administrative system that remains the least adapted to the requirements of modern, efficient government in Western Europe.

In 1987, the year of the *sorpasso* in which Italy actually surpassed Great Britain as economic power, the government added an extra 18 per cent to its estimate of Italy's national income. Italy's GDP became 10 per cent bigger than Britain's in 1986, and its GDP per capita 9 per cent larger. These figures shook up the industrialized West. The average Italian was shown to be richer than the average Briton when standard of living was compared using the ownership of consumer goods. In Italy 76 per cent of households have a car, compared with 58 per cent in Britain; 81 per cent have washing machines and 14 per cent have dishwashers, compared with 77 per cent and 3 per cent respectively for British families.

It seems that Italy understood at the end of the '70s what Americans have not yet understood today: "flexible production," that is, a new, more cooperative way of organizing relations between firms; a populist sense of who has useful knowledge about how to manufacture things; a recognition that small firms with highly motivated, skilled workers can be more responsive to market changes than multibillion-dollar institutions with dozens of layers of supervision and hundreds of volumes of operating manuals. Mass production in large American industries had created a monopoly of expertise in management at the top, and the polarization of corporate rewards–the top executives who make as much as Madonna, and the unskilled workers who increasingly earn little more than welfare mothers–have corroded the work ethic of the majority who are required to keep the machine working and working properly. Moreover, "flexible production" can respond better to consumer markets where tastes change rapidly because a premium can be put on design qualities and craft skills, on workers who can take the initiative. Flexibility enables workers to develop craft skills, to reacquire the technical knowledge monopolized by management.

In Italy, "flexible production" has featured the rise of "SMEs"–small and medium-sized regional enterprises. Emilia-Romagna now has over 300,000 SMEs; nearly 70,000 are industrial firms. The leading sectors are machine tools, agricultural equipment, ceramics, metalworking, mechanical engineering, garment and textiles. A lot of the same industries that New York City planners wrote off as too small and too high-cost to compete globally fared well in Italy. Firms in Bologna, Modena and Forlì exploited their flexibility; they moved products from design to market very quickly. Instead of New York-style yippie networking, the Italians formed industrial networks: strategic alliances, buyer-supplier partnerships, joint ventures. In the garment industry they went "upmarket" to escape competition with low-cost producers. These sub-giants have formed cooperative networks that compensate for the lack of large sums of capital and have been the industrial engine that brought about the resurgence of the manufacturing industry in some cities. The more successful firms have invested intelligently in new equipment, have pushed productivity up and have given technical innovation its head. As a result, Italy has moved into the forefront of advanced technology, able to export massively both her products and her know how.

Some of Italy's cities, like many American cities, had experienced a big loss of blue-collar jobs in the second half of the 70s. Third world competition, rising energy costs, high wages and rigid union rules were the cause for the big decline of the manufacturing sector. To relieve unemployment and replenish dwindling revenues, many cities gave up on industry and looked to services, such as banking and insurance. But bold policies in some cities showed that there was no need to give up on manufacturing. The economic resurgence came about through very small, flexible enterprises organized around multiple-use, automated machinery. The tiny shops became intermediate producers, which link together in varying combinations and form networks to carry out complex manufacturing tasks for world markets. Frequent subcontracting within networks makes it easy to upgrade product specifications and even change product lines rapidly in response to market signals. Moreover, the small-scale industrial enterprises have bridged the distance between artisanal and modern production methods.

Development of this system of flexible network manufacturing is encouraged by local governments across the country. City and regional governments pitched in with municipal land, credit, child care, public transport, advanced industrial training. Many municipalities provided affordable work-spaces in converted factory buildings and mini-industrial parks. Local schools turn out well-trained apprentices and keep shop owners up-to-date through evening programs. Publicly subsidized research centers provide assistance in product innovation, technology transfer and export marketing. The emphasis on innovation and quality means that experimentation and education are encouraged. There is continual upward movement as former apprentices open their own firms. And rigid work rules make no sense where machine operators must contribute willingly to the constant revision of processes and products if the shops are to prosper. The basic features of this Italian industrial system are very much in the American grain. It stresses entrepreneurship, self-employment, the pleasure of making things, creative challenges and good income.

Manufacturing is the largest sector of the economy, comprising 35 per cent of GDP and employing 30 per cent of the labor force. However, there are signs of a lessening of Italy's industrial strength. Footwear and textiles have experienced a gradual decrease in export business. That loss must be compensated by a growth in other industrial sectors such as machinery, transport equipment and chemicals. Products from the metalmechanical industry account for 25 per cent of total exports; textiles, clothing, leather goods, and furs with 19.5 per cent; metallurgy with 8.8 per cent; and chemicals with 8.5 per cent.

Luckily for Italy, Italians seem never to lack solutions. Look at how the country reacted to the major crisis at the end of the 1970s. What gave impetus to the second "economic miracle" was certainly the **decentralization of production.** The process of such decentralization was mainly caused by the sharply rising labor costs and an expanding social welfare which burdened large companies. Social security contributions and related payments to the state meant that the total cost of labor to an employer escalated to be more than double the net salaries. All salaries were linked to inflation, and it was virtually impossible to lay off workers.

By the early 80s, it had become clear that labor union demands and a strong state presence in the economy, which had created the basis for the "welfare state" in the 60s and 70s, were now crippling the nation. Lack of vigor in the banking world, an out-of-date fiscal system, poor liaison between pure and applied research, excessive State bureaucratic interference in private industry, all were problems that needed to be addressed. Clearly, the state and the labor unions' strong role in the economy had fulfilled their original mandates, but now their excesses needed to be corrected. Gradual political changes and visionary entrepreneurship brought about a remarkable shift and turnabout in economic direction. The remarkable success of the small and medium-sized industry was a blow to the powerful labor unions and served as a clear message to *excessive* presence of the state in the economy.

As part of the process, Italy started a program of ***privatizzazione*** following a pragmatic approach in adopting a set of measures: transfer of activities from public sector to private through share offerings; utilization of private companies to manage services previously in the hands of state or local governments; introduction of a "fee" for services previously offered and financed through taxes. These measures were not entirely based on the standard of what was best for Italy, however. There were some political motives involved, for the center-right wanted to build up the electoral support of a body of small-scale capitalists who benefitted from the liberalization of market.

At first the privatization programs affected mainly large enterprises. In addition to industrial and financial restructuring, the state giant *IRI*, in its strategy for recovery, followed the path of privatization and partnership, which means "divestiture of enterprises." It considered putting up for sale three kinds of enterprise: first, marginal ones, which were not integrated with other *IRI* companies, and therefore had no "mission" to accomplish inside the *IRI Group*. Second, companies which were operating in the red. And, finally, enterprises, or even subholdings of IRI, which were or could be profitable, and even form an integrated whole, but did not appear to be consistent with the group's basic long-term objectives. Between 1983 and 1992, over 30 enterprises of different size from big Alfa Romeo to small Ducati (motorcycles), from banks to washing-machine producers, have been divested. The process of divestiture slowed somewhat in 1985, but starting in July 1986, regained steam and has touched every sector of the economy, including services.

Small-Sized Firms and Underground Economy

One of the most striking peculiarities of the Italian economy has been the remarkable strength of the export sector, which in some ways is a paradigm of Italy's economic performance. In the fashion world Italian clothing, furniture, and textiles have emerged as world leaders, while in some industrial areas, such as machine tools and robotics, Italian products have earned an outstanding reputation for quality and won a growing share of the world market.

Because of their exceptional ability to sense changing consumer demand and to produce attractive goods, Italian exporters have been highly agile in shifting into new markets and alternative products. The Italian export industry is remarkable for its ability not only to move quickly into new geographic areas but also to change into the production of items for which demand is on the rise.

The achievements in this area are all the more impressive since exporters have rarely received help from the government, either through assistance in penetrating world markets or through export credits. The trade policy, as a result of free-for-all agreements, greatly helped the Italian economy.

The principal question concerning the Italian economy is whether giants like the state holding companies (*ENI* and *IRI*) and private giants like FIAT and Olivetti will be competitive without state protectionism after 1992. Although FIAT currently maintains 15 per cent of the European car market share, its dependence upon the protected Italian market makes it especially vulnerable to European competition after 1992. The same may be said about textiles, a historically vital sector of the Italian economy, accounting for 38 per cent of the clothing imports of the EC as of 1988 and Italy's third largest industry. There is no question that the successful international performance of *Benetton*, *Stefanel*, and fashion designers such as *Armani*, *Versace*, and *Valentino* shows no signs of letting up. *Benetton* is recognized as a leader in the "Europreparedness" stakes, having established a vast chain of shops throughout Europe and the US by the early 1980s. Similarly, Versace is aiming to go public and thereby raise enough capital to expand its already multinational operation. However, there are serious doubts as to whether the Italian textile industry as a whole will be able to compete with the newly industrialized countries such as Taiwan, Korea and Brazil which are able to exploit "mature" manufacturing technology with cheap labor.

The success achieved by the medium and small-sized industries has given evidence that Italy will be able to sustain the assault that will be coming from Third World countries. In fact, this industrial sector, which was behind the economic boom of the 80s, became the most outstanding trait of the country's current industrial structure and the most dynamic anywhere in Europe and has caused mass social changes without precedent in Italy. Originally most of these companies were set up to escape the trade union regulations that followed the "hot autumn of 1968," since firms with fewer than fifteen employees need not be unionized or pay standard wages and social benefits. They therefore operated at great cost efficiency and high productivity and without risk of strikes. There was still another impetus. Firms with annual incomes below approximately $75,000 were not required to make their books available to income-tax authorities. The astonishing consequence of this has been that starting in 1984 fully 95 per cent of Italian firms declared incomes of less than that figure!

Since the production of these small firms escapes official records, the country's real GDP and export statistics are appreciably higher than official accounts would indicate. It is estimated that the "underground economy" employs anywhere from 2 to 4 million persons and produces fully 20 to 30 per cent over the official GDP.

This small-business sector has changed the industrial map of Italy. No longer does the Italian economy entirely hinge on the old industrial triangle Milan-Turin-Genoa. The new firms are not in large cities but in provincial towns in former agrarian areas. And they have spread from Emilia-Romagna, the Veneto, and Tuscany into the Marches and on to Umbria, Abruzzi, Puglia, and the area south of Rome. They produce clothing, leather products, shoes, furniture, textiles, machine tools, agricultural machinery, toys, car parts, and jewelry. The manufacturing sectors are regionalized: in the Northwest there is a large modern group of industries; in the Northeast there are small enterprises of low technology but high craftsmanship; in the Center and South the two forms exist side by side. Thanks to low price, and high quality of their innovative products, these firms are remarkably resistant to the ups and downs of the international economy.

Among the distinguishing features of these decentralized, but integrated industrial districts is a seemingly contradictory combination of competition and cooperation. Firms compete vigorously for innovation in style and efficiency, while cooperating in administrative services, raw material purchases, financing and research. "A rich network of private economic associations and political organizations...have constructed an environment in which markets prosper by promoting cooperative behavior and by providing small firms with the infrastructural needs that they could not afford alone."[1] These networks of small firms combine low vertical integration and high horizontal integration, through extensive subcontracting and "putting out" of extra business to temporarily underemployed competitors. Active industrial associations provide administrative and even financial aid, while local government plays an active role in providing the necessary social infrastructure and services, such as professional training, information on export markets, and so on. The result is a technologically advanced and highly flexible economic structure, which proved precisely the right recipe for competing in the fast-moving economic world of the 1980s and 1990s.[2] The degree of success of these firms is higher in the Emilia-Romagna region because of the higher level of civic traditions, of contemporary civic community, and of high-performance regional government. Most observers have demonstrated that what is crucial about these small-firm industrial districts is mutual trust, social cooperation, and a well-developed sense of civic duty—in short, the hallmarks of the civic community.[3]

Public Indebtedness and Democracy

The success of medium and small-sized industries has had a positive impact also on the private heavy industry sector, for the industrial giants, by subcontracting to the smaller industries, was able to overcome certain labor demands and, consequently, produce goods more cheaply. However, occasionally big industry has chosen to expand abroad rather than at home. Industrialists like Carlo De Benedetti of Olivetti have been leading the way.

Situations like this could signal very serious problems for the average Italian worker, but in the Italian scene it is always difficult to assess just how changes will impact on workers' rights. In economic, as in social reforms, Italians have gone from one extreme to another, and they are still struggling to find a happy equilibrium. They find salvation in the fact that they are great lovers of drama; whether in opera, politics or soccer, they swing from the depths of depression one moment to excessive optimism the next. Italians have long proved their ingenuity in the face of apparently insurmountable obstacles.

Italy has long been famed for its hidden economy--that mysterious underworld of tax dodging, illegal employment of foreign workers and students, and civil servants who moonlight in the afternoons when their offices close. Rigid labor laws, high taxes, social security contributions and a general willingness to break the law are the reasons for the largest underground economy in the industrial world.

Italian wage-earners are the ones who have to carry the national fiscal burden. Statistical data indicate that the total "tax burden" for the average Italian reaches only 22.7 per cent of his income, a rate lower than the average for citizens of the European Community. Worldwide, Italy places ahead of Switzerland (21.8 %), USA (20.6 %), Japan (19.5 %), and Spain (16.9 %), but well behind the Northern European countries where taxation is heaviest: Denmark (47.4 %), Sweden (38 %) and Norway (37.9 %). Because Italians prefer to stage life, tax cheating too, either for its blatancy or its pervasiveness frequently makes big headlines. Italian movie stars get in the news because they claim to make less than the sanitation employee; industrial magnates report little more than some of their clerks and secretaries; doctors, lawyers, dentists, architects, accountants are shown to be reporting, on average, less income than is paid to skilled industrial workers. The owners of well-known restaurants and cafes regularly report less income than they pay to their chefs, waiters and dishwashers. Much of this collusion is based on the implicit assumption that the fiscal laws are not fair, that they are not rigorously enforced against everyone, and that the state, in its imperious way, has so defrauded the ordinary taxpayer that it is entirely natural and acceptable that the latter should return the favor in kind. In a nation where the overwhelming majority of the population regards its democratically elected political leaders as a bunch of *ladri* (thieves), anyone cheating the government may be sure of general benevolence. "None of my money for that rotten system," most of tax dodgers say. There is something fundamentally democratic about tax evasion; one way or another, the practice extends to a very large proportion of the adult population. It is true, of course, that those on fixed wages and salaries cannot evade, but this applies only to one's first–not second or third–job. Those who are working in the second and unreported economy include hundreds of thousands of blue-collar workers or members of their families as well as professionals. The practice of auto mechanics, plumbers, carpenters, physicians, dentists, lawyers wanting payment in cash and willing to be prompt and accommodating when told the customer doesn't need a receipt is commonplace in Italy as it is in America.

In 1992, the Italian Finance Ministry published a list of about half a million alleged tax dodgers in an attempt to shame evaders into paying. The "Red

Book" report included well-known actors, businessmen and journalists. The total amount of unpaid taxes was 33 trillion lire ($25 billion) which would have covered about twenty-five per cent of Italy's budget deficit. The government has passed stiff laws to combat tax dodging. Customers by law have to walk out with a *ricevuta fiscale* (register receipt) from any premise where goods were bought or service was rendered (from the purchase of a *cappuccino* to a hair cut). But, even though fines are heavy and are given rigorously, Italians enjoy the thrill and the satisfaction of tax evasion.

In the official economy, the Italian worker is well rewarded with high wages, good benefits and many paid holidays. In 1992, the average employee in the industry and services sectors worked about forty hours per week, 1,622 hours per year (compared to 1,847 in USA); s/he received 40 1/2 paid holidays and vacation days (compared to 23 in USA and 31 in Britain). While the cost of each hour of manufacturing labor, including benefits was $19.49 (compared to $13.70 in Britain and $15.39 in USA).[4] All this places Italy on the high side as far as growth in unit labor costs, even though the country ranks toward the top among leading nations as far as growth in labor productivity.

The question, again, is, how come the state does not collapse? Some convincing reasons were given by the respected weekly of London, *The Economist*. The first reason is that unlike governments in America, Belgium and Denmark, which have financed a large chunk of their borrowing abroad, only 3 % of Italy's public debt is owed to foreigners. Second, Italian households are among the thriftiest in the world. They save some 23 per cent of their disposable income, even more than the Japanese, and thus provide a large pool of cash from which the government can finance its deficit. In contrast, America's budget deficit has caused such problems because American households save less than 4 per cent of their income. Unlike Americans and Britons who happily mortgage themselves up to the hilt to buy a house, the two-thirds of Italians who own their homes save up much of the money first. The old tradition of parental support is also still very much alive. In Italy there is a strong family tradition not to fall into debt—learning how to save rather than how to spend is taught from childhood. But savings cannot be relied upon forever; consumers are starting to overcome their aversion to debt and are being wooed by new financial intermediaries. The third reason is that the **Bank of Italy** remains staunchly independent and highly respected. The central bank has thereby helped to maintain investors' confidence. Governors of the bank are appointed for life and so are free from political interference.

Nevertheless, the government's huge budget deficit which is almost as big as America's, even though America's economy is seven times larger, has brought Italy to the verge of collapse. Historic inefficiency and waste in the public sector, huge welfare costs, especially on the health provisions, and corruption of politicians and government officials at every administrative level have forced the country to a rude awakening. The need to bring closer national tax systems and the limits on public deficits and debt contained in the Maastrict treaty made the problem not just a national priority but a European community requirement.

Other Serious Problems

In the early 1990s, public services represented the most dismal feature of the Italian economy because they reflected and compounded, more than other sectors, the still unsolved, or only partially solved problems of a traditionally poor and underdeveloped country, and the new problems besetting a nation which, only recently and very hastily has become affluent and demanding. Public services in such key areas as health care and railroads, social security and the mails, justice, schools, and airports needed profound changes to be improved. By and large, these services are more expensive than in many other Western countries while they often operate at a loss and their performance is generally well below the standards required by a modern democracy.

Although Italy has a marvelous highway system, its rail system is in dire need of modernization. This situation may not be important for passenger transportation because Italians have a love of their *macchina* (car), but it spells trouble for the effective transportation of goods. The state railroads' freight service is so unsatisfactory that today less than one-eighth of all goods moving in Italy are shipped by rail. Trucking in Italy costs three times as much as shipping by freight train, but farmers and manufacturers usually put up with this higher expense for the sake of speed and reliability. One striking example is that Southern fruit and vegetables cannot be sent by rail to northern markets because the trip may take three weeks instead of one day!

Mail service, notwithstanding recent improvements, is still a serious problem. It may take half an hour to buy stamps at the postal office, or it may take a week to have a letter cross Rome. These difficulties persist despite a slackening demand due to the increasing appeal of fax machines.

Moreover, in the early 1990s, welfare was still one of the most problem-plagued sectors of Italian social policies. One factor is the extremely early retirement age, for men 60, for women 55. In most countries men retire at age 65 and women at 62 if they do not follow the same age limit as men. The only country that has a lower retirement age than Italy is Turkey where men retire at 55 and women at 50. Yet in Turkey the average longevity is at least ten years lower than Italy. Among industrialized nations only Japan has the same retirement age eligibility as Italy. However, Japanese pensions are calculated on the earnings average of one's entire career, whereas in Italy the average is based on the last five years of work. Italy's generosity in its pension system needs fine tuning. In five years, 1985-1990, social security expenditures went from 182,975 to 308,493 billion lire and revenues went from 192,161 to 323,839 billion lire, with an increase, as compared to GDP, respectively, from 22.6 to 23.6 per cent and from 23.7 to 24.8 per cent.

The large population of "invalids" also has to be re-examined. Toward the end of each month, one out of every ten Italians runs to the post office to collect the pension that the state pays its army of invalids. With 5.5 million certified *invalidi* (including about 700,000 people officially wounded or who suffered some bodily harm during WWII), Italy would seem to be one of the world's most hazardous countries. Yet Italians on average live longer than do Britons, French, or Germans.

Few of the 5.5 million supposedly handicapped Italians are incapacitated to work. The overwhelming majority of those who receive monthly invalidity pensions are well-nourished and are fit to work. By far the major part of the spurious infirm live in the South. Since Southerners have a hard time finding jobs, to be pronounced officially invalid guarantees them a state pension which is like having a minimum wage or unemployment compensation. Abuses persist: for years, candidates for elective office have been busy obtaining disability status and pensions for reputedly disabled constituents.

Social security absorbs 42 per cent of public expenditure, while at least three quarters of the deficit is due to the social welfare programs of the state. Moreover, the system of social security contributions for public employees, differing from the private one, legitimatizes unequal treatment.

In 1992 the country's balance sheet was horrendous. The budget deficit had risen to 11 per cent of GDP, above the 10 per cent average of the previous two decades. The public sector debt (including both the central government's and localities') had ballooned to 106 per cent of GDP. (To give some relative terms, in the US, the public debt is about 37 per cent of the country's GNP). Just to service this 1,469,831 billion lire debt, equivalent to over $1.2 trillion, the government spent an amount equivalent to 10.2 per cent of the GDP.

Hard Choices Ahead

The Maastricht Treaty, in an attempt to establish a monetary union in Europe, imposed unequivocal rules. Italy did not have any choice if she wanted to continue to belong to the European Community. The European linkage, first of all, meant a commitment to a sound economic system in tune with the European Community and the international market. To meet Italy's commitment, and ensure the country's continued participation in the European Community's economic unification program, and the monetary union in particular, the government had to reduce the budget deficit to 3 per cent of GDP, and the national debt to under 60 per cent of the gross domestic product. These were difficult goals to achieve because accomplishing them would create an additional hundreds of thousands of jobless workers, on top of an already high 11 per cent unemployment rate.

Italy is one of the countries furthest from meeting the conditions for participation in the final phase of EMU (the European Monetary Union). For years she was unable to eliminate an inflation differential due entirely to domestic factors, or to resolve the imbalance in the public finances. The consequence was the loss of competitiveness, an astronomical deficit and the growing tendency for production to be transferred abroad.

To respond to the gravity of the situation, the Italian parliament supported for prime minister Giuliano Amato, a Socialist and a Columbia University-trained lawyer, a man of integrity, intelligence, character. He had to head the first Italian government after the collapse of Communism and had the thankless job of steering an economic course for the country that would enable it to comply with European Economic Community (EEC) requirements for continued full membership after the single European market was established 1 January 1993. Premier Amato's task was to form a government promising less to its citizens and at the same time asking more from them. Amato was seen as a Gorbachev-like figure, an innovator, though still attached to the old system. The guidelines approved by his Council of Ministers in July 1992 were intended to begin to plug the enormous shortfalls of the budget; they were intended to be the beginning of a plan to return to a rational and responsible financial system.

The government engaged in a policy which would wage war against tax evasion, and the growth of public debt, while attempting to hold inflation to a level close to the rates prevailing in the most stable European economies. It also made recommendations on how to improve the efficiency and productivity of public services. The package of economic measures consisted of three separate areas. The first, dealing with fiscal policy, outlined ways to raise $26 billion through tax and excise increases, and the imposition of a 0.6 per cent levy on all monies held in bank deposits as well as on residential real estate. The second set of measures was destined to save the Treasury tens of billions of dollars in future years by raising the retirement age for workers covered by the nationwide pension plan operated by the Government, to 65 years for both men and women (as pointed out earlier, under current laws, women can retire at 55 with full pension benefits, and men at 60). At the same time, the cost to the treasury of Italy's universal health care system was also cut. Third, the government would speed up the privatization of two of Italy's public sector companies, *IRI* and *ENI* (estimated to account for some 40 per cent of the country's GDP and the foundation of the nation's powerful patronage system managed by political parties) through consolidation of all major groups of government-owned business into two giant holding companies. It was decided to dismantle *EFIM*, the other state holding, rather than privatizing it, because of its very precarious financial situation, (it owed its bankers about $8 billion, including about $3 billion in principal and interest to foreign lenders). This action would reduce the relative size of the country's government-owned industry to 10-12 per cent of the GDP. The government proposed also to privatize the *Istituto Mobiliare Italiano*, the country's oldest and most powerful merchant bank, as well as *Banca Nazionale del Lavoro*, a commercial bank.

Between EC and the Regions

Since Europe does not want to remain the offshore battleground of consumer superpowers Japan and the USA, it is forging a single consuming and producing entity that can offer the world a third alternative. In this struggle Italy has to raise herself to the level that will enable her to play a primary role. The success or failure of the challenge is like life and death.

However, the road to European integration is full of obstacles. One of the principal impediments is the fact that within the borders of the 12 EC member countries and their non-EC neighbors see the hundreds of years of social, cultural, and moral differences. Some, such as language, are profound; others, such as ritual lunch hours, can be downright amazing.

Geographically, two countries, the United Kingdom and Greece, do not even touch any other EC member's borders, although the UK will soon connect with France via the Channel Tunnel. Two non-members countries, Austria and Switzerland, drive a geographical wedge into the EC between Germany to the north and Italy to the South. The 12 countries speak 8 languages, though they would claim 13. The UK and Ireland, alone among the EC states, drive on the left-hand side of the road. Work habits also differ sharply. The Germans arrive early, take a short break for lunch at noon, and leave the office at 4:00. By contrast, in many parts of Italy, most stores close for the midday meal from 1:00 to 4:00 p.m. and do not shut their doors until 8:00 in the evening. Public offices in Italy operate in an even less efficient way: most of them close for good at 2:00 p.m.!

The EC has to break down centuries of physical and cultural barriers. Besides the hard obstacles—which include the different and, at times, conflicting laws, procedures, and administrative practices that dominate each individual country, EC has to solve soft obstacles—which encompass the cultural and social methods, morals, and mores that have kept Europe a patchwork of separate states since the decline of the Roman Empire. Interestingly, the EC finds the soft issues the hardest to address.

The unification implies the elimination of tariffs among EC members and therefore profound adjustments. For instance, because of tariffs, a BMW priced at $25,000 in Germany retails at over $40,000 in Italy. Obviously, the Italian government wants to limit the numbers of BMWs its citizens buy to encourage the purchase of its own high-priced cars–tariffs have traditionally aimed at protecting indigenous industries from cheaper or more attractive foreign competitors. Nevertheless, the unification is going to take place, it will eventually be beneficial to Italy, and will have a profound effect throughout the world.

Not less important, certainly, is how Italy, a very centralized nation, continues to delegate power and authority to the regions. The process of administrative reform and renewal is taking a long time because the Christian Democrats were opposed to the decentralization of power. Even though the Constitution called for the immediate formation of regional governments, the DC governments or governments of coalitions dominated by the DC refused to implement regionalism because they feared that it would make it easier for Communist regional control. When regional governments were finally approved in 1970, the fears proved to be unfounded. By 1980, out of twenty regions, the Communists were in control of only three–Emilia-Romagna (centered on Bologna), Tuscany and Umbria.

By the beginning of the 1990s, the new governments, barely two decades old, were spending nearly a tenth of Italy's gross domestic product (only slightly below the figure for American states).[5] Total funds available to the regions had grown rapidly–from roughly $1 billion in 1973 to roughly $9 billion in 1976 to roughly $65 billion in 1989. All regional governments had gained responsibility for such fields as urban affairs, housing, agriculture, public works, hospitals and health services, vocational education, and economic development. On paper, the twenty regional governments are virtually identical and potentially powerful. However, the social, economic, political, and cultural contexts into which the new institutions were implanted differ dramatically.

Some regional governments have been consistently more successful than others–more efficient in their internal operations, more creative in their policy initiatives, more effective in implementing those initiatives. The regions in the South have been less effective. We agree with Robert D. Putnam that the main reason for the lower level of effectiveness must be found in the lower level of civic virtues in southern society.[6] The fact that Southern Italians, argues Putnam, tend to pursue personal interests and be less civic community minded, make the South less successful in its quest for socioeconomic modernity. The same attitude makes life easier for criminal organizations, the Mafia and Camorra, to enter the structure of government.

Nevertheless, the Italian South has to find new energy and resources in the new wave of regionalism. Of course there are dangers in the process of regionalism. The individualistic character of the Italians could certainly create parochialism and entrenched local autocracy. The regions are now competing more vigorously with each other–not just by lobbying for favors from Rome, as in the old days, but by seeking their own solutions. The new system can in time produce a new and dynamic generation of younger local leaders and could provide a lively new focus for local loyalties and energies. While this seems to be a positive factor, there is a danger that more force will be expended on local issues rather than on the larger, national scene. Another problem is that poor regions may fall further beyond. It will be up to the state to provide them with good roads, telecommunications, research centers and so on–and then hope that the new industries will develop on their own accord.

Overall, the process is positive, for it releases new local energies and may allow Italy to capitalize on the richness of its diversity. The drawback is that the competition could lead to some waste and duplication of effort and that it could accentuate the disparity between the rich dynamic regions and the poorer ones. The decentralization has created new vitality and self-awareness in many towns and their regions. The cultural revival of many towns has been striking: new theaters, concerts, art galleries help to make life more exciting, and the influx of new populations has created a more open and varied society.

Thus, economically and socially, Italy has gone through a profound change. The percentage of those employed in industry and agriculture in Italy has decreased, while the tertiary sector has grown to include half the working population. The numerical importance of the working class is in diminution and Italy is fast becoming a 'post-industrial' society like other advanced Western countries. However, in Italy there remains the issue of an astronomic deficit, a very corrupt political class, and the problem associated with full participation in the EC. Underneath all of these difficulties lies an even more serious obstacle to Italy's future success. It is an issue which differentiates Italy from every other European nation and we will deal with it in the following chapter.

Notes

1. Mark H. Lazerson, "Organizational Growth of Small Firms: An Outcome of Markets and Hierarchies?" *American Sociological Review* 53 (June 1988), 331.

2. Patrizio Bianchi and Giuseppina Gualtieri, "Emilia-Romagna and its Industrial Districts: The Evolution of a Model," in Robert Leonardi and Raffaella Y. Nanetti, eds., *The Regions and European Integration: The Case of Emilia-Romagna*, (New York: Pinter, 1990), pp. 83-108. See also Robert N. Putname, *Making Democracy Work*, pp.

159-162.

3. See especially Pyke, Becattini and Sengenberger, eds., *Industrial Districts and Inter-firm Co-operation in Italy* (Geneva: International Institute for Labor Studies of the International Labor Organization, 1990).

4. "High Pay For A Short Week In Seven Industrialized Countries," *Italian Journal*, (vol. VI) 1992, no. 4, p. 57.

5. The establishment of the regions did not make the Italian system of government fully federal, for the constitutional and political status of the Italian regions is less autonomous than, for example, the American states or the German *Lander*.

6. Robert D. Putnam, *Making Democracy Work* (Princeton: Princeton University Press, 1993), p. 86-91.

VII

The Two Italys and the Southern Question

Drifting Apart

Even though in many ways Italians are more closely knit than they have been in over a thousand years, Italy remains a divided country in material well-being. Because of that difference, Italy increasingly gives signs of coming apart. The old resentments of the prosperous North toward the less developed South have acquired such dimensions as to generate serious concerns.

Northerners would like to think of themselves as being closer to the continent than to the peninsula: to France which has had much influence in Piedmont, to Germany through old ties to the Austro-Hungarian Empire which provided efficient administration for so long, to Switzerland to which many of those on the borders commute. They feel that the Southerners have ruined their dream of being the richest country in Europe.

In the last few years, the kinds of anti-South slogans normally reserved for wall graffiti have found their way into the political discourse. There have been calls for a division of the country in three republics or making it a federation of states. Some northern autonomist groups have even advocated conducting municipal business in local dialects to limit the influence of Southerners.

The first political party to articulate a political discourse autonomist views was the *Lega Lombarda* (Lombardy League), an autonomist party of Lombardy. When it started in the early 1980s, autonomism appeared to be purely anachronistic and reactionary. The symbol of the *Lega Lombarda*–an armored knight with sword raised aloft–seemed to be more a nostalgic appeal to a vanished past with its reference to the old Lombard League that defended Northern Italy from the barbarians in the Middle Ages, than a sign of a political movement with a future.

The Lega's broadside attack on high taxes, poor government services and the parasitism of the government in Rome–and its proposal to split Italy into three separate republics: North, Center and South–quickly found a willing audience among many ordinary Italians. The success was such that other autonomist parties in other northern regions also made significant advances. Such parties have now banded together to form the *Lega Nord* (Northern League). The parliamentary elections of Spring 1992 showed that the *Lega* had clearly become a strong national political force, gaining 8.7 per cent of the national vote in the Senate (carrying 55 seats) and 8.2 per cent in the Chamber of Deputies (carrying 25 seats).

The local elections held in June 1993 confirmed and in some ways magnified the trends emerged since early 1992. It was the first test of the new system calling for direct election of the mayor in larger cities and middle sized towns with a runoff between the two candidates polling most votes if no one gets a straight majority on the first round. The Northern League won in Milan, and in most other cities and towns of the Po Valley; the number of Northern League mayors went from 12 in 1992 to 74 in 1993. The *Lega* has become the largest party in the north. The overtly anti-South rhetoric of the Lega is due, in part, to widespread disappointment with 45 years of state assistance to that part of the country. The leaders of the *League* feel that despite hundreds of billions of dollars poured into its economy, some areas of the South still have little or no running water, unemployment is at 20 per cent, per-capita income is half that of the North's, and state funds seem to disappear into a black hole of political patronage. They contend that while the northern portion of the country enjoys a standard of living that perhaps only Switzerland can match, the South's economic development has slipped below that of Greece, Portugal and Ireland. And with trade barriers disappearance in 1992, a number of northern industrialists are worried that Italy's cumbersome bureaucracy and inadequate infrastructure will prevent it from competing on an equal footing.

In a country where the state consumes 52 per cent of the gross national product, a frontal assault on big government, corruption, patronage, waste and red tape resonates across the political spectrum. Since all the traditional parties have participated in a system by which money and jobs in almost everything from public-works projects to television stations, from banks to art museums have been openly divided up along party lines, it is not difficult for a party like the Lega to score high points with the public. Its support, therefore, has come from the erosion of support for all the old major parties. About a quarter of the Lega's votes have come from people deserting the Socialist and the ex-Communist parties; but it has also attracted votes from the *D.C.*

To survive the changing mood, the major political parties not only changed their names (*D.C.*, *P.C.I.*, *P.S.I.*, and *M.S.I.* disappeared from the political nomenclature) but worked hard to dissociate themselves from the hated Rome "partitocracy." "Neo-regionalism" was the political fashion of the early 1990s. The Italian Socialist Party, for example, launched the idea of becoming a federation of regional socialist parties. The Democratic Party of the Left also proposed granting greater powers of taxation and administration to the regions. The Christian Democrats sought for able leaders from the North to shed their image as the party of southern patronage.

It is most unlikely that the Lega will succeed with its proposal to create three separate republics within an Italian federation. It had, however, the effect of scaring the traditional parties into adopting some of its more moderate ideas, such as reforming aid to Southern Italy, eliminating patronage and political corruption and finally getting serious about the fight against the Mafia.

The Historical Division

The reasons that the South is lagging so far behind the North are not just geo-cultural; they are also historical and political.

Only 21 per cent of the South is classified as plain—aridity, poor soil, and erosion have disadvantaged agricultural activity. The southern half of the country has also been less favorably disposed because of its isolation and distance from the industrialized and prosperous market of northern Europe.

In addition, the South has a history markedly different from the North and the Center. It is a history not only of high culture and prosperity, but also of exploitation and poverty. It is often hard to realize how Southern Italy was virtually part of Greece for hundreds of years before the Roman conquest. It was called *Magna Graecia* and many Greek legends actually had their setting in Southern Italy. **Greek** settlers built large urban centers and religious shrines and established a brilliant civilization. City states like Taras (now Taranto), Syracuse (Siracusa), and Akragas (now Agrigento) flourished. Many place names are of Greek origin, including Naples, derived from Neapolis, a Greek word literally meaning new city and Gallipoli in southern Puglia. Pythagoras, Herodotus, Aeschylus, Euripides, and Plato visited at various times what is now called the Mezzogiorno in much the same way world artists visit Central Italy today. The philosopher Empedocles belonged to the ruling clan of Akragas. Archimedes, the greatest mathematician of antiquity, was a native of Syracuse. Some of the most splendid remains of Greek temples in the Mediterranean are in Southern Italy: at Paestum, near Salerno; at Agrigento, Syracuse and Segesta, in Sicily. In Bova, a village in Calabria, the inhabitants speak a dialect based directly on ancient Greek.

In ancient times the South was the most prosperous part of the peninsula. Under Roman rule it became an expanse of enormous farming estates, the latifundia, where a slave population worked the soil, enabling the absentee landlords to regale themselves in Rome. Then came raids and invasions by Germanic tribes and centuries of domination by Byzantines and Arabs, and by Norman, German, French and Spanish rules.

It was during the domination of the Normans, at the court of Frederick II that the first Italian literary school, *La Scuola Siciliana*, started to produce a literature with a national character. The *Scuola Siciliana* preceded the well-recognized Tuscan school, *Il Dolce Stil Novo*, by about half a century.

Refugees have also played a part in the southern culture. There are twenty-six Albanian villages which originated from Mehemet II's invasion of Albania after he had taken Constantinople in 1453.

Between the fifteenth century and the *Risorgimento* of the nineteenth the South was subjected to foreign rule and exploitation numerous times. Colonialism imposed a strong tradition of strict class structure, reinforced by the presence of a powerful and oppressive feudal organization that was abolished much later than those of other European countries, creating certain socio-cultural barriers to development.

With the unification of Italy things did not improve. Count Camillo Benso di Cavour, the diplomatic architect of Italy's unification, was not interested in liberating the South or making it part of Italy. Since Garibaldi's march from the South made this an accomplished fact, Cavour did not have choice in the matter. However, as prime minister, Cavour never even bothered to visit the South.

Consequently, Southerners quickly gained the feeling that they were not citizens of a new Italian state with the same rights and opportunities as the Northerner, but instead had become subjects in a colony. The new institutions, laws, and economic policies were generally alien to the customs and contrary to the interests of the South. Taxes became ruinous, the area's economic base was undermined while the industrialization of the North perpetuated and even deepened the division. Economic conditions were so hard that in the fifty years before WWI roughly half the southern population–5 million people–emigrated.

Under Fascism the South was still regarded as a no man's land, and despite some spotty reforms, it continued to lag behind. Instead of channeling the nation's energies and resources into the Mezzogiorno, Mussolini sought to conquer an African empire. When Fascist authorities wanted to dispose of "dangerous" individuals, they would exile them to the South. As previously mentioned, while in Basilicata, writer Carlo Levi, one such individual, wrote a stunning book, *Christ Stopped in Eboli* (1945), in which he represented the primitive society and pattern of life he found in a land which he felt Jesus had never touched. Another stunning representations of the precarious conditions of the southern peasants was given by Ignazio Silone in his novel *Fontamara*:

> the same earth, the same rain, wind, the same feast days, the same food, the same poverty--a poverty inherited from our fathers, who had received it from their grandfathers, and against which honest work was of no avail. The life of men and beasts, and of the land itself, revolved in a closed circle... There has never been a way out. At that time, a man could perhaps save twenty or thirty *soldi* a month, and in summer perhaps even a hundred, so that by the autumn he had thirty *lire*. They disappeared at once—in interest on some loan, or to the doctor, the pharmacist or the priest. And so one began again, the next day. Twenty *soldi*, a hundred *soldi*...[1]

In the same book, Silone gave an ironic picture of the hierarchy of the region still pervaded by strong feudalism:

> At the head of everything there's God, the master of Heaven.
> That everyone knows.

Then comes Prince Torlonia, the master of the land.
Then come the Prince's dogs.
Then come the Prince's guards.
Then nothing.
Then, still nothing.
Then come the *cafoni* (the peasants).
And that's about all.(p. 29)

Fontamara eloquently represents the hopeless world of the Southern *cafoni*. *Cafone*, explained the author, means "flesh accustomed to suffer."(p. 43) Silone was well aware that the name *cafone*, in Italy, was an insult. "But I use it in this book in the certainty that when in my country suffering is no longer something to be ashamed of, it will become a title of respect, perhaps also of honor." (p.6)

Even after World War II, the Italian government did not move quickly to change its policy. Its head from 1945 to 1953, Alcide De Gasperi, rarely visited the South and seemed to distrust its potential for economic and cultural development, even though southern specialists kept insisting that the *Mezzogiorno*–basically the six southernmost regions of the Italian peninsula plus the islands of Sicily and Sardinia–might one day become the California of Italy.

Nevertheless, the mood was now ripe for change. Some of postwar Italy's leading writers–Domenico Rea, Leonardo Sciascia, Saverio Strati, and the above mentioned Carlo Levi and Ignazio Silone–were publishing eloquent novels on the plight of the South. These authors understood better, felt more deeply, and conveyed more powerfully than the politicians what life there was really like. Finally the government had no choice but to act. The new republic undertook one of the largest and most ambitious regional development programs in Western Europe to solve the "Southern Question." It followed three courses of action: land reform, infrastructure development, and industrialization. The single most important institution to become involved in this process was the Fund for the South (*Cassa per il Mezzogiorno*), founded in 1950. Its main source of funding was state revenue, but it also drew on foreign loans. Initially, the fund concentrated on infrastructural projects in agriculture, sanitation, and transportation; in 1957 the focus shifted to an effort to industrialize the south. That year the government approved legislation obliging state holding companies to locate a substantial share of new investment in the South and providing one of the most generous investment incentive packages in Western Europe.

By the early 1990s the state had poured into the *Mezzogiorno* an estimated $150 billion of public funds. Approximately two-fifths of this expenditure went to public works, the remainder being allocated primarily to investments in agriculture, industry, and tourism. As result, thousands of miles of new streets and hundreds of bridges, many new schools, universities and hospitals, and a network of modern hotels, restaurants, and service stations were built. Running water, electricity, and telephone service was brought to even the smallest hamlet; and a few large, new industries, like the Taranto steel mills and the petrochemical complexes at Brindisi and on Sicily's east coast were built. Infant mortality declined by three-quarters and illiteracy among youngsters has been practically eradicated as well, and while the overall character of the South has remained rural, its principal cities have greatly expanded. Their historic cores are now surrounded by vast belts of condominiums and new housing projects. The countryside is also full of elegant new housing.

Surprisingly, however, the economic gap between the *Mezzogiorno* and prosperous Northern and Central Italy continued to widen. By the early 1990s the South—an area the size of Greece, with 40 per cent of the country's land area and 30 percent of its population—accounted for only 20 per cent of G.D.P. and has an official unemployment rate of nearly 20 per cent of the labor force, against 5 per cent in the North. The per capita income in Southern Italy was still barely 60 per cent of the average in the rest of Italy, while the per capita income was more than 80 per cent in the North.

Industrialization without Development

No one denies that the southern development, despite a number of isolated successes, fell short of all its original expectations and goals. Economists and political scientists have given many possible reasons:

1. Physical disadvantages of the South, including distance from markets, unfavorable terrain, and lack of natural resources.

2. Misguided government policies, especially in the late nineteenth century, including, in particular,

(a) trade policy (first, free trade that killed off fledgling southern industry and later protection that encouraged northern industry);

(b) fiscal policy (high taxes on the South, and spending to benefit the North, on education, defense industries, and land reclamation—although by the end of the nineteenth century total taxes were proportionally no higher in the South and the national government had already begun investing substantial sums in public works there); and

(c) industrial policy (which served northern interests by promoting an alliance between heavy industry and large banks).

3. Market externalities, the "economics of agglomeration," and "learning by doing" that magnified the North's modest initial advantages.

4. The "moral poverty" and absence of human capital in the Mezzogiorno, along with the culture of patron-clientelism.[2]

However, the major causes for failure have to be mainly attributed to political reasons and to Southern socio-cultural factors, especially to lack of civic traditions. It would also be safe to say, however, that throughout the 1950s the South was not conceived of as a center of industrialization and that the new government had planned to continue the same policy of pre-war governments, that is, to keep the South agricultural.

It was in 1949 when southern peasants started occupying some of the *latifondi*, or large estates, that the government was forced to deal with the problem of the South. At that time over half the population of the South–compared to a third in the rest of Italy–earned its livelihood from the soil as small holders, tenant farmers, or day laborers. These peasants barely made a subsistence living. In the face of the spreading discontent, the government enacted a modest land reform program in 1950 to buy out some large estates and sell the land to the peasants. During the first dozen years, from 1950 on, the government, through the *Cassa per il Mezzogiorno*, concentrated its attention and roughly 78 per cent of its money on agriculture, with most of the remainder going to related infrastructure. Land reclamation, construction of dams, irrigation, aqueducts, and a vast extension of the road network gradually changed the face of the South. Technical experts introduced new farming and marketing methods. Malaria, which had afflicted the fertile lowlands in many parts of the South, was finally eradicated. The state intervention contributed to the end of latifundia system and the birth of a new small-scale peasantry.

However, when the program was largely completed in 1962 a mere 1.5 million acres had been transferred to some 85,000 peasants. For many, especially in the mountainous areas, the redistribution amounted to no more than a small plot of poor soil, insufficient to maintain a family. In the South as a whole, land holdings –half the average size of those in other Common Market countries–were too small to achieve fully modern and low-cost production. The real income of the average farmer did not increase much. As a consequence, in the course of the postwar years the share of those employed in agriculture in the South declined from 57 to 27 percent of the work force. Soon enough it became clear that efforts to improve agriculture had not reduced unemployment, raised incomes, or narrowed the overall gap between the South and the rest of Italy. So the flight from the land intensified. Tens of thousands continued to leave the farms and poured into the labor market in the cities both in the South and the North. As in the previous hundred years, the state intervention in the South was subordinated to the interest of the industrial economic groups.

In fact, the massive migration from the South which could supply cheap labor for the North was not the result of 'natural' causes but it was politically determined. Angelo Costa, President of the Italian Employers' Confederation (the *Confindustria*), in the course of an investigation conducted by the government explained that he thought that the adoption of policies for the localization of industry along the UK model would be detrimental to the Italian economy. He asserted that it would be preferable to "move people" rather than things.[3] In other words Costa was in favor of internal immigration rather than the location of industry in the South. This implied that the role of the South in post-war reconstruction would have to be that of providing the northern industries with the necessary supply of low-cost labor. The development of the North was thus financed by the systematic drainage of the South's sole resource: human labor. In exchange the South was given a constant stream of state funds. This policy was spearheaded by the DC because, through the process, it could establish a strong patronage system and would have underpinned the stability of its regime. The Christian Democrats cooperated with Costa, who accepted the need for public works program in the South provided that the wages in the southern public-sector programs would have to be inferior to wages in the industrial northern sector in order not to compete for labor with private industry. Thus, there was a conscious political decision to intervene where private industry is reluctant to intervene and to do so on the basis of a low-wage policy.

Costa's plan of assuring cheap Southern labor for the North was sustained by a consciousness that the Southern Italians, unlike workers in other underdeveloped countries, had a cultural level, however low it may appear to some, already structured by the ethics and the mentality of the technological world. It is this cultural aspect which permitted the transformation of the Southern peasant into a high-productivity, assembly-line proletarian in a couple of weeks, whereas such a transformation is unthinkable in a similar space of time in the majority of underdeveloped countries.[4] Thus government policy protected a section of the southern population and more or less forced the rest to seek a life away from the land.

The agrarian reform and the creation of the *Cassa per il Mezzogiorno*, while intended to restrict the numbers of absentee landlords, created a large class of small land-owning peasants and united them in a political bloc which stopped the communist advance in the South. However, it would be difficult to demonstrate that the non-industrialization of the South was part of a political design to keep the conservative land-owning peasants from becoming progressive urban proletarians –the great majority of Southerners who became Northern factory workers became communists.

When the agrarian reform began to be criticized for its failures, the *Cassa* embarked on large-scale projects to create infrastructures. The strategy of public works programs which was in the hands of the *Cassa* and other state agencies was meant to consolidate the infrastructures, strengthen the agricultural sector and develop tourism. State intervention could be accepted by the North because it developed a market in the South for northern produce without increasing the competitiveness of Southern industry. It obtained the favor of southern political and business leaders because it helped to expand the building industry, sustained a vast network of small peasant properties, and created a sector of dependent public employees. In fact, through the development of the state sector a large class of white-collar workers was also created which with time became a clientele system for the leading party of government, the *D.C.*[5] However, in reality, government action in the South helped the North more than it did the South. First, by increasing Southerners income through a public works program, it expanded the market for Northern industry; second, the moneys spent on the infrastructure, e.g. motorways, helped Northern industries both directly and directly.[6] Moreover, in the process, the *Cassa* programs also created a sector of marginalized workers who were marginally trained. Those who had left their land to work in one of the *Cassa* projects could not return to it when the project was terminated; they, too, had to move further North. The massive decrease in employment in agriculture was partly due to the change in emphasis in the direction of state intervention in the agricultural sector. This became clearer with the second *Green Plan* (1966): small farmers were discouraged and public intervention went increasingly towards electrification and irrigation projects which were meant to favor existing entrepreneurs in rural areas rather than the marginal farmer. [7]

Many experts had insisted all along that only rapid industrial development would create jobs and prosperity needed to break the vicious cycle of unemployment and poverty. Put simply, industry was to be moved to the area of surplus labor rather than labor's moving to the area of industrial activity. The shift of state investment funds from agriculture to industry paved the way to a serious attempt to the industrialization of the South.

The *Cassa*'s spending on infrastructure was therefore cut from 42 percent in 1957 to 13 percent in 1965 while assistance to industrial enterprises was stepped up from 48 percent to 82 percent. To encourage private investment the government offered generous credits and tax incentives. It also required the state holding companies *IRI* and *ENI*, to invest increasing amounts of capital in the South. *IRI*, the major investor, injected over $20 billion into the South between 1963 and 1978.

The industrial policy for the South had two political motivations: first, to enable local entrepreneurs to become full-fledged industrialists instead of remaining craftsmen or farmers. Second, to attract northern investment. The state intervened with large public projects through its enterprises: *Istituto per la Ricostruzione Industriale* (*IRI*) established giant steelworks near Taranto while *Ente Nazionale Idrocarburi* (*ENI*) located large petroleum refineries in Sicily. In this way came about a steel industry (at one time the most modern in Europe) at Taranto, an Alfa Romeo plant near Naples, and giant petrochemical factories in Sicily and Sardinia. The volume of industrial development in the South during this period was remarkable.

However, even though some of these investments were productive and profitable, the all-out heavy industrialization program did not turn out to be the magic solution to the South's problems. The new industries were not labor intensive and created relatively few jobs. The managerial and technical personnel were recruited from the North and later returned there, leaving the South without an indigenous managerial and technical class. And the industries themselves were subsidiaries of northern companies which never developed links to the local economy. These large-scale, technologically advanced plants had no connection with the rest of the southern economy. They were a sort of colonial enclave with little if no contact with the small local firms. They did not generate ancillary small and medium-sized enterprises in their areas; on the contrary, they maintained a direct connection with the North. Moreover, the *Cassa* began to finance basic large-scale enterprises, both private and public: electricity, steel, paper, chemical, gas–all industries which are fairly capital intensive but which contribute little to employment.[8] Italians speak of the solitary industrial giants in the South as their *Cathedrals in the desert*. Some factories in the South were apparently built only to collect the state subsidies for economic development in the region. Furthermore, many firms from the North were able to obtain considerable funds from the State in the form of subsidies, low-interest or interest-free loans as well as direct grants as a part of invested capital. Consequently, the cost of the *Cassa* often went back to the North. Northern firms got subsidies for starting up factories in the South and then went bankrupt and re-exported their machinery to the North. One example Southerners frequently cite is the Taranto steel works, where all the overalls used were imported from the North and paid for by government subsidies which should have gone to the South. Or the firm which went down to Maratea, in the Calabria region, bringing its old machinery, and then started a new factory in the North purchasing new equipment with its government subsidies.

Often these new southern industries could not compete in the international market or withstand changes in economic trends. The steel plants at Taranto and Naples-Bagnoli were dragged down by the decline of the entire European steel industry in the 1970s. The huge petrochemical plants on the coast of Sicily and Sardinia were based on cheap petroleum sullies; after the price increase in 1973, they, too, failed.

Overall, by 1980, the old South had changed. About 2,400 new factories employing over 305,000 persons had settled in designated industrial estates. However, new industrial jobs were concentrated in a limited number of sectors; 73 per cent of southern factory employment in 1980 was in the chemical, mechanical, or metallurgical industries. Most of the firms in these sectors were large, state-controlled, capital-intensive units. In 1982 *IRI* accounted for 52.5 percent of employment in southern manufacturing plants having over 1,000 workers. Other state holding companies represented another 11.5 percent of employment compared with 36 percent for the private sector.

However, at the beginning of the 80s a continuing problem was the fact that industrial development in the south was confined not only sectorial but geographically as well. The bulk of development was concentrated in three main areas: Naples and its neighboring provinces, the Bari-Brindisi-Taranto triangle, and the Syracuse-Augusta axis of eastern Sicily. 80 per cent of the funding of the *Cassa* went to only four regions–Puglia, Sardinia, Sicily, and Campania. Spending was also extremely concentrated within the regions. For example, two-thirds of Puglia investments was directed to Taranto.

The government had enacted laws in 1971 and 1976 requiring the *Cassa* to concentrate on a new range of intersectorial and interregional projects. These included the further development of industrial infrastructure, the exploitation of natural resources, social projects in metropolitan areas, water-reclamation projects, cleaning the Gulf of Naples, extending the road network into remote mountainous areas, reforestation, and promotion of citrus fruit production. Many of these programs had to be scaled down or scrapped as a result of the economic crisis following the oil price increase after 1973. Some of them were gigantic fiascoes.

Emphasis then shifted to the selective encouragement of small and medium-sized firms, which in the early 1980s accounted for over 90 per cent of the projects and 85 per cent of the investment of the *Cassa*. Unfortunately this has met with limited success. Only Abruzzi and Puglia have witnessed the growth of a dynamic sector of small firms similar to those that have developed in Northeastern and Central Italy.

As a result, the private investment that was to follow the development initiated by the state never came. Private investors had to cope with the so-called "Southern Italian risk," that is, worker absenteeism, low productivity, labor unrest, and low labor mobility. A concrete example of such "risk" was the Alfa Romeo plant constructed near Naples in 1972. It was so afflicted by labor strife and absenteeism that it ran up losses of $700 million, which had to be covered by the parent company in the North. For many years every "Alfa Sud" car on the road was sold at less than its production cost.

Potential investors, Italian and foreign, consequently often decided that the South was too great a hazard and in fact, in the late 70s and 80s there was a net decline of foreign companies investing in the South. Even the investment which did occur in the South did not do much to reduce unemployment because industrialization and employment were not entirely compatible goals. This problem was typically faced through the expansion of the bureaucracy and on the public purse.

Development had been the victim of bad planning, bad economics, and above all, bad politics. The emphasis shifted from agriculture to infrastructure development, to large industry, to small and medium-sized industry, and back to agriculture. The whole development process went ahead, Gianni Agnelli, president of FIAT, remarked at a conference of southern experts in 1980, either in "the good faith of error" or in "the bad faith of political 'necessity'."

By becoming an employer even in the industrial sector, the government entered into a compromise with the social groups by establishing clientele relations. Through the development of the state sector a large class of white-collar workers was also created. This class owed its existence to the *D.C.* and did not–as in other countries–appear to be the natural consequence of economic development.

The diminution of employment on the land and the relative failure to industrialize the South brought about a considerable expansion of a protected sector in the economy of the South: a sector where the State played the leading role through direct use of public spending. This was achieved through a kind of welfare assistance through pension and disability policy and again through the expansion of the bureaucracy. Disablement pensions increased at a phenomenal rate in the mid 1960s. Unlike old-age pensions, disablement pensions depend on 'subjective' factors such as a certificate from a compliant doctor employed by the pension fund controlled by the small farmers and funded by the State. By 1974 the pension funds paid disability pensions to nearly 1.5 million small farmers against 625,000 for old-age pensions. (Ibid., p. 60) Fifteen to seventeen million welfare benefits and pensions, in a population of 57 million, are paid out mainly to Southerners.

The South did not derive any particular benefit from the effects of the decentralization of production towards the hidden sector which permitted Italy to achieve a growth-rate higher than most industrial nations in the early 1980s. The small and medium-sized firms of the hidden sector were located, on the whole, in the Center and in the North, with very few in the South. Therefore, when the larger firms, both public and private, decreased the rate of growth of their investments, the South was hit harder. The state resources which could have been used otherwise had to be directed towards enabling existing firms to pay their debts or reorganize existing plants.

But the South suffers mainly because of its own faults. In the Mezzogiorno, the observation made by Pasquale Villari in 1883–"One feels too much the 'I' and too little the 'we'"–is still very much valid.[9] Civic traditions and civic engagement alone do not account for the big difference between North and South, but their very weak presence in the South have made a profound difference. Civic traditions help explain why the North has been able to respond to the challenges and opportunities of the twentieth century so much more effectively than the South.[10] The most relevant distinction is not even between the presence and absence of social bo nds, but rather between horizontal bonds of mutual solidarity and vertical bonds of dependency and exploitation. The Southerner has sought refuge in vertical bonds of patronage and clientelism, employed for both economic and political ends.

Let's not Despair

The future of the South lies in its ability of becoming of a mature civic society and in the prospect of seeing the young generation fully integrated into a productive Italy and Europe. The Italian government has finally undertaken a serious effort in this direction without placing politics as the first item on the agenda. In order to create entrepreneurs in the new generation of the South, under a 1986 law, the government established the *Committee for the Development of Young Entrepreneurs in the Mezzogiorno*. The financial assistance provided for under the law is aimed only at residents of the *Mezzogiorno* under 29 which also happen to be the largest unemployed age group. In spite of limited financial and human resources, the Committee has shown that it is possible for a state agency to help train skilled, young entrepreneurs even in the *Mezzogiorno*. The task of the Committee is to assist young people with good ideas and imagination who do not have the necessary capital and structures to back them up.

The Committee has won its gamble on creating young entrepreneurs in The South, thanks in part to the support systems which are tailor-made for each of the new enterprises. The new business is accompanied during its first year of activity by another company, a tutor, (Isvor-Fiat, Hewlett Packard, Ferrero, Elea-Olivetti, Enidata, to name a few) which helps it to overcome the thousands of obstacles a novice could otherwise stumble over and risk not getting back up. The relationship between the Committee and the tutor is formalized only after this teacher-company has presented a valid plan of action for the new company. This plan must mainly diagnose what is needed to launch and then nurture the new venture. The tutor pays for the study out of its own pocket, and in some cases it does not bear fruit if the Committee judges the proposals inadequate. If the tutor's plan is accepted, the tutor goes to work and is bound by contract to make a report every three months on the work accomplished. To the recipients of the Committee's financial aid the term "advance payment" is unknown. They receive the state's money only after the person in charge of the project has demonstrated to have truly done what was stated in the project. However, once the go ahead is given, they receive the financing in a short time, approximately seventy-six days.

Over forty million dollars were approved for these training. By mid 1991, the project had funded over 15 million dollars in investments and created 13,000 jobs. There are already over 350 companies open for business, 650 projects have been approved with another 450 presently under evaluation. The experiment shows that young entrepreneurs can actually be created in the *Mezzogiorno* and that the suspicions about the lack of professional training available and the impossibility of overcoming obstacles with initiatives funded through state agencies is still very possible.

Southern Italians have demonstrated their competence in many fields throughout the history of modern Italy. They make shrewd lawyers, able administrators, sharp police investigators, and consummate diplomats; they excel in philosophical speculations or mathematical theory. The plays and novels of Luigi Pirandello Nobel Prize-winner (1934) for literature provide penetrating psychological insights into the South.

Beyond any doubt the South has been transformed and the social changes are very striking. The *Mezzogiorno* is no longer isolated; Southerners have gradually gone through a process of "Americanization" or modernization. Their outlook and mores—the secularization, the standards of consumer society, with all its defects, and the social values—have come close to those of the Northerners. The South is now linked to the rest of Italy not only through radio and television, but also through one of the most advanced networks of roads and highways in Europe and a web of economic relationships.

Thus in the 1990s the "Southern Question" is not a matter of simple modernization, or of an increase of state funds. It cannot be addressed by pointing fingers at southern shame or northern guilt. The "problem of the South" cannot even be understood purely in terms of the Italian North, but must be thought of anew in terms of the relations between Italy and the rest of the EEC and the Mediterranean.

Notes

1. *Fontamara* (Milan: Mondadori, 1974), pp. 7-8.

2. Robert N. Putnam, *Making Democracy Work* (Princeton: Princeton U.P., 1993), pp. 158-159. For a good assessment also read Gianni Toniolo, *An Economic History of Liberal Italy: 1850-1918*, trans. Maria Rees (New York: Routledge, 1990); Vera Zamagni, *Industrializzazione e squilibri regionali in Italia: Bilancio dell'età giolittiana* (Bologna: Il Mulino, 1978).

3. In L. Villari, ed. *Il capitalismo italiano del Novecento, vol. II* (Bari: Laterza, 1975), p. 486-7.

4. Marcello De Cecco, "Lo sviluppo dell'economia italiana e la sua collocazione internazionale," *Rivista Internazionale di Scienze Economiche e Commerciali*, October, 1971, p. 982.

5. Mariano D'Antonio, *Sviluppo e crisi del capitalismo italiano 1951-1972* (Bari: De Donato, 1973), p. 236.

6. Guido Fabiani, "Agricoltura e Mezzogiorno," in *AA. VV. Lezioni di economia. Aspetti e problemi dello sviluppo economico italiano e dell'attuale crisi internazionale* (Milan: Feltrinelli, 1977), p.158.

7. Giuliano Amato, *Economia, politica e istituzioni in Italia* (Bologna: Il Mulino 1976), p. 52.

8. Vittorio Valli, *L'economia e la politica economica italiana* (Milan: Etas Libri, 1979), p. 107.

9. Cited in Tullio Altan, *La nostra Italia*, p. 13.

10. For a convincing argument see Robert N. Putnam, *Making Democracy Work*, especially chapter 5 and 6.

VIII

Emigration, Migration, Immigration and Social Transformation

In Search of a Better Life

Because Italy in the mid-1950s was still, in many respects, an underdeveloped country, Italians, mainly from the South, were still emigrating by the thousands in search of a better life. Emigration was still a way of life for many just as it had been for the previous three or four generations. Naturally this had a profound impact on the economy of large areas of the country, on family life and structure, and caused the socio-transformation of many villages and small towns.

Migration has been massive and it has not been unidirectional. The currents have flowed overseas, within Europe, from southern to northern Italy, from poorer rural areas to richer rural areas and/or to cities, and back home from abroad. But the primary motive for migration has always been economic and social: poverty, unemployment, land hunger.

The invention of the steamship certainly gave impetus to the movement across the ocean and made emigration a big business. Agents acting on behalf of steamship companies or foreign employers were eager to enlist laborers because they were getting a cut per head. Moreover, the small-town "political class" had a vested interest in emigration because it was an important unofficial source of income. Lawyers, teachers, politicians, travel agents were all involved in arranging for passports, booking the passages, lending the money for the fares (often at usurious rates), and finally selling off the peasants' land and houses. Such "businessmen" were often not much more than venal speculators and traffickers in human flesh. By the 1890s the Southern middle class was busy enrolling peasants, hiring ships, and making money on those whom it had previously been exploiting the most. Sometimes it even managed to export its social dominance across the Atlantic, to reappear in America as "bossism."

For millions of Italians especially from the South, America, as a dream land, offered hope for a better future. The Italians who immigrated into America took pick-and-shovel jobs, entered the building trades, provided manpower for the waterfronts, worked for municipal sanitation departments. Some managed to scrape together enough money to open small restaurants or groceries. The women became seamstresses in the sweatshops and factories of the garment industry.

Many who had left their families behind dreamed of going back to the old village one day to buy a piece of land which would give them independence. Quite a few did go back, sometimes twenty or more years later, when the children they had last seen as infants were adults. Most, however, changed their minds and had their wives and children join them. Although the bulk of them were originally from rural areas, in the US they tended to cluster in cities and suburbs, forming "little Italies;" this kind of relocation, of course, caused problems for those who did attempt to re-establish their roots back in Italy.

Many of the immigrants from the South were virtually illiterate and the country's cultural heritage had no meaning for them. In a sense, many of them had left Italy before becoming Italians. If this situation was contributing to a negative impression of Italians, it did not really matter for the United States because the growing country needed large numbers of sturdy laborers for the heavy construction work. And the Southern Italians played a key role in building America, for they dug the ditches, toiled in the mines, laid the rails and carried the bricks and mortar. They tacitly gave their sweat and blood in laying the material foundations of America.

Those Italians who stayed home generally welcomed the exodus because it was seen as a remedy to social problems. In the 1890s, Prime Minister Francesco Nitti described emigration as a "powerful safety-valve against class hatred." Sidney Sonnino, another prime minister of the exodus period, maintained that to prevent emigration would be a clear attack on the poor. Nevertheless, emigration was controlled in some areas of the South where the big landowners controlled local government and wanted to preserve the system of exploitation. There were others who were opposed to emigration because of the way emigrants were being treated abroad or because of the impact that emigration was having on family structure. Edmondo De Amicis (1846-1908), a Socialist, aroused much indignation by representing emigration as shameful in the account he gave in a very moving book, *Sull'oceano (1889, On the Ocean)*. The Catholic Church was also not supportive of emigration because of the effects it had on family life (families were split for many years and very often were never reunited) and on religious belief (thousands of emigrants to America became Protestants, often Pentacostalists). In fact, Protestant groups actively conducted missions in an effort to convert Italians. At one time there were almost 300 Italian Protestant missionaries engaged in full time work. Prominenant figures like Leonard Covello, Fiorello La Guardia, Ferdinand Pecora and Charles Poletti were Protestants.

Nationalists were also opposed to emigration because they worried that Italy was losing too many of her potential soldiers; they believed that Southern overpopulation should have been remedied by colonies in Africa, not through emigration to America. Thus after 1907 the debate on emigration gradually changed and was combined with imperialistic ideas. In the 30s, stories about America in the depths of the depression certainly weren't favorable to emigration, and the fascist regime also did its best to keep people at home by making emigration regulations more bureaucratic. Mussolini wanted to build up the male population to fight his wars and had to increase the over-all population to justify its colonial expansion and its imperialistic dreams. The "great safety-valve" had suddenly been shut. Not only was emigration discouraged, but during the depression Mussolini was sending ships to New York to pick up any Italian who wanted to return to Italy. Depressing accounts of those Italians who came back thinking to escape the American depression are given in novels mentioned earlier, *Cristo si è fermato ad Eboli* (*Christ stopped at Eboli*, 1945) by Carlo Levi and *Fontamara,* 1933 by Ignazio Silone.

Postwar Rural Exodus
After WWII the exodus resumed, especially from the South. And it was again a consequence of deep disillusionment, and this time it was probably due also to impatience.

In the 1951 census, agriculture was still by far the largest single sector of employment; it accounted for 42.2 per cent of the working population nation-wide, including 56.9 per cent for the South. But the agriculture was still rudimentary and the livelihood it provided, especially in the South, was still very poor: in 1950 the income per capita was about 60 per cent that of 1924! Emigration was again an escape from the crushing poverty; however, now it took different forms; people left the countryside by the thousands but most of them remained in Europe.

Between 1951 and 1961 about 1.75 million people left the South; this increased to 2.3 million in the following ten years. These are net figures and do not include seasonal workers. The figures of total emigrants that include those who returned to the home areas are understandably much higher: 7.5 million emigrated from 1946 to 1976 (net emigration of 3.5 million); 4 million from the South alone.

Because of the full awareness of their social situation and the prospect of better conditions in the urban industrial world, farmers flooded the cities of their own country. Those who were more adventurous and could not be absorbed by the expanding Italian economy went abroad. One shocking statistic is that Italy is the only country of the advanced industrial world which suffered massive emigration while sustaining rapid economic growth.

The most dramatic form of emigration was overseas, to the Americas and Australia. Between 1946 and 1957 the numbers of those leaving Italy for the New World exceeded by 1,100,000 the number of those returning: 380,000 had remained in Argentina, 166,500 in Canada, 166,000 in the US, 138,000 in Australia and 128,000 in Venezuela. They were for the most part artisans and peasant proprietors rather than landless laborers; nearly 70 per cent were from the South.

Initially (1946-54) there was a certain balance between emigration towards other European countries and that directed towards other continents, but after 1955 Italian emigration was essentially European.

Emigration to Western Europe

In a silent mass migration that made no headlines either at home or abroad, 6 million southern Italians–nearly one-third of the population of the Mezzogiorno– moved northward. Between 1946 and 1957 the numbers heading to northern Europe exceeded by 840,000 the numbers of those who came back: France took in 381,000, followed by Switzerland with 202,000 and Belgium 159,000. The emigrants to these countries tended to go for short periods, six-month or one-year contracts, and regarded work abroad a temporary rather than a permanent solution to their problems.

After 1955 emigration from the rural South was directed both towards countries of Western Europe and to urban areas of Northern Italy, which by now had taken their place among the world's advanced industrial centers. The movement became easier in 1968, when citizens of the EC were given the right to free movement within EC boundaries, however, migration to Europe had already peaked in 1961. In Northern Europe, the emigrants provided manpower for large and small industries, went down into coal mines, worked as ditchdiggers and bricklayers, as hotel maids and waiters, as cooks and dishwashers. Many made good quickly and became foremen in factories and construction firms, or opened their own pizzerias or restaurants.

This export of labor continued until 1973. In that year for the first time in the history of modern Italy more Italians returned home than left: between 1973 and 1978 the 'balance of labor' showed a gain of nearly 68,000 people.[1] In fact, starting in the early 1970s and until 1981, repatriation was proceeding at a higher level than emigration. The return of Italian emigrants was mainly due to the international economic crisis which hit construction and manufacturing, particularly assembly-line work in the car sector. This led countries such as West Germany to "unload" some of its surplus laborers by sending them back.[2]

The emigration to Western Europe is notable for some peculiar features. Not only were emigrants disposed of like any other surplus goods, but the host countries had saved all the expense of educating the imported workers and providing social assistance for their families. Since many came when young and able-bodied and without their families, they saved the host country expenses associated with schooling, pensions, health services, etc. In other words, foreign workers were putting into the economy far more than they were getting out of it in terms of social services.[3]

Migration to the North and to the Cities

During the period of the "economic miracle," many Southerners migrated to the North of Italy. This internal Italian migration acquired, from the very beginning, a form of permanent immigration. This was a new phenomenon because until the mid-1960s migration was still illegal because the fascist laws had not yet been repealed, and officially the migrants needed a job to get housing and housing to get a job. It had been the fascist way to preserve the social stratification. But with the new laws, Italian citizens could move freely both geographically and between categories of work. The workers who left the countryside for the northern industrial triangle of Milan-Turin-Genoa had citizenship rights equal to those of the local people. Unlike those emigrating abroad, they could not be discriminated against politically or isolated by language barriers or risk being expelled.

However, the problems of adjustment and integration were not less severe. Many Southerners met the same unfriendliness, slights and hostility in the North as did those who emigrated abroad. In Italy's North the standard disparaging nickname for any native of the *Mezzogiorno* became—and still is—terrone, a word derived from terra (soil). Terrone suggests less a yokel than an uncivilized but cunning fellow, an individual who is clannish and anti-social. For northern Italians, the terroni are the causes of all Italy's ills. Northerners' antipathy for Southerners has found increasingly less subtle expressions especially in the northern news media. Newspapers in Turin, Milan, Venice, or Bologna often make a point of noting that an arrested robbery, burglary or murder suspect was born in Palermo or some other place in the South. Northerners do not hesitate to openly accuse the bureaucrats of the nation's capital and the Southerners of stealing and squandering the tax money that they contribute out of what they earn through their efficiency and hard work. However, official estimates show that many more millions are lost through the tax dodgers in the North than through waste in the South; moreover, the scandal of the tangenti has shown that Northerners, especially politicians, public officials and industrialists are no better than Southerners when it comes to compromising morals or civic values.

The adjustment to the northern environment has been difficult for southerners of every age-group. Even for the youngster, for whom social and cultural adjustment was easy, integration was difficult. A very perceptive representation of that condition has been given by many artists in their films and literature. *Rocco e i suoi fratelli* (*Rocco and His Brothers*), by Luchino Visconti, a movie released in 1960, focuses upon the migration of Southern Italians to northern industrial areas and the struggle to survive in an environment that demands profound adjustments. Visconti concentrates upon the dramatic clash of differing value systems—that of the traditional southern peasant family and

its archaic code of honor and family loyalty on the one hand, and a more individualistic and contemporary morality reflecting industrial society, on the other.
Although Rocco omits much of what a historian or a sociologist would consider
essential to a discussion of urban migration in Milan –unions, strikes, racism,
crime, and so forth–it does give a penetrating picture of the effects of rapid
cultural change upon the ancient values of traditional Southern Italian families.[4]

For Southern Italians, the absence of collective festivals, of the piazza as
a meeting place, of street-living and inter-family visits had a profound impact.
On the one hand families suffered in the stifling atmosphere of a shanty town,
on the other hand, each nuclear family unit tended to be more closed in and less
open to community life or to forms of inter-family solidarity. The problems
and inadequacies that emerged from these environmental and familial shortcomings were not to be underestimated.[5] Certainly, the younger members of
the family found greater opportunity for social pleasures in the new urban
settings. Bars, dance halls, soccer matches, etc. did offer new freedoms and
pastimes. Moreover, authority structures within the family became less rigid,
as did paternal control over family finances.

Unlike the emigrants to Germany and Switzerland, the Southerners who
emigrated to Northern Italy brought along their families, their demands, their
right of influencing political organizations and trade unions, and, in 1969, they
could be in the forefront of the events leading to the "hot autumn." With emigration the "Southern Question" was not solved, indeed, it became more complex. Its reserve army of labor fed the Italian "economic miracle" and when
this came to an end the tension remained, grew and exploded.

However, in a sense migration worked. Besides relieving rural overcrowding, the prosperity of immigrants and repatriated emigrants, and the substantial
remittances received from relatives who had emigrated had a strong impact on
the economy. Within the local social system the remittances of emigrants have
been responsible for the rapid rise in the standard of living of many. It could
be said that both, those who have migrated and those who have stayed behind,
have been affected positively. Indeed, it could also be said that the most visible
changes in the South came through emigration. At last, the poor became up-
wardly mobile, unfortunately, while becoming outwardly mobile. Despite the
often appalling conditions of emigrants' life and work, it was better than stay-
ing at home. Moreover, migration served to expose more and more Italians to
life beyond the village. Returned migrants brought back new ideas and new
ways of looking at the world. Those who remained were not forced to unac-
ceptable terms of sharecropping. The huge disaffected rural proletariat, the
braccianti, could find work at last and make demands.

Unexpectedly there were also some ecological benefits. The abandoned
hills began reverting to pasture and forest, just what Italy needed. After years

of deforestation and reclamation, mountains and hills were increasingly surrendered to nature and were spared from the constant dangers of landslides and
erosion.

However, emigration had also a profound negative effect on the social
structure which was more apparent in the towns than in the countryside. The
cities became overcrowded. Turin, for example, had to cope with 700,000
immigrants in fifteen years, and by 1970 had more Southerners than any other
city except Naples. Rome, with 1.1 million inhabitants in 1936 and 1.6 million
in 1951, passed the 2 million mark in 1960 and had over 3 million at the end
of the 70s. Dreary tenement housing arose everywhere in city outskirts, most
hastily erected without benefit of planning and often without adequate roads,
schools, electricity or even sewage systems. Parks and open spaces were destroyed. The hopeless immigrants were often put into huge blocks of flats, with
densities of 500 people per hectare in some parts of Rome. In short, Italian
cities became "Americanized."

Since most of the immigrants to Northern cities were Southerners, they
aroused much resentment and even racial hostility among natives. The immigrants, as usual, were blamed for crime, illiteracy, sponging on the welfare, and
overloading the available public services–transport, public housing, schools,
hospitals, etc. Because of the new political and social awareness, the immigrants did not accept tacitly the negative reactions to their presence and responded by voting Communist at the general elections.

All this was part of the cost of "making Italians." Millions of Southerners
were being assimilated into 'Northern' cultural values, although the process
must often have seemed to be working the other way around.

The cost to the emigrant and the community he/she left was higher than
that incurred by those who hosted them. The cultural shock for the emigrant
on entering a new way of life was considerable. Considering the fact that most
emigrants were moving from an agricultural to a urban setting, the adjustment
process usually called for a complete change in life, from habits, to customs,
traditions, use of language. The separation from home and family created
serious psychological as well as social problems for many: the problem of
identity, the price of assimilation, the pain of discrimination.

A film directed by Franco Brusati, *Pane e cioccolata* (*Bread and Choco-
late*, 1973), captures these problems in poignant images. The protagonist,
Giovanni Garofali, a classical Southern Italian worker in Switzerland, is pathet-
ically out of place in his "guest-country." The clean, tidy, but cold nature of
Swiss culture is juxtaposed to the more exuberant and humane, although somewhat tacky Latin culture. The urban life with its rules but also social benefits
is in marked conflict with the old habits enjoyed in the rural setting which is
more relaxed but always accompanied by deprivation and suffering. Every

time Giovanni starts home towards Southern Italy, the sight of singing immigrant workers on the trains turns him back to Switzerland. It is a desperate situation, one experienced not only by hundreds of thousands of Italians abroad but by millions of others in Europe as well: forced to leave their homeland and their cultural roots, these workers fail to discover anything abroad to replace their old values and attachments. Like Garofali, they are trapped between a world which forces them to leave to escape poverty and a world where prosperity is given at the cost of identity.[6]

Immigration

Because of the economic success which Italy was achieving, a strange turnabout was soon to take place in the matter of Italian emigration-immigration. By the early 1980s Italy had ceased to be a net exporter of workers: there were an estimated 800,000 immigrants (mostly illegal) in Italy; by the early 1990s the number had gone well over one million. They were coming from Sub-Saharan Africa (Ethiopia, Somalia, Nigeria, Senegal, Cape Verde), the Middle East (Iran, Iraq), Asia (India, Sri Lanka, China, the Philippines), Latin America (Brazil and Argentina), and Eastern Europe (Poland and Yugoslavia).

Since returning Italian emigrants were not willing to take the jobs in domestic service, hotels, restaurants, and seasonal agriculture which paid low wages and were perceived as being too demeaning, immigrants from the Third World were allowed to fill them. Their most visible activity, dominated by the Moroccans, is the selling of poor-quality clothes, bags and trinkets on streets and beaches up and down the peninsula. But they are also engaged in a large number of other poorly paid irregular jobs in agriculture, domestic service and manufacturing: from the Filipino female domestics in the big cities to the Egyptian foundry workers of Emilia, from the Tunisians in the Sicilian fishing industry at Mazara del Vallo to the Eritreans and Ethiopians working as dishwashers, porters and building workers in Milan. The humiliations and suffering of the Italians in Northern Europe in the 1950s and 1960s are now those of the Africans in Italy.

Until recently, the word "immigrant" bore connotations of refugees from the Third World. But with the upheavals in Eastern Europe and, more particularly, in the Balkans, Italians had to face a new tide of economic refugees from across the Adriatic Sea. The flood of Albanians strained Italy's self image as a land of tolerance for immigrants and of welcome and benevolence toward the dispossessed.

The Albanian exodus started in July 1990 when about four thousand refugees landed in small boats in the port of Brindisi. In March 1991 the refugees started coming by the thousands. The Italian government responded by relocating some of them to the other regions like Friuli, Piedmont, Liguria and Campania.

It soon became evident, however, that as the refugee total topped 28,000 with more still coming, the Italian authorities would have to find other solutions. Pressed to put an end to "the inferno of Bari"–where conflicts arose between Italian police officers and angry, disillusioned Albanians held in a soccer stadium–the government made the decision to repatriate 15,000 Albanians and to restrict more boats from landing in Italian ports, pledging to help Albania's plight by sending $70 million in food aid and other emergency needs.

This decision may have strained Italy's image as a nation of tolerant, welcoming people, but for many it remained the only solution to a problem of international dimensions. Albanians were fleeing poverty more than repression, Italian authorities felt that letting them in would have been an irresponsible invitation to other economic refugees or asylum-seekers searching for a place on a crowded continent. As of August 1991, Albania was well on its way to becoming a democracy. Few Albanians could convincingly argue that it was political oppression that drove them to flee to Italy rather than a search for consumer paradise, which they were seeing on Italian television programs reaching their country.

Italy has been caught totally unprepared politically, psychologically, culturally, bureaucratically in its attitude toward immigration. Moreover, job-seeking immigrants overlap with two million Italian unemployed. This condition has given rise to murkier sentiments, displayed in racial tensions between some Italians and immigrants. Italians have long prided themselves on being less racist and less anti-semitic than other nationalities and are considered politically progressive and tolerant, but there are some who are falling into the trap of racism when confronting immigrants who, not being provided with proper housing and work, appear to be idlers, thieves and a nuisance to the community. Tolerance and open-heartedness are being put to the test. A series of incidents involving immigrants reflects not only a certain level of hostility of Italians towards newcomers, but also the dependence of many immigrants on criminal organizations which exploit them in illegal occupations such as prostitution, drug-dealing and robberies. Fifteen per cent of Italy's prison population is made up of immigrants, of whom 52 per cent, many of them North Africans, have been convicted of selling drugs.[7]

The left takes a positive approach and, therefore, favors it. They argue that immigrants–particularly illegal immigrants–accept wages and working conditions that citizens, even poor citizens, would not. The center-right, on the other hand, has been more cautious and has been pressing for more control. It maintains that the low-skill immigration of recent years has not helped the economy of the country; if anything, it has helped a few businesses that have profited from the supply of cheap labor, leaving the community at large to pick up the social costs. The right also argues that what most immigrant pay in taxes, when they work legally, does not cover even a fraction of the services they receive; moreover, it claims that the downward trend in immigrant skills has been accompanied by an upward trend in their use of public assistance. Immigrants compete with citizens for drastically reduced public services. It further argues that no immigration policy can remedy the failures of other nations to meet the needs of their poor, so it is both sensible and moral to base Italy's national policy primarily on the needs of the country: generating an economic revival and raising the standard of living of the nation's poorer citizens. On the other hand there are those who argue that immigrants arrive with a high level of desire and drive, so much so that their basic contribution could be felt in the stimulation of the natives to do better. Immigrants usually live, at least in the beginning, in areas where the lesser achievers live; their presence may become a social and economic reawakening force.

Many are also genuinely concerned about the impact that the flow of immigrants will have on Italian culture–in its psychological, social and anthropological dimensions–since the immigrant groups are characterized by ethnic, linguistic and religious diversities that pose completely new cultural and social problems. Considering the high number of races, languages and dialects that make up the people coming from the very same country (e.g., Ethiopia, Senegal, Nigeria), some Italians perceive in the immigration flux a potentially explosive mixture, especially where conflicts present in the country of origin are transplanted in Italy.

In the mid-1980s, Italy made it easier than ever for illegal immigrants to enter the country. At the very moment when other European countries were becoming more restrictive, Italy loosened up visa requirements. This action was taken totally *alla garibaldina*, that is, with cheerful audacity, little advance planning, and plenty of gambling. Many things in Italy are launched *alla garibaldina*: sometimes they succeed beyond reasonable expectations, but most of the times they end in shameful failures. The handling of immigration belongs to the second category. There was no mechanism to match the kind of jobs available with the people being allowed into the country. Until 1991, there were no funds available for counseling or housing new arrivals, no Italian-language or job training courses. At first no government ministry was responsible for immigration. Then the newly created Ministry of Immigration had only a skeletal staff and an essentially advisory role.

However, as usual, State failures are compensated for by individual inventiveness. There is a growing tendency among the public to promote a culture of acceptance. This attitude of acceptance animates the work of numerous voluntary associations which have either sprung up to offer help to immigrant workers or existed before the influx of foreigners and have subsequently changed their priorities. Among these last there are widespread national service networks, of a religious or trade union character, which operate all over Italy involving the immigrants themselves.

As a result of Italy's generally liberal immigration policy, there is concern in many European nations that with the free movement throughout the European Community began in January 1993, Italy will serve as a port of entry for an influx of illegal immigrants from Asia, Africa and South America. The Italian government would prefer to see uniform European immigration laws, but it may be forced to institute visa requirements in the near future. As the overwhelming demographic and economic disparities between Europe and the developing nations grow, the movement of desperate job-seekers will certainly increase; so too, however, may the series of anti-immigrant violent acts.

Meanwhile Italy is adopting a policy of economic aid to countries in its proximity that are in distress. One example previously mentioned is the decision to repatriate part of the Albanians in 1991 that was accompanied by a pledge equivalent to $70 million in food aid to Albania to tide it over three months of acute shortages, in addition to other emergency help.

Italian immigration problems may be solved only with policies linked to those of EC. One of the major steps adopted by EC is to abolish all internal controls, and at the same time to strengthen security at the external border points. The community members are trying to put into effect a strategy which would harmonize the issuing of visas and adopt a "one-chance rule," under which asylum seekers can apply to only one of the countries; denial by one means denial by all. In the words of former Belgian Interior Minister Joseph Michel: "We run the risk of becoming like the Roman people—invaded by barbarian peoples such as Arabs, Moroccans, Yugoslavs and Turks. People who come from far afield and have nothing in common with our civilization."

Many economists and most people feel that the recent influx of immigrants has helped fuel much of the economic growth during the past decade. And, while some perceive foreigners as taking jobs away from native-born Europeans, those who have studied the matter say recent immigration has had little impact on the employment opportunities of people born there. New immigrants, these experts say, tend to go into low-wage industries, where native-born groups don't usually compete for jobs.

One of the consequences of immigration has been the surfacing of some racist feeling, directed mainly against the colored immigrants. This has been fuelled above all by rising unemployment. It is all very sad and perplexing because the Italians always enjoyed the reputation of being less color-conscious than most West Europeans and, in an other respect, a good deal less nationalistic and chauvinistic. Their legitimate patriotism has taken on a more modern flavor; except at international soccer matches, it is difficult to see Italians displaying their flag as an expression of passionate nationalism. And the sight of that flag never creates tears in the eye or vibrates strongly nationalistic heart-strings. They are less insular than the British and less chauvinistic than the French. Italians have traditionally been less xenophobic towards other people and more open to outside influences, more aware of belonging to a wider community. Clear evidence of this may be seen in news coverage by the national media. International cultural or sporting events tend to be under-reported by the British media, while in the Italian media they get much fuller coverage. In France it is done with a strong emphasis on the French role. The Italians do seem to think of themselves in terms of a wider community, and in conversation will often talk of "we in the West" or "we in Europe" where an Englishman may still say "we in Britain."

Therefore, apart from the very few isolated incidents of antagonism against immigrants, Italians do not have discriminatory feelings. In the same vein, Italian attitudes to the Third World are rather positive. Italy today spends large sums on overseas aid; and I would say that the Italians are at least as ready as most other European nations to play their part in helping poorer nations.

Notes

1. Claudio Calvaruso, 'Rientro dei migranti e condizione delle collettività italiane in Europa,' *Civitas*, vol. 31, no. 1, 1980, p. 34.

2. In 1982 there were 296,200 Italians classified as workers and a total of 601,600 Italians in West Germany; 41,400 Italians entered West Germany, and 81,800 left that country. A favorite destination from 1950 to 1980 was Switzerland, which in 1982 had 233,100 Italian workers with annual contracts, who with their families totaled 412,000. In 1982 some 11,800 Italians entered Switzerland, and 20,200 Italians with annual permits left that country. France had attracted migrants early and in the 1940s and early 1950s became, along with Belgium, a major target. In 1982 France had 136,800 Italian workers and 441,000 Italians, including family members. Rinn-Sup Shinn, *Italy, A Country Study* (Washington: The American University, 1985), p. 110.

3. Bruno Trentin, *Da sfruttati a produttori* (Bari : De Donato, 1977), p. xi.

4. Peter Bondanella, *Italian Cinema: From Neorealism to the Present* (New York: Ungar Publishing Co., 1983), p. 199.

5. For a valuable assessment of this phenomenon see: L. Balbo, *Stato di famiglia* (Milan: 1976).

6. The plight of emigrants has also been repeatedly represented in compelling literary works by Rocco Scotellaro, Mario La Cava, Nino Palumbo and especially Saverio Strati.

7. In 1992, one third of Rome's criminals were said to be immigrants, with an overwhelming majority of them born outside the European Community. The foreign-born criminals, which in that year numbered about 1,000, were not spending time in jail for having committed a violent crime. Rather, of the approximately one thousand, 543 were jailed for drug-related charges, and 339 for petty theft. Most of the criminals were arrested in the city's historic center, particularly in the area surrounding the city's train terminal.

IX

Democratizing the Education System

Education Only for an Elite

Like every other institution and aspect of Italian life, Italian education has drastically changed in postwar Italy and, like everything else, it had to be rebuilt in every aspect. Because of the socio-political changes caused by the war, in a sense, the new government faced a condition that demanded a restructuring and a revamping similar to those needed after the unification of 1870.

Education under fascism and under the liberal regime which preceded it was the ideological and cultural reproduction of a narrow ruling class.[1] Not only was an élite student body taught by an élite teacher corps, but the education system was built in such a way that it preserved the established social class structure.

The destruction brought about by the war, demanded and, ironically, permitted a complete reshaping of that system. Not only was it necessary to rebuild the physical infrastructures, but everything else including the outline of the studies, curricula, syllabi, teaching methods, school management system, the responsibilities of the administrative offices and operators at all levels had to be profoundly transformed.

At the end of the war most of the school buildings were severely damaged, if not destroyed; the classrooms that were available were very crowded, had no heat, had scarce furniture and lacked proper sanitary conditions. In some areas of the country, especially in the South, many children could not attend school because they even lacked proper clothing. In mostly agricultural areas of the South, many parents were still keeping children on their farm to help with the daily tasks. There is a moving scene in the Taviani brothers' film *Padre Padrone*, set in the 1950s, when an authoritarian shepherd comes to school to physically remove his son from the classroom. Based on a true story, it gives a stark picture of the Sardinian families so completely dependent upon their herds that their children had to be kept home to help with the work.

As late as 1951, as many as five million people (about 10 per cent of the population) were still illiterate! The new democratic government had the overwhelming task of rebuilding the infrastructure and of reorganizing the system on a democratic base, that is, giving the right to every citizen to reach the highest levels of education, even though lacking the financial means. To achieve this democratic principle, steps had to be taken to put every citizen in condition to acquire that common level of education deemed indispensable to participating knowledgeably in the life of the country.

These changes also involved re-shaping the general attitude of teachers, who had to become more conscious of their need to keep up-to-date and of the necessity of regarding their profession in a new light in order to raise their professional level with the knowledge that the progress of schooling depends on the personal progress of all teachers.

Changes were possible across the country because the system was highly centralized. The Ministry of Education had and still has central control of curricula, syllabi, hiring and salaries of teachers, and much of the financing; even financing of buildings came from the Ministry of Public Works, as well as the Ministry of Education. By the early 1980s the system had completely changed its character. The expansion of education not only increased the number of educated young people but also changed qualitatively, not always uniformly, the education system in Italy.

In few other areas has Italy advanced more since the war than progressing from a disastrous to a relatively modern educational system under which practically everyone goes through the upper-school and a very high percentage continues to the university. Despite these advances, progress has been slow and much remains to be done.

Reforms and the Student Revolt

In the immediate postwar years, reforms were still conducted in a very conservative way. Although there was clearly a need for a profound change that had to span from the lowest to highest levels of education, the changes made during the first fifteen years were just window dressing.

The first substantive reform came about with the establishment of compulsory secondary schooling until the age of fourteen and the establishment of a single system of middle schooling. The basic reform law which triggered this transformation process, approved in 1962, abolished the old lower secondary school (*scuola media*), attended by students intending to continue their studies, and the secondary technical school (*avviamento*), attended by those intending to enter the job market as soon as possible. It instituted a new lower secondary school (*scuola media unica*) equal for everyone with training and guidance characteristics. It was an important reform socially and democratically, since it enacted the constitutional norm, which established a period of compulsory education for at least eight years equal for every student. It also tried to ensure that another constitutional norm was applied, whereby the most able and deserving were entitled to reach the highest levels of education, by assuring that everyone enjoyed the same opportunities at the outset. The two main aspects of the new system–training and guidance–were an attempt to achieve through the reform greater social justice.

However, the reform of the very regressive structure could not be easily implemented because many middle-school teachers remained hostile to the new law because, it was claimed, it watered down the curriculum (Latin became optional) and threatened discipline; implicitly, the teachers did not want to see the old élite middle school "destroyed." Consequently, to a certain extent, the curriculum remained archaic until the end of the 60s when radical changes swept through the entire academic system. However, in bringing to eight the number of mandatory school years, the state made an heroic effort to make education accessible to everyone, including the children of farmers who for economic, cultural and social reasons had stayed away in large numbers. In the 1960s and 1970s the government spent billions of dollars in this effort; schools were built in even the most remote hamlets, sometimes serving only a few dozen children. With these new schools came all the other supportive facilitation: roads, electricity, free transportation.

Consequently, the number of students and the make-up of the student population changed radically. For the first time in Italian history children from every social background had the same opportunity and treatment in getting a basic education. The impact of the changes brought about a cultural revolution. Indeed, the material bases of the explosion of protest in the Italian universities and high schools of the late 60s are to be found in the education reforms of the early 60s. The mandatory reforms for the middle school opened the road to demands for mass education beyond the eighth grade. The number of students, which rose rapidly, for the first time included a high percentage of girls and children from the low, middle and working classes. Many of them, especially from the middle classes, decided to continue their studies and go on to the university. Legislation of the 1960s made this easier: in 1961 access to science faculties was opened to students from technical institutes, and in 1965 entrance to university by examination was abolished. By 1968 the number of university students totalled over 450,000, compared to only 268,000 in 1960. The number of women students had doubled in the same period, but in 1968 still constituted less than a third of the new students beyond the mandatory years.

This new generation of university students entered a university system which was still terribly antiquated. The expansion of infrastructure carried out in secondary schools had not been continued at the higher level. The number of universities had remained the same and all had maintained their essentially feudal structure. Worse still, many of the professors were rarely present in the university. Their obligations to the universities were limited to fifty-two hours of teaching per year; once their obligation had been satisfied, they could attend their "main" profession, that of being doctors, lawyers, engineers, architects, chemists, and, above all, politicians. There were no seminars, no tutorials, and no faculty-student contact. Not surprisingly, the number of students who failed their oral exams was very high. In 1966 81 per cent of those with a secondary school diploma went on to university, but only 44 per cent succeeded in graduating. In this kind of situation, the poorer students faced the highest odds of success. Even worse, most of the sons and daughters of the "new" university society, mostly from the expanding urban middle classes, who succeeded to graduate, suffered a series of disillusionments when trying to enter the job-market. It seems that the university continued to operate a particularly subtle form of class-based selection. The Left in government had succeeded in opening up the doors of the university to everyone, but had not been able to prepare the system for the new student population.

This kind of environment, nourished by ideological issues that were brewing in many parts of the world, led to the student revolt of 1967-68. Many students of the mid-sixties were doubtful of the values that had become predominant in the Italy of the "economic miracle"–individualism, the exaltation of the nuclear family, consumerism. Education had made them more analytical of society's failures and the need for social justice. The dream based on achieving success through talent and hard-work was revealed to be just a myth for many students coming from the lower classes. Social structure and connections (who you know) seemed to remain the big factors for success. The power of social structure was recognized as the major constraint to life changes. By finding the door of the university open, the major influence of father's or mother's occupational attainment on son's or daughter's occupational attainment had been overcome, but the effects of social origin on academic success and occupational achievement and mobility remained significant. Students' questioning of this situation was carried out by leaning on the current Catholic social doctrine and Marxist thinking; values of solidarity, collective action and the fight against social injustice and social division were juxtaposed to the individualism and consumerism of "neo-capitalism."

Some world events certainly had their impact on this situation in ferment. The Vietnam War changed the way a whole generation of Italians thought about America: the image of a powerful and destructive America had replaced that of an America that offered opportunity and realizable dream in the 50s. The Cultural Revolution in China in 1966-67 was interpreted in Italy as being a spontaneous anti-authoritarian mass-protest movement; Mao's invitation to Chinese youth to 'open fire' on headquarters was interpreted in Italy as a cultural revolution which had to be carried out from below. Finally, there was the teaching of radical South American priests who sought to reconcile social Catholic doctrine and Marxism. This should explain why the first university revolts took place in strongly Catholic institutions. The explosion which started in the Autumn of 1967 (long before the French unrest) at the University of Trento, followed by those at the Catholic university at Milan and at the public university at Turin set the stage for a cultural revolution which swept through the nation. Students questioned not only what was being taught, the "canon", and the way the mental process was put to work, but also the individualistic ways of presenting one's image. Students changed the way they dressed and looked. Men grew their hair and beard, and abandoned jackets, ties and somber-colored clothes in favor of jeans and other casual attire; the women gave up make-up, dresses and high heels in favor of jeans, pullovers and boots. The movement reached its climax in spring 1968 but continued throughout the 70s.

The most unfortunate aspect of the democratization process was the deterioration of quality. The open-enrollment policy aimed at eliminating the privileged situation of some schools (*licei*) was supposed to be temporary. The awaited reforms at the upper secondary school level and those undertaken in universities were supposed to bring some balance to the system. To date, however, this long-awaited reform has not yet seen the light of day. The extended period of open enrollment has had profound effects on the entire university system. The open enrollment policy instituted in 1969 proved to be only a ploy of the left to demonstrate another victory for the masses, without in reality providing a real gain. The **democratization** of the school system has transformed the system from a university for the élite into a university for the masses, but the transformation has taken place more to satisfy a political necessity than to prepare a society of highly educated and skilled citizens; it was done more to fulfill a political agenda rather than to raise the level of education of the nation.

In the mid-seventies, when the welfare state was being instituted in a most bizarre way, the education system was experiencing the same turmoil as the rest of Italian institutions. The principles at the base of the Workers' Statute and other social insurance laws which were aimed at bringing about considerable equality of conditions were also at the base of the democratic reforms in education. In education, too, equality of opportunity was meant to be also equality of results; in the democratic spirit, regardless of how well-prepared students were, everyone was expected to be passed and graduated. Once enrolled, students were expected to graduate as a matter of right. Thus, great pressures were placed on professors to relax the stringency of the oral examination system that prevailed throughout the system. During those chaotic years, not only did the quality of students and academic standards decline, but those who taught moved politically to make their own jobs permanent as a matter of law. Several legislative reforms had the effect of granting tenure, in one fell swoop, to thousands of academics, irrespective of their qualifications as scholars and teachers. Although not all of these got to be full professors (*professori ordinari*), they all joined the ranks of millions of other public servants in public-service jobs who had life-time job security.

The state also responded in a very confused way in meeting the serious problems created by overcrowding. Although the state opened many more universities throughout Italy, this new generation of university students entered a system which was still grossly inadequate. Overcrowding strained all academic facilities. In the 1991-92 academic year, the state universities in the three largest Italian cities (Rome, Milan, Naples) enrolled over 40 per cent of the total university population; nine university centers throughout the country are so over-crowded that each enrolls more than 40,000 students. In the mid-1980s the University of Rome, "La Sapienza," had an enrollment of 160,000 on a campus built for about 33,000. Some professors lectured to audiences of more than a thousand students. Rome's medical school was supposed to train 23,000 students concurrently; many of them never made it to the anatomy laboratory. To secure a library seat, students had to line up early. However, most Italian students (especially in the humanities and social and behavioral sciences) did not bother to go to classes; they expected to accomplish more by studying in the comfort of the home atmosphere instead of going to a class where seats were scarce and professors frequently cancelled classes. As some form of standards started to be reapplied, not surprisingly, many students failed their exams with the complaint from the left that the reforms had not satisfied the aspiration awakened by the social changes. Indeed, the Italian university system unintentionally started to operate a subtle form of class-based selection; while it was supposedly open to all, the odds remained heavily against poorer students earning a degree or finding a job.

Ideology and Academic Freedom

The system never found the correct balance in the democratization process. Like everything else the system became highly politicized. Politics seeps into every area of the educational system—from bottom to top, from nursery and elementary schools to the high schools and universities. Schools actually produce in some students and reinforce in others clear-cut political predispositions.

Needless to say, university student bodies are politicized as well. In the late 1960s and early 1970s they represented the prime recruiting ground for political terrorist organizations, particularly those of the left. Several founding members of the Red Brigades were contemporary students of sociology at the University of Trento. Even the most "normal" organizations are typically organized along the same lines that define Italy's political parties. Italian student organizations are in line with European student practice. They are vigorously active bodies with, very often, formal ties to the political parties within which many students will pursue political careers or from which they intend to seek support when they go out to look for jobs. Italians cannot conceive of student organizations American style, that is, ones having just social and cultural aims.

Unfortunately, many students become *professional students* who, supported by political parties, make a living out of being political agitators. The system is so absurd that in theory it is possible for a student to spend up to twenty-five years getting a degree. Not surprisingly, only one-third of all students who enroll in Italian institutions of higher learning ever graduate; the other two thirds remain "professional students," eventually dropping out to look for some job or swell the unemployment lines. On the other hand, it could be argued that the Italian university system anticipates the time when, as in all industrial countries, further education will probably be encouraged as an alternative to unemployment. The system gives hundreds of thousands of young people a chance to educate themselves, and a sense of belonging to society. The Italian government has come to understand that it is cheaper to pay for an education that is a "parking place" than to be forced to pay for other social services, or even detention institutions as consequence of the lack of employment.

Besides being political and social, the problem is also ethical. Even though the prospects of finding a job with a degree in the humanities are remote, the largest percentage of students enroll in those disciplines because they are easier than the sciences. Very few enroll in physics notwithstanding the high demand for physicists and other scientists. Physics still enjoys the reputation of being the heir to an illustrious tradition, but also produces statistics that are unattractive to students who are not highly motivated: of those who enroll only about 30 per cent graduate and most of them take five or six years instead of four. The enrollment in medicine is also very high in spite of the high number of doctors scrambling for jobs. Italy has the highest ratio of doctor/inhabitants in the EC because politicians have pursued more a policy of employment rather than one which assures that doctors are professionally prepared.

Since Italian life is politicized at every level, changes cannot be implemented easily and in some cases are even impossible. The answer seems to lie in a selection system for applications for enrollment as well as in a suitable strengthening of structures and premises which should also be evenly distributed throughout the country. The state has tried to respond to the overcrowding by opening new universities. Although between 1970 and 1990 about 30 new universities were opened, some in large urban centers already with one or two universities, most in areas never touched by academic life, the overcrowding in the old centers was not alleviated. Most students preferred to enroll in institutions with a tradition and which are associated with names of scholars and scientists who have made a long-lasting impact in many fields throughout history. No one can convince students that a degree from a new University such as that of Calabria is worth as much as that of a University with an illustrious past such as that of the University of Bologna or Pavia. Students are also very aware that the new centers attract only the young professors who accept those first appointments as a "parking place" while they wait to move to an older university as soon the opportunity presents itself. In a country where traditions still have meaning, it becomes even more difficult to reduce their significance when they are attached to a glorious past. Italy has the oldest university tradition in the world. Salerno was the first, founded in the ninth century by "four masters": a Jew, a Greek, a Saracen and an Italian. In the twelfth century, before Oxford or Cambridge colleges were founded, Bologna University, opened in 1088, had ten thousand students. The University of Padua was founded in 1222, Naples in 1224, Rome in 1303, Pisa in 1342, Turin in 1404, Catania 1444. Some of them are among the oldest and most distinguished in the West. Many boast centuries of humanistic and scientific achievements. Even today, despite the intrusion of politics into the system, several universities remain islands of intellectual rigor and innovation that rival similar institutions anywhere else in the world.

Today, however, the troubles of the system stem from the strong power achieved by the students and by the old autocratic faculty system. Students have become so powerful, or the government has conceded so much power to them, that reforms have been difficult to come by. When in November 1984, the prefect of Rome suggested that all universities should limit enrollment in the medical schools to 70 per cent of the previous year's number, there was such a political uproar that no one who had been contemplating the measure was willing to support it. In 1985, in reaction to a proposal by Minister of Public Education Falcucci to increase tuition by about $100, the students of the left organized such a general protest that the government backed off. The problem was not that Italians are overburdened with a high cost of higher education (today even the poorest university student spends $100 in a week-end out for pizza); students assumed the position that education should be completely free. On that occasion the lack of political maturity of students and their politicized positions became more evident than ever. No student organization leader responded to the government with a counter proposal or with constructive critical assessment of the university system and how it should be improved if additional fees were accepted. No student-group responded to the government that the extra $100 would be paid provided that they would be spent in the university system, say, to improve the libraries which at the present time, as we have tried to indicate, are a disgrace.

When another attempt was made to reform the system in Spring 1990, the system was practically shut down for almost two months. Reaction to a proposed law, which would give individual campuses more autonomy to set course requirements than they now have under a highly centralized system and which would also allow individual universities to sign contracts and start other joint projects with private companies, brought back memories of the late 60s and mid 70s. Students worried that big corporations may be given a free hand to reshape the country's schools to fit their own needs. While the sciences and engineering are likely to get adequate financing they argued, the liberal arts will fall by the wayside. In American universities, good science departments, through the grants they bring to the campuses, may also enhance the life of humanities and arts divisions. Usually real scientists support university policies to share the "indirect costs" charged by the universities on grants with every academic area of the campus because a good comprehensive university needs humanists and artists to prepare a more "humane society" especially in a scientific age. In Italy, however, laboratory researchers joined the protests because they also felt that they will lose their independence and become tools of industry. Large companies, it was also argued, are more likely to invest in the well-developed Italian North, further widening the considerable gap with the relatively poor South. Not coincidentally, the campus protests first erupted in Palermo, where the unemployment rate is over 20 per cent, three times that in Turin. Objections to the plan reflect widespread cynicism about the concentration of economic and political power in the hands of a few industrialist titans like Giovanni Agnelli of FIAT, Carlo De Benedetti of Olivetti, Raul Gardini of the Ferruzzi-Montedison agrobusiness group, and Silvio Berlusconi, a television magnate.

However, today's students are very different from those of the late 60s and 70s. Protest may flare up over specific grievances, but gone is the old political idealism. The vast majority share the current Italian disillusionment with ideologies; the few politically active ones are either on the extreme Right or extreme Left.

How Democratic Can a System Be in the Hands of *Barons*?

As we have previously mentioned, one of the major problems of the Italian university system, like the entire education system, is the high level of politicization. Professors are openly concerned with politics and are openly lined up with political parties. Despite arguments about the importance in a democratic society for intellectuals to remain relatively autonomous, either aloof from political parties or with politics kept at a distance and in perspective, so that they may be honest critics of social and political arrangements, in Italy the situation is completely the opposite. "By and large, Italian intellectuals not only shun any such effort; they thrive in political works. Far from being the critics of political parties and party factions, they are often the latter's major spokesmen. Far from seeking a modicum of space, in a politicized society that admittedly offers very little of it to anyone, they hanker after the rewards, including public offices, that the parties can distribute to the faithful."[2]

Although no academic institution can and should be immune to political fermentations, the Italian system thrives on ideological confrontations. Political parties find it prestigious to have candidates or ministers who are university professors.

What is even more damaging to the entire system is that the universities are firmly in the hands of autocratic senior professors, unfondly called *baroni*. As La Palombara underscores, the Italian "barons" are not just playing academic politics; they are intricately a part of the bigger political game as well. In the bargains the "barons" strike, in the trade-offs they concoct, and in the "balance" they seek to establish within the university community, political and ideological considerations that reflect the politics of the nation. The political coloration of the competing candidates weighs at least as heavily as their professional quali-fications, and sometimes more.(p. 72) So, despite appearances to the contrary, professors practice the same division of the spoils enjoyed by the political parties in the patronage system which almost brought Italy to ruin. Italian professors are known as *baroni*, not only for the prestige they enjoy and the influence they exercise, but also for their authority and independence. Still today, they can choose the date of when to begin the academic year; they can delegate their work to a host of assistants that each one of them has; and until recently, they could freely take up another post. Efforts have been made to induce professors to devote less time to their private affairs and more to their academic duties. For instance, if a professor is elected to parliament or receives another important public appointment, it has been established that s/he be placed on leave of absence from the university. However, efforts to induce professors to hold one position, to reside in or close to the cities of their chair, and to teach and undertake research in their universities have been only par-tially successful. It is not uncommon in Italy for professors to reside two or three hundred miles away from the university where they teach!

Moreover, as in most universities throughout the world, there are no tests on the actual ability to teach or lecture. It is inconceivable that an Italian uni-versity professor would allow students to evaluate his/her classroom experience the way we practice it and value it in the American university system.

A law was passed in 1980 to restructure the ranking of the academic body and to create some 45,000 new positions. These would be divided into three categories–the *ricercatore*, "researcher," the lowest position, which is appointed through a *concorso*, a state competitive examination and assessment of publications, and three years teaching experience; the next stage, *professore associato*, associate professor, which can lead to the last stage, full professor, *professore ordinario*, both of which are achieved through a national competition. These changes which were meant to break the feudal system have met with only partial success.

As in the American university system, there is an overemphasis on research and a corollary distaste for teaching. This research is "make-believe scholarship," which charge can be confirmed by how infrequently a researcher's work is cited by others within five years of publication. In the sciences, fewer than half the articles published were cited in that period of time. In the social sciences the "uncitedness" index rises to 74.7 percent, in religion to 98.2 per cent, in literature to 99.8 per cent! It's not difficult to conclude that much research is self-defensive and self-indulgent.

Today there persists much controversy about what role a university should play. Should it be primarily for research or for teaching? Italian universities are certainly distinguished by the former rather than the latter. Can it still fulfil the Renaissance ideal of producing the well-rounded, cultivated individual? Or, in this age of the masses that is also an age of specialization, should it become more vocational? Should it teach for "culture" or for professional ends? There are many who believe that it can and should do both, but that its courses should distinguish more clearly than at present between these two ends, instead of blurring them. On the whole, Italian universities emphasize culture, and the classical tradition is still strong.

The most serious problem that the Italian university system faces, and one which has slowed down any reform because of its implications, is that of its independence as an institution. The question is: should the constitutional norm, which recognizes the right of universities to be autonomous organizations, be applied in a complete way? It is in fact obvious that the problem of autonomy for universities is connected with innovation and the development and programming of university studies. The very future of the university lies in finding the balance that permits accessibility and affordability while providing a sound education.

There Can be no Democratization without High Standards

Primary and secondary schools have also been democratized while sacrificing quality education. Curricula were not only reformed because of the emergence of new fields–aeronautics, electronics, marketing, computer science, linguistics–but above all because the middle-class values of the system did not match those of many of the users. The school had to respond to the problem of how to equalize educational opportunities for all children, regardless of their socio-economic background. The new breed of students during the militancy of the early 70s had engaged in a socio-cultural revolution. They not only asked for curriculum reforms, but also questioned the old methods of teaching based on *nozionismo,* the accumulation of knowledge without relating it to a practical context. It was also propounded that a less authoritative teacher in the class-room would make the learning process more effective. In a series of memos after 1968, the government's education authorities directed high school teach-ers to take into consideration the entire personality, intellectual commitment, and mental process of a student, not his or her performance on a specific test. This was an implicit rejection of *nozionismo*, and it encouraged students to cultivate the old Italian penchant for rhetoric. The testing, mostly through oral exams throughout the whole educational system, certainly allows the teacher and pupil to cover more ground, since speaking is obviously so much faster than writing, and if the student's thinking is woolly the teacher can question more searchingly. It should also be said that in Italy personal communication has always been highly prized.

As result, at the compulsory levels, a new method of assessment of stu-dents was introduced. Progress reports based on numerical markings was re-placed by brief analytical reports. Moreover, in planning class activities and programs, teachers were asked to take into account not only needs of the group but also of individuals. In this regard, it should be pointed out that special efforts have been made to integrate handicapped children into regular classes in elementary and lower secondary schools. ***Special education*** was seen as demeaning and negatively affecting the potential learning abilities of students, therefore, it was limited to the severely physically and mentally handicapped. Consequently, remedial teaching activities for pupils with problems, foreseen by law, were reinforced and provided through the support staff properly trained in special two-year specialization courses. It must be said that the situation of these experiences is not uniform throughout the country due to the diversified social context in Italy. While some are well advanced, others are facing diffi-culties and contradictions. This process of integration of the handicapped into normal classes would seem to be irreversible, and is no longer questioned. However, there is still some discussion on how to achieve this integration; that is to say, on how to plan teaching activities and how to organize all the other aspects connected with the presence of a handicapped child in the class.

The evenness of the quality of the system is guaranteed by the fact that public school teachers are considered state employees and get their jobs through state competitive exams, *concorsi*, administered by the Ministry of Public Education. They are assigned or transferred without consideration of the exigencies of the individual schools. In Italian public schools, teachers can not choose the schools they prefer, and no school can choose its own teachers. Contrary to the American system, which is classist (separatist) because of the close connection of real estate value with school district prestige and the internal selection of students in each school through the creation of honor sections, AP courses, etc., the Italians do not use tracking system. Italian educational authorities feel that students tend to stay in their track throughout their schooling years, and that remedial students develop poor self-images and are alienated from schooling. Students in a tracked-system do not learn better, and the content and quality of education offered in each track is very different. Students form self-concepts, social relationships and aspirations reflecting the status of the track in which they are placed. In America this problem is alarming because the racial and socio-economic makeup of students in different tracks tends to mirror the race and social class stratification of the larger society. In Italy instead, on the whole, everyone from the son of the doctor to the daughter of a waiter mixes in the same class. Indeed, because of the reforms of the 60s and 70s, the social-class distinction in education was wiped out. This does not imply that elitism has been completely eradicated. The most prestigious high school is still the *liceo classico* which, notwithstanding all social changes, still attracts for the most part children from an educated background. Indeed, some educationists criticize this system. However, Italy has understood that in today's high-tech world of work, countries cannot overemphasize college and demean technical training. Italian school officials help the non-college bound students to pursue a more demanding curriculum than the "general" course so many American kids choose. It spares Italian industries and businesses from spending more money on training workers and it spares colleges from spending so much on remediation of ill-prepared freshmen, who may not belong in college at all.

The democratization of the system did not eliminate gender preferential divisions which are determined by tradition and social predeterminations. As most studies show, girls are very selective in the choice of the type of school they attend. Their number is greater than that of boys in professional schools leading to elementary school teaching (girls comprise 90 per cent of the total enrolment in these schools), in art schools (64 per cent), in technical schools preparing for clerical occupations (53 per cent), and even in those schools for children of the upper and upper-middle classes. Girls are more numerous in the "liceo classico," centered around literature and philosophy (53 per cent), than in the "liceo scientifico," based on mathematics and natural sciences (38per cent). The same situation can be found at the university level where girls account for only one-fourth of the enrolment in medicine, economics and law, one-fifth in physics and chemistry, less than 10 per cent in engineering, but 60 per cent in biology and 75 per cent in literature and philosophy.

Flirtation with educational practices that skip rudiments, inflate basic concepts and hurry to results has had detrimental effects. Secondary schools have been moving towards the American school model where fun-and-games, talk-ins and so-called self-expression take the place of real intellectual training. Experimental teaching methodologies to find easy way to make the learning work less laborious and demanding abound, while the use of audio-visual machinery has become more desirable than subject matter. As in everything else, Italy has been looking at the US for an improvement of its education system; unwittingly, it has been looking at a system that has been in search of its own easy fix!

On the positive side, when compared to other countries, Italy presents a favorable academic picture. Italy has 210 class days compared to 180 in America. It has the lowest teacher-to-student ratio of Europe; between 1980 and 1992, the enrollment in the first eight years went down by almost one and half million students while the number of teachers grew by about one hundred thirty-five thousand teachers. Parents still play a key role in the learning process of the students at home. Another important feature of the elementary school is the inclusion, among the new subjects, of foreign languages as a means of understanding and comprehension and as part of the overall framework of linguistic education.

Teachers Must Be More Accountable

Many teachers and parents alike are simply left bewildered by the spate of often contradictory reforms and tinkering over the past thirty years, and are skeptical as to whether any solution will succeed. But it is clear that no new system or reform will ever work effectively without a more flexible commitment and generous attitude on the part of the teachers. In and out of class, they remain the key to the whole problem. They have certainly evolved since the late 60s, in terms of more relaxed human contact with their students. But one of their handicaps is still their lack of up-to-date training: they were taught to instill academic virtues, and few of them have much knowledge of modern teaching methods, of child psychology, or of what might be called education for civics and leisure. But the teachers' attitude remains the most serious problem. Few are the teachers who are ready to put their hearts into the kind of work usually accepted as a basic part of the job in Britain or America. It is the usual Italian problem: teachers complain about State control, but then have no idea how to use their freedom when they get it. Too many of them lack any initiative, except that of protest. No educational system can attract quality faculty if it must indiscriminately pay its teachers/professors the same regardless of talent, potential, or performance.

Like other professions, the teaching profession includes three general groups: the excellent, the good, and the bad. Since unions bargain for pay increases as if all teachers performed at peak levels, excellent teachers become consistently underpaid while poor teachers become consistently overpaid. The cost of carrying poor teachers falls on the backs of the large middle group of good teachers. If the unions supported a *merit pay* structure, as it is done in

USA, they would lose their clout overnight. Unions argue that since teaching is a subjective art that cannot be accurately measured, a merit system could not possibly work. The argument may be sound, logical, and fair, but it completely misses the point. All institutions, both public and private, in a free market system evaluate performance on subjective as well as objective bases. Politicians win elections, executives capture promotions, and consumers buy goods and services, not just because they meet strictly measurable standards, but because people vote, work, and spend their money by whim and perception as much as by fact. Periodically, the education process itself looks rather subjective from the students' point of view. Grades, test scores and most evaluations all reflect subjective criteria to some degree or another. To improve quality in a real sense, schools should be allowed (the impossible dream) to ruthlessly expel teachers who do not perform to set standards. Doing so would traumatize a system that has long protected and promoted its incompetent labor force, but in the long run, such paring of the inferior will better prepare the system, its teachers, and students to compete in an age of global knowledge network.

The situation has been changing. On the one hand, the Ministry of Education has been trying to overhaul teacher training, making it less purely academic, with a new stress on modern pedagogic techniques. On the other, the education system has reacted positively showing great reserves of vitality. There is a growing awareness at the grassroots level that billions of lire alone cannot improve the quality of democraticized school system. High academic achievements and a relevant education is achieved through revision of course content and up-dating of teaching methods which must be carried forward by the teachers themselves with the full involvement of the community and individual parents. But in the politicized Italian world, such a transformational process from the grassroots level has raised some concerns–the left has raised the smoke of inequalities that such initiatives may cause. That is to say, while such initiatives toward reform are developed in some areas where the situation is favorable, it may be lacking in other areas. Here lies perhaps the most important challenge facing the government and school administrations in the coming years. Instead of imposing new global reforms from above, the on-going reform process should be better monitored and guided in order to infuse the system throughout the country and stimulate those weaker areas less aware of the needs for such initiatives.

A Reform that Works

Because of needs posed by social changes, pre-schooling was instituted and gradually, as the industrialization level of the country increased, was expanded. However nursery school, *asilo nido*, and kindergarten, *asilo infantile*, for children from 3 to 5 years of age were only optional, since they serve more as preparation for the compulsory school, though both are of special social importance, providing as they do babysitting service for working parents. Since it is not mandatory, such service is not funded by state government but run either by the municipalities or by private bodies; therefore, once again, it became either available privately to those who could afford it, or publicly by only those municipalities that were financially stable. Public nursery schools are in short supply, and even those run by the local public administrations, can be expensive to support. Therefore children of mothers who have jobs are given preference. In urban centers like Milan and Rome, more than one third of the demand is unsatisfied.

At this level, Italy has instituted some very good school reforms from which United States' educators could borrow some ideas. One such system is the pre-school program in Reggio Emilia which has received world wide praise. Departing from the basic concept that each child is unique and different, the school system works on the assumption that in pre-school, teachers should only be concerned with the physical, emotional and social aspects of development to provide children with a rich and stimulating environment that is, at the same time, warm, loving and supportive and create in them a solid sense of security, positive self esteem, and a long-term enthusiasm for learning.

The program is designed to foster young children's learning, representation, and expression through exploration and mastery of many symbolic media.

Reggio educators believe children have preparedness, potential curiosity, and interest in constructing their learning, in engaging in social interaction, and in negotiating with everything the environment brings them. Creativity is seen not as an exceptional occurrence or a separate mental faculty, but as a characteristic way of thinking, knowing and making choices.[3] Children's work is not casually created, but rather is the result of a guided exploration of themes and events that are relevant to the life of the children and the larger community. Classwork is organized around themes that allow children to learn a variety of skills and help them understand their world. What looks like art, for example, is actually a science, math, and art lesson. The classroom space is utilized in a manner that encourages creativity and individual freedom.

These schools are tax base supported, however families with children enrolled in the childcare (*asilo nido*) pay a monthly fee of $69-$269 based on the family's ability to pay. Disabled children and single parent children are admitted automatically. Other admissions are based on interviews.

Many features of the Reggio Emilia pre-school reflect Italian values. The relationship that is created between parents and teachers is similar to the roles played by the Italian extended family. Parents, teachers, and other members of the community have worked together to produce a unique pre-school/day-care program that proves that children learn and grow in a social atmosphere outside of and in addition to the home. The emphasis on the arts and aesthetic insights expresses an appreciation of detail and sensitivity to design that is in the mainstream of the Italian cultural tradition of being creative. And so, amid endless debates, the struggle goes on to find solution to the education system for a new age.

Student Life Today: Less Political but not Civic Oriented

Incidents of the last few years indicate that students are very different from those who stormed the barricades in the late 60s. Protest may flare up over a specific grievance, but it is not the old political idealism. The vast majority share the current Italian disillusion with ideologies; the few politically active ones are usually extremists.

As individuals, Italian students are hard-working, serious-minded, worried about their own futures; they are not indifferent to the world's problems, but they are skeptical and have lost faith in the ability to improve even their university or school environment, let alone society. Significantly, only a tiny percentage of university students even bother to join a student union. And a severe setback to the 1969 ideals of 'participation' is the fact that very few students vote in the new university elections or come forward as candidates. So students stay quietly in the background, their noses in their textbooks, obsessed by the hunt for diplomas (*laurea*) that may stave off unemployment.

Even in their leisure lives many feel isolated, for Italian universities and secondary schools are not warm club-like communities American style. Unlike in Britain and the USA, the tradition is that students go to their local university; therefore, the great majority live at home, where they at least have the comfort of family and a nucleus of existing friends. But others, whose homes are too far away live in rented rooms or dormitories, and here they can be very lonely.

The paucity of clubs and organized social life has always seemed–to an American or Briton–a striking feature of Italian universities which have no equivalent to the big American "student union" building, a focus for community. Many large universities do not even have any student drama group or orchestra; and attempts to start them have been growing ever rarer, now that students are so preoccupied with work, exams and job prospects. Consequently, students seldom show any enthusiasm for the university or school and their lives.

Whose fault is that? Not altogether the students'. The building of campuses has not helped. Until the late 1960s nearly all universities were down-town. Here the students crowded the local *caffè*, deriving some warmth from the town and adding to its liveliness in return. But, with the growth in numbers, many departments are now scattered throughout the cities or have been transferred to big new campuses on the outskirts. Some of these are quite attractive, and they have eased working conditions; but the students are now more isolated than ever. For both universities and secondary schools, the problem is still institutional. Neither local faculties nor the state Ministry since the end of the 60s have made much effort to turn a school or university into more of a real community, a focus for loyalty, a fun place for students to stay around when classes are over. That is not the Italian tradition. A school, and to a large extent the university, are facilities for the transmission of knowledge and the passing of exams, and nothing more. There is nothing like the American clubs and teams life. Photography clubs, drama societies, concerts, plays, recitals, sport events, and other cultural or recreational events are unheard of in most Italian universities. The Ministry pays lip-service to the need for more out-of-class activities, but in practice puts them near the bottom of its budgetary priorities. It does not even provide proper funds for libraries, which even in the best licei tend to be miserably small and ill-stocked.

If out-of-class activities such as clubs are so few, it's also because so few teachers are prepared to stay on after hours to help organize them. A teacher does not see this as part of his/her job; in fact, most likely he belongs to a union that militantly opposes this kind of unpaid overtime. The average professor/teacher regards the school as a kind of office job: s/he arrives, holds her/his classes, maybe with donnish brilliance, then goes home. The student's out-of-class lives are not his/her business. True, this attitude is changing a little among younger teachers; but it is still widespread. School/university activities are considered marginal to the academic life. Real life for students is what they get from outside, from travel, television, friends, family.

Training in democracy, leadership, and civic feeling help students feel part of a living community and allows them to share responsibility for it. But in Italy, the traditional thinking is that it is the family's responsibility not the school's to train character. Parents look on school as an academic utility, which should not compete with them as a center of loyalty; and if a school were to attempt training in leadership or civic responsibility, this would be resented as an intrusion into their own sphere. From an Anglo-American point of view, this leaves a void in the youngster's full education.

In conclusion, it is easy to be impressed by Italian students' resilience and their apparent ability–helped no doubt by their *home background*–to survive the system to which they are subjected. Yet, one is equally sure that a system that would attend to the formation of a social conscience might go a long way towards healing the maladjustments in Italian society and Italian public life. This is true of secondary schools; it is even more true of the universities.

Notes

1. G. Vacca, *Quale democrazia?* (Bari: De Donato, 1977), p. 168.

2. J. LaPalombara, *Democracy Italian Style* (New Haven: Yale University Press, 1987), p. 68.

3. For an informative report and assessment of the Reggio Emilia pre-school system see: R. S. New, "Excellent Early Education: A City in Italy Has It," *Young Children*, vol. 45, 1990, n. 6, pp. 4-10; (N.C.), "The Ten Best Schools in the World," *Newsweek*, 2 December 1991, pp. 50-58; P. Hinckle, "A School Must Rest on the Idea That All Children are Different," *Newsweek*, 2 December 1991; D. Newbold, "A State Nursery School That is Simply the Best," *Time Educational Supplement*, 14 February 1992, p. 15; B. Rankin, "Inviting Children's Creativity: A Story of Reggio Emilia, Italy," *Child Care Information Exchange*, vol. 85, 1992, pp. 30-35.

X

Secularization of State and Society

Is the Church still in Control?

One of the most radical changes that Italy has undergone in the last twenty-five years is the secularization of every aspect of life and the consequent change in the relationship between state and Church. Being rooted in a peasant society and culture, the profound change in Italian Catholicism was inevitable with the rise of industrialization and economic development. While the authority of the Church as an institution has diminished, a new-style liberated spirit of religion is very much alive, and takes the most diverse form.

At the end of the 1950s, still primarily an agricultural people, the Italians outlook toward the Church and religion was basically that of many centuries before. Italy was still the geographic center of the Catholic world. The Vatican was an Italian institution and the pope himself was Bishop of Rome and primate of Italy. By the terms of the Italian constitution, the church enjoyed privileges unique among democratic countries. Catholicism formed a profound and natural part of the social fabric of the nation. Catholic values had played, both anthropologically and culturally, a decisive role in shaping individual lives and collective behavior. For the average citizen church ceremonies were both social and religious events and the profession of faith was still felt with strong passion. Religion, in the form of adoration of a host of local saints in a widely diffused pagan religiosity, offered especially the peasants a sustaining refuge from the harsh realities.[1]

The Church's presence in the life of the citizens was strong at every level also due to its education and welfare activities. The parish priest was the center of the community life–he was lawyer, adviser, teacher, psychologist, and social and spiritual healer–he had responsibility for the local nursery schools, for bible classes, oratories, the parish library, etc. Over many decades the Church had built up an impressive network of hospitals (the most popular bearing the name "Fate bene fratelli" "Do Good Brothers"), nursing homes and old people's homes, staffed by various religious orders. In addition, the POA (*Pontificia Opera di Assistenza*) organized a large number of educational and recreational institutions. These varied from seaside and mountain camps to kindergartens, to *doposcuole* (afternoon activities for six-to twelve years-old), to "*case del fanciullo*" and "*della fanciulla*" for runaway teenagers. In the absence of state provision for old people, families turned with gratitude to Catholic welfare institutions.

In the 1950s Italian parishes were spilling over with activities. In 1956, 69 per cent of adult Italians said that they were going to church on a regular basis.

The great number of masses, confessions and communions in each parish each week testified to the church's vigorous state of health. So too did the number of organizations associated with parish life, especially Catholic Action, which represented the "civic" face of Italian Catholicism. However, Catholic Action was two or three times stronger in the civic, more association-prone regions of the North than in the less civic areas of the South. In Italy, as Robert Putnam demonstrated, organized religion was an alternative to the civic community, not part of it. Vertical bonds of authority were more characteristic of the Italian Church than horizontal bonds of fellowship.[2]

This world largely vanished in the course of two decades or so. By the mid-70s, with the rapid secularization of Italian society and turmoil within the Church following the Second Vatican Council, the presence of the Church in society diminished rapidly and the power structure of the Church changed immensely.

The process, begun in the early 1960s, had as a most significant development the gradual transformation of the Church from a Eurocentric body, in which Italy was the leading country, to an international body whose center of interests spread far more to the rest of Europe and to the Third World, particularly Latin America. When Pius XII died in October 1958 the College of Cardinals had 55 members of whom 36 were Europeans, half of those Italian, and Europe had the highest number of baptized Catholics. When Montini became pope (Paul VI) in 1963, 52 of the 80 cardinals were Italian. After the mid-sixties the size of the body was expanded and the number of Italians in it declined through attrition. By 1971 there were 120 cardinals, of whom only 28 were Italian. For the first time the Italians were not a majority.

At the same time Paul VI had reduced the importance of the Italian hierarchy in other ways. In the second half of the 1960s the Italian dioceses were consolidated and the number of bishops reduced from 315 to 270 a still disproportionate number when compared to France's 88 and Spain's 65. This measure was accompanied by an effort to place some distance between the Holy See and the Italian hierarchy. With the pope as Primate of Italy and the curia essentially Italian, the Vatican and the Italian Church had always been inseparably interconnected. In 1966, for the first time in history and about one hundred years after similar bodies had been established in other countries, an independent conference of bishops, the *Conferenza Episcopale Italiana* (*CEI*), was established. When John Paul II was elected twenty years later in October 1978 the College of Cardinals had doubled in number (110) with 56 non-European cardinals, 44 of whom came from the Third World, and Latin America had the highest number of Catholics (40%). Therefore, the election to pope in October 1978, of Karol Wojtyla, Archbishop of Cracow, the first non-Italian to ascend to the throne of Saint Peter since 1522, although somewhat dramatic, was not unexpected. The election of a Pole to pope also implied that the Church was going to play a much less important role in Italian affairs than in the past and that the time was approaching for a re-negotiation of the relations between State and Church.

The Solution of the "Roman Question"

The formal basis of church-state relations in Italy is the Lateran Treaty of February 11, 1929, signed by Mussolini and Pope Pius XI. With that accord the Church and the Italian State brought to an end a conflict that had begun with the unification of Italy. Italy had been unified on liberal, secular principles and, in keeping with Cavour's famous principle of "a free church in a free state," most of the church's legal privileges had been abolished. When Italian troops entered Rome in 1870 the pope ceased for the first time in centuries to be a temporal sovereign. In anger he shut himself into the Vatican as a self-proclaimed "prisoner" of the Italian state. The church refused to recognize the new state, excommunicated its monarch, and forbade the faithful to hold public office or vote in national elections. In assuming such a position, the Church not only fostered a widespread popular alienation from the state but also isolated itself and its faithful from the vital forces of society.

The *Roman Question* was not settled until Mussolini saw advantage in gaining church support and was willing to pay a high price for it. The Pacts of Lateran were in three parts. One was a treaty creating an independent Vatican city-state of 108 acres and giving the Holy See possession of a number of churches and palaces in Rome, a papal summer residence at Castel Gandolfo, in the outskirts of Rome, basilicas at Padua, Loreto and Assisi, and custody of all catacombs in Italy. The pope was recognized as juridically sovereign and the Vatican was accorded the attributes of a sovereign state, with the authority to maintain its own police, postal system, bank, radio. In return the pope recognized the Italian state and renounced the Holy See's claim to the former papal territories. With mutual agreement, crimes committed on Vatican soil would be tried in Italian courts and be subject to Italian legal penalties.

A second accord was a concordat that established Catholicism as "the sole religion of the state" and gave the church sweeping privileges in civil affairs. Catholic religious instruction was compulsory in both elementary and secondary schools. Church marriages were deemed legally valid and did not have to be followed by a civil ceremony; their dissolution was solely the responsibility of ecclesiastical courts. Religious institutions were authorized to hold property and were exempted from taxes. Seminarians and priests were exempted from military service, and those expelled from the priesthood were banned from teaching, government employment, and any position that brought them into contact with the public. Priests were also banned from party membership and political activities. The state was given the right to approve the appointment of bishops.

A third accord dealt with the financial settlement that gave the Holy See over 750 million lire, plus a further one million lire in Italian state bonds, as compensation for the loss of the pre-1870s territories; this huge indemnity in time became the basis of a financial empire, first in Italy and then abroad. Moreover, in its few years in office, Mussolini's government increased clerical salaries, granted several million lire for damaged churches, restored the Crucifix in classrooms and law courts, rescued the (Catholic) Banco di Roma during the depression, closed down all brothels and anticlerical journals. It also set up a national examination system to enable Church school students to graduate on an equal footing with those from state schools, and recognized degrees given by the new Catholic University of the Sacred Heart in Milan.

Unquestionably, Mussolini did settle the *Roman Question*, but he settled it at the expense of the separation of church and state which had been at the core of the *Risorgimento*. But for all the legal concessions, the Fascists did circumscribe the activity of the church in civil life with the result that relations between the church and the government were at times strained. For example, under Fascism there was great hostility to Catholic Action as it was regarded as a vocal alternative rather than a support of the regime. Many leading Christian Democrats such as Aldo Moro, Amintore Fanfani and Giulio Andreotti were closely linked with the Church and had been leading members at the time Cardinal Montini, who later became Pope Paul VI, had an influential role. With the fall of fascism, and the supremacy of the Christian Democrats in political affairs in the immediate post-war period, the Church became very powerful politically and established a strong grip on every aspect of Italian life. Its activities were facilitated by the fact that the Constitutional Assembly, by a vote of 350 to 149, supported the incorporation of the Lateran Pacts in the new constitution. That decision, in fact, set the stage for the subsequent course of church-state relations: a nearly organic relationship, almost in symbiosis, between the church and the Christian Democrats.

The Church and Italian Politics

At the end of the 1940s, the hierarchy of the Church identified itself closely with the ruling upper-bourgeois class and protected its interests by defending the social *status quo*. In rural areas priest and gentry were natural allies. Although the Church was anti-temporal, it did meddle in politics. Priests were taking an oath to devote their lives to the re-Christianization of the working class.

Many Catholics, especially younger ones, felt that it was time for the Church to broaden its role and to share in building a better world; and with their ardent faith they set about this task. Strong faith, they claimed, was necessary in order to defend belief from the possible influence of satanic political doctrines. In its determination to fight communism and to create a society consistent with Catholic doctrine, the Vatican, the hierarchy, and the laymen's organizations worked together to mold Catholics into a political bloc and to tie that bloc to the Christian Democratic Party as necessary alternative to the dreaded Communist Party. At election time the church, from pope down to the parish priest, stated that it was a religious duty to vote for the *D.C.* That party was greatly helped by *Azione Cattolica* (*AC*), an organization based on the parish and not on the party. Azione Cattolica was open to members of both sexes, but women always prevailed: in 1946 AC had 151,000 men and 370,000 women, by 1969 it had 183,000 men and 459,000 women. Church and AC provided the strongest basis for women in the *D.C.*

If one looks closely at any of the grass-roots movements of post-war social reform, in nearly every case one will find that some nucleus of Catholic militants played a very important role. The new militant social Christian action took many forms but always with the purpose "to build the Kingdom of God on earth," something the Church, it was claimed, never used to care much about. The Church had also developed a political ideology known as the "social doctrine," a fairly vague set of principles which could be used for social and political activity and which could be constantly reinterpreted by the Church. Its central idea was class reconciliation.

The political actions of the Church became strong as the war ended. During the early postwar period Pope Pius XII, through his fear of Communism and desire to create a "Catholic Italy," recognized virtually no limit on the church's political involvement; he was the one who declared it a matter of religious duty to vote for the Christian Democrats. On July 13, 1949, Pius XII issued a decree which prohibited Catholics from joining the *P.C.I.*, and from writing, reading, publishing or distributing any communist literature. Those engaging in any of these activities could be excommunicated and would not receive any of the sacraments. Two weeks later the Vatican explained that excommunication would apply not only to those who joined or supported the Communist Party but also any of its associated organizations or allies including the trade union CGIL and the Socialist Party.

All this had a deep social impact. By injecting itself into every aspect of civil life and dividing the political world into saints and devils, the church reinforced the country's historic problem of social division. As La Palombara commented, the Church's massive political intervention had the same effect after 1945 as after 1870 by separating "loyal Catholics" from other Italians.[3] This action resulted also to be a mistake because it did not stop the growth of the Left over the next forty years, nor did it prevent the ***rapprochement*** between the *D.C.* and the *P.S.I.* in the 1960s. Indeed, the conservative position of the Church up to the end of the 1950s did not have any positive results either on the spiritual or the political level.

The election of Angelo Roncalli, as Pope John XXIII in 1958 signalled the desire of the Church to move with the times. The new pope had an acute sense of how fast the world was changing, and how important it was for the church to understand this change and adapt to it. In his brief papacy he dedicated himself to an *aggiornamento*, a modernization of the church. Where Pius XII tried to erect barriers, John XXIII sought to open doors. As a first step designed a strategy to revise Church relations in three areas: (1) towards Eastern Europe; (2) toward non-Catholics including Marxists; (3) toward capitalism.

Certainly, the political changes in Eastern Europe were just as important. Historians will eventually assess the kind of direct and in direct role or influence the Church might have played in the fall of Communism in Eastern Europe. The process of *détente* with Eastern Europe was initiated with a series of symbolic acts. Pope John's meeting with Khrushchev's daughter and son-in-law was symptomatic of that new mood.

While the Pope himself began to look at the larger world picture, Italian political affairs were being delegated to the Italian bishops. And as a consequence of this change the church intervened more, not less in Italian politics. In May 1960, in a leading article in the *Osservatore Romano*, the official Vatican daily, the Church hierarchy attempted to establish its supremacy in Italian affairs by making some "basic points":

1. the Church must guide the faithful in both ideas and practice;

2. the Church cannot be politically neutral;

3. the Church must be the judge of whether political cooperation between the faithful and the non-believers was permissible;

4. the Church cannot allow believers to cooperate with Marxists. Meanwhile, however, the Pope was making some very radical pronouncements. In the encyclical letter *Mater et Magistra* (*Mother and Teacher*, 1961), he began to question the support given by the Church to Capitalism. Concentrating on the social teaching of the church, he rejected the free play of market forces, emphasized the need for greater social justice and called for the integration of the disinherited into the social and political order. This position coincided not only with the debate on the modernization of the Italian economy, but also with the debate on the constitution of a center-left government of the *D.C.* in alliance with the *P.S.I.* The 1963 encyclical *Pacem in Terris* (*Peace on Earth*) called for international conciliation based on neutrality of the church and its refusal to accept the barriers of the Cold War. The encyclical was addressed to "all men of good will," not just to Catholics, and argued the need for cooperation between people of different ideological beliefs. In addition, the encyclical

stressed the need for the betterment of economic and social development of the working classes, the entry of women into public life and the justice of anticolonialist struggles in the Third World. The possibility for a dialogue between Catholic and Marxist worlds had been opened.

The repercussions in Italy of *Peace on Earth* were very strong, for in practice the Pope had given his effective blessing to the new coalition.

The changes in the Church were also underlined by the papal decision to convene an ecumenical council (the twenty-first in the history of the Church and the first since 1870). The Council, known as Vatican II, was called to modernize the Church as an organization, develop better relations with other religions and face the problem of modern society. *Vatican II* opened in October 1962 and closed under Paul VI in December 1965. As a result of the council, the position of the bishops was considerably strengthened by instituting synods of bishops to be elected by the national Churches. The distinctive contribution that the laity could make to the Church was recognized and encouraged.

The new pope, Paul VI, continued the policy of détente with the East and vigorously pursued a policy of dialogue with the Third World. As the Vatican became more international in body, it also became less of a "Christian Democrat" supporting system. The important encyclical *Populorum Progressio* (*Progress of the People*) (March 26, 1967) stated that the Christian principles are incompatible with a political system which puts at the base of everything the pursuit of private profit and competition and the absolute right to private property. The encyclical also asserted that even though revolutionary insurrections can be evil they may be necessary in exceptional circumstances such as the struggle against a permanent and cruel form of despotism.[4] In the *Octogesima Adveniens* (May 14, 1971) Paul VI asserted in stronger terms his belief that no social system could be derived from the "social doctrine" of the church. If there was no "Christian political thought" then it followed that there could be no "Christian political party." This meant that Catholics could be active in various political parties.[5]

The implications for the Italian political scene are obvious. After 1968 some clergy had already started to assume political aims; they felt that Christianity needed to be liberated from the Church which they regarded as still a tool of the bourgeoisie. Social issues became their main focus. "Priests don't talk about God any more, they talk about the housing crisis," was an often-heard complaint of many older Catholics.

The autonomous role of the Church in political affairs was parallel to the autonomy declared by the lay Catholic organizations. Organizations such as the Association of Italian Christian Workers (*ACLI*) and Catholic Action (*AC*) officially cut their political affiliation with the *D.C.* When the *D.C.* sought to abolish the divorce law through a popular referendum, expecting the Vatican's support, the Vatican delegated to the Italian bishops the anti-divorce campaign. The attitude of the Vatican could not but encourage Catholic dissent in Italy. The youth branches of ACLI came out in favor of divorce, ACLI itself refused to take a position and so did a number of leading bishops and some important cardinals. Many Catholic intellectuals fought openly on the side of the divorce parties, and during the campaign loosened their ties with the *D.C.* For some of them the difference created such an emotional and ideological split that in the next political campaign they ran and were elected to parliament as candidates on the *P.C.I.* or *P.S.I.* lists. In the referendum held on May 12, 1974, the opponents of divorce were able to muster only 41 per cent of the vote.

The *D.C.* had come to rely on the formidable organization of the Church and, through it, to establish a presence in virtually all sectors of society, but by 1975-76 the *D.C.* had lost its monopoly over Catholic representation. The Church and the *D.C.*, the two institutions that dominated postwar Italian society, had lost their power; a decisive majority of Italians had stated implicitly that religious doctrine was not to be the basis of the country's laws or social life. The 1970s were in fact a traumatic period for the Catholics in Italy and the world. As a result of the cultural crisis of the 1960s, the end of the "economic miracle," the workers' unrest, the growth of political dissent, the students' movement, the birth of feminism, the changes within the Church itself, young Catholics became attracted by new forms of internationalism and particularly by the "new theology" coming from Latin America as well as by new anti-authoritarian form of organizations. At the base of these reactionary forces there was both an anti-establishment attitude and an inner desire to improve the world. Many of the groups were community-based and active in helping those who were at the fringes of society, like the handicapped or drug-addicts; others assumed more an international posture and campaigned for world peace, anti-nuclear policies, Third-World economic assistance.

A Catholic lay organization which assumed a very important active secular and political role is the ***Movimento Popolare*** (*Popular Movement*), founded in 1976, which represents a more militantly political Catholic element, ready to oppose the Left, take part in demonstrations and heckle at Communist meetings. With the intent to work at the socio-political level, the members of the Popular Movement have worked to take control of student assemblies in schools and universities and have created hundreds of cultural centers. Although fervent Christians, they are an independent community.

Ambiguity, conciliation, and passivity were not the traits highly prized by John Paul II with his Polish experience, and in the course of the 1980s a change of style and direction in the papacy became increasingly evident. From the start the hallmark of his office was the affirmation of a monolithic, authoritarian, and aggressive church. Appalled by Western secular and materialistic values, he pursued a mission of promoting traditional–and conservatively interpreted–social and ecclesiastical values.

The pope was very critical of the Italians' religious practice: a secularized society afflicted by a "de-Christianization" of mentality and morals caused by a "practical materialism" abetted by atheistic ideologies. The substance and manner of John Paul's approach contrasted starkly with the conciliatory stance of the majority of the hierarchy. For the first time in modern history there were substantial differences between a pope and most Italian bishops, and it wasn't just that they did not speak the same language! The central disagreement was over the church's political and social engagement. It is very important to make clear the difference between the Vatican as the center of the world organization and the Italian Church. In the past, this distinction hardly seemed to exist. Although the ultimate head of the Italian Church is the Pope, it is the cardinal who presides over the Italian Episcopal Council who has the day-to-day responsibility of running the Italian Church. The new system, a quarter of a century old, originated with John XXIII and gives the Italian Church its own identity similar to the French, Spanish, German, American or any other national Church.

Yet the Church remained a strong presence in Italian political life with its approximately 28,000 parishes performing about 160,000 Sunday services attended by several million people. Its cultural apparatus is responsible for producing several hundred books every year, as well as a daily paper, *Osservatore romano*, over fifty weeklies (one of these *Famiglia cristiana* is the largest circulation weekly in Italy), well over two hundred monthlies and several hundreds of parish bulletins.[6]

Secularization of Society
The drastic population shifts from the land to the cities and from the South to the North destroyed the centuries-old social order. And one of the most dramatic effects that the process of urbanization and industrial development had was the secularization of society.

Migration, especially, had such a profound impact because there was a marked difference between Northern and Southern religiosity. Southern migrants missed the local customs, patron saints and feasts of their village churches and could not reconcile themselves to the somewhat barren and arid life of the northern churches. Some Northerners denounced the Southerners for leaving their religion in a totally superficial way, more as magic and bigotry than in a truly Christian manner.[7] Moreover, as the growth of the Welfare State made state and local authorities more responsible for social services which for years had been the prerogative of the Church, the social functions of the Church contracted remarkably. Not less important, the American model of a consumer society unquestionably helped to erode Catholic values. Political parties, clubs, social circles, sporting associations could provide outlets for a host of activities which were once primarily centered around the church.

How extensive and how fast was the secularization process? In 1956, 69 per cent of the population attended mass regularly; twenty years later the figure had declined to 37 per cent, and by 1985 it had fallen to 25 per cent. In a 1974 poll, 59 per cent of those questioned characterized themselves as "indifferent" to the church and 11 per cent in "opposition" to it. Only about 30 per cent described themselves as practicing Catholics. Another indicator was the number of couples who had only civil marriages. Before 1970 there were very few of them; by 1980 the figure reached 10 per cent and in Rome 25 per cent. The number of abortions soared during this period. A 1980 survey by the Diocese of Rome on sexual morals, abortion, and divorce showed that even among practicing Catholics, 60 per cent approved of divorce, 47 per cent of abortion, and 52 per cent of birth-control methods. More surprising were the results of a poll conducted in 1984 by the Regional Episcopal Council of Piedmont. It showed that only 9 per cent of the Catholics in the region attended mass every Sunday, with another 21 per cent going to church at most once a month. Although 89 per cent had a religious wedding and 92 per cent had their children baptized, only 12 per cent shared the views of the church on sexual morals and a mere 6 per cent opposed abortion. In step with the times, in 1970 the Constitutional Court annulled a law making adultery a crime and several months later canceled a prohibition of contraception and public dissemination of birth-control information.

The process of secularization is also very evident in the rapid decrease in the number of clergy. Between 1961 and 1981, while the population increased by about 2 percent, the number of priests declined from 43,000 to 40,600. In 1961, 601 persons took holy orders, in 1980, the number was down to 347. Not only has it become increasingly more difficult to recruit new priests, but the diocesan clergy has become an aging body ever less able to cope with a growing and changing population. Today the priest is no longer the center of the community as he once had been; in a society in which roles were more diverse, he can easily be lonely and isolated.

The most startling indication of the changes that can occur in religious belief is the public's stand on abortion. In 1978 parliament enacted a liberal abortion law. Despite a Catholic campaign against it, abortion became widespread. It is calculated that in the 80s the abortion rate was 800 for every 1,000 live births. When the Pope and the DC forced a popular referendum (May 1981) on the issue, merely 30 percent voted for repeal. To the surprise of everyone, women in the conservative South voted to retain abortion by roughly the same proportion as those in the North.

Religion is no longer a matter of social convention but of real conviction, and so it is now more sincere. A young man's faith is no longer so "protected" by the environment of family and parish. It has to pass through the ordeal of contact with atheism, and if it survives, it may be more real than in the old days. While social action continues, if less widely than in the 1960s, simultaneously many people are now turning back to the true spiritual sources of Christianity, to the fundamentals of prayer and worship. In some cases this is due to a feeling that social action for its own sake had gone too far and that Christ was in danger of being forgotten. It may also be due to the fact that in this new anxious age people feel greater need for spiritual consolation. At any rate, the trend is widespread, but it does not, however, take the form of a return to traditional church services. Like some other countries, Italy has seen the rise of the so-called `charismatic' movement, whereby informal groups meet regularly for prayer and discussion, often in private homes. It is all vaguely revivalist, very different from old-style Catholic worship. Often no priest is present. Prayers are spontaneous, expressed in everyday language, a complete break with the ritual rosary-type prayers of Catholic tradition

Therefore, there has also arisen a number of religious communities of a new kind, often formed by laymen who find the traditional parish context inadequate. These are not enclosed and tightly disciplined centers like the old monasteries, but informal meeting-places where laymen can come together in their leisure time, maybe under the guidance of a priest, or maybe not. These groups represent a new desire of laity and priests alike for more self-expression, for finding their own ways to God and to Christ.

The hierarchy of the Church in Italy has reacted warily to the new trends. On social issues it projects, sincerely, a liberal image. At the same time, partly under the Vatican influence, it is now outwardly adopting a much tougher line on abortion, birth-control, pre-marital sex, and even divorce. Its problem, like that of the Vatican, is that its doctrines are no longer in tune with the actual behavior of the majority of Catholics. The Church may preach against birth-control, yet most younger Catholics practice it and do not find it inconsistent with their Christian faith. Indeed, it may not signify any waning of real Christian belief, but does certainly have serious implications for the relationship between church hierarchy and the laity.

Farewell to the Catholic State

This high level of secularization of Italian society indicated that the 1929 concordat had become a relic of the past and the time was ripe for a new agreement. It was signed in February 1984 by the Vatican Secretary of State

Agostino Casaroli and Bettino Craxi, the Italian Prime Minister, the first from a party of the left. In the three most important articles—dealing with marriage law, religious instruction in public schools and tax exemption of church organization —the church did not retain much power. Although a religious wedding retained its validity in civil law, the act of marriage had to conform to the legal requirements set by the Italian laws. Marital annulments by ecclesiastical courts were subject to approval by Italian courts. Religious instruction in public schools was made purely voluntary. The issue of state salaries to priests and the taxability of church property required more time for a complete solution. The Vatican had for years claimed exemption from taxes both on the property of Church organizations and on the Vatican's shareholdings in Italy. When under parliamentary pressure it was forced to pay taxes, the Vatican sold off its Italian stocks; but it continued to lobby for tax exempt status for some 50,000 ecclesiastical organizations and properties that were used at least in part for commercial purposes–such as monasteries that rent rooms to tourists. At the end it was agreed that only church properties of a strictly religious nature would retain their tax exemption. The stipend to the clergy (which amounted to $175 million in 1984) as well as funds for the construction of churches was phased out by 1990, leaving the church dependent on voluntary contributions which are tax deductible as in the United States.

The most difficult problem to resolve was finding a way to control the activities of the Vatican bank, which operates as a normal commercial bank for depositors of the ecclesiastical order, and has always been very secretive about every aspect of its affairs. Not being subject to Italian banking regulations and exchange controls, the bank has operated "freely." Until the end of the 1960s the bank's investments were in a broad range of Italian industries and in vast real estate holdings. With the taxation pressure on its stock dividends from the Italian government, in 1968 the bank moved its assets into financial shareholdings outside Italy, especially in the USA. In transferring these funds, the bank's president, Archbishop Paul Marcinkus, an American with no financial experience, depended heavily on the assistance of two Italian bankers, Michele Sindona and Roberto Calvi. The two bankers turned out to be first-rate financial swindlers who brought embarrassment and huge financial losses for the Vatican.[8]

Secularization, defection of the laity, and virtual disestablishment by the state have left the church adrift in Italian society, more so perhaps than at any time since early in the century. In searching for a proper place for the church in the country's rapidly changing social and political environment, most bishops have assumed a conciliatory position in political ideology. However, the bishops and the curia still have the firmest links with the *cattolici popolari,* thedescendents of the old *DC.* It is that party that the church sees as its last best hope of finding a defender of its worldly interests. The bishops know that the *cattolici popolari* need Catholic electoral support as much as ever but they recognize that each side can do less for the other. The church's interest in politics and its influence on them have declined. Although remaining an important factor in national life, the church can no longer command the allegiance of the majority of Catholics on any issue of public life. In practice the area in which the church and state interact has steadily diminished and is now quite small. What has evolved is a church-state relationship of the sort Cavour originally intended back in 1870.

In the process of secularization, the number of clergy has decreased considerably, especially in the figures for male members. Nuns constitute more than three-quarters of the ordained or consecrated Church personnel. From a total of about 155,000 nuns in 1971 the figure declined to 129,000 in 1991; meanwhile the male clergy in 1991 had fallen to only about 25,000. In the South and the islands, there is one nun for every three hundred women over the age of twenty, in the Center-North the ratio is one for every one hundred-fifty. About two-thirds of them work in the center-north engaged in hospital work, teaching, and social assistance. To fill the vacuum being created by the fall in number, some religious orders are recruiting novice nuns in Africa and Asia.

In the face of these deep social and ecclesiastical changes, the bishops have shifted their attention to pastoral matters, in particular religious renewal at the diocesan and parish level. The conviction that the past obsession with anti-communism had led to a fundamental obfuscation of reality–that it was not Marxist materialism but the materialism of the consumer society that, in the wake of secularization, had weakened the church's position.

A New *Modus Vivendi*
Practicing Catholics are now a minority of only 30 percent in Italy. In today's increasingly urban society the struggle is between faith and apathy. There is a lack of interest in religious problems, and a rejection of Christ and the Gospel because it is felt that neither the Gospel nor Christ has anything to say to a modern man. The loss of faith is partially the consequence of a cultural crisis, the result of the shattering of many successive illusions in the last two hundred years, from the eighteenth-century faith in Reason, to that in Progress, Nationalism, Development. And the fall of Marxism, for many, is the fall of yet another god.

However, among those who do practice their religion, there has been a re-examining and sharpening of faith, and a major shift of emphasis away from old-style pious liturgy and towards social action and private prayer. Moreover, although most Italians do not go to church on a regular basis and regard Church laws as any other laws, which means, therefore, they can be broken (contraception, divorce, abortion), their spiritual adherence to Christian teaching is still very strong. They have an almost innate sense of what is right or wrong, and a capacity to view everyone as people with individual souls, to feel that there may, perhaps, be a purpose in this life because it leads to another one. The Church has helped to give Italians much of their humanity, their balance between spontaneity and restraint. In every village, the Church and its bell-tower, *campanile*, dominates the town square, looking down from above like a guard guaranteeing order and calm. In fact, the Italian word *campanalismo* means local patriotism, love of one's village. In times of joy, it is a welcoming inn crowded with celebrants of christenings, weddings; in time of sorrow, it is like a black hearse, followed by weeping relatives.

The Church's worldly role today is mainly to help those in trouble. Instead of just providing hand outs for the poor, the Italian Church and Italian Catholics are involved in many projects to assist the needy and those living on the fringe of society, such as drug addicts and homosexuals. The Church still staffs hospitals, schools, old people's homes, mental asylums, homes for the handicapped. *ACLI* still runs universities and trade unions, while the *Movimento Popolare* finds work for its members and has centers where they sell food at a discount to poorer people. The Church involvement in Italian society still stirs an active conscience both in the individual and in society.

Notes

1. The various cults of the South, from the *tarantismo* ('dance of the spider') analyzed by the famous Italian ethnologist Ernesto De Martino to the 'festivals of the poor' described by Annabella Rossi, were different expressions of an autonomous culture, separate from the structure and social doctrines of the Catholic Church. This was a world which offered the possibility of trance and release, of mass pilgrimages and miraculous cures. E. De Martino, *Sud e magia* (Milano: 1959), and *La terra del rimorso* (Milano, 1961); A. Rossi, *Le feste dei poveri* (Bari, 1969).

2. Robert N. Putnam, *Making Democracy Work* (Princeton: Princeton University Press, 1993), p. 107.

3. *Democracy Italian Style* (New Have: Yale University Press, 1987), pp. 60-65.

4. For more on this encyclical see Lucio Lombardo Radice and Luigi Pestalozza, `Intervento sulla *Populorum progressio*,' in *Problemi del socialismo*, vol. 9, n. 18, May 1967.

5. Gianni Baget-Bozzo, *Il partito cristiano e l'apertura a sinistra. La DC di Fanfani e Moro 1954-1962* (Florence: Vallechi, 1979), pp. 128-9.

6. Carlo Cardia, "L'area cattolica dopo il 20 giugno 1976," *Critica marxista*, vol. 17, no. 1, 1979, pp. 48-52.

7. Church-going plummeted especially on the peripheries of the big cities, where the new urban population was most concentrated. See A. Monelli and G. Pellicciari, "Comportamenti di voto e pratica religiosa," in G. Pellicciari, ed., *L'emigrazione nel triangolo industriale* (Milano: 1970), p. 334.

8. For an account of the financial scandal in which the Vatican was involved, see: Luigi Di Fonzo, *St. Peter's Banker: Michele Sindona* (New York: Franklin Watts, 1983).

XI

Family: Tradition and Change

Crisis of the Institution

While secularization has brought about a significant revolution in the relationship between Italians and their Church, it is not uncommon to hear older Italians complain how modern times have brought sweeping changes also in the family structure and family values. The traditional picture of the Italian family as the institution where the individual finds consolation, help, advice, provisions, loans, weapons, allies and accomplices remained unchanged for many centuries. Changes in the structure of society have undermined the social stability and effectiveness of both the extended and the nuclear family. After Italy became a welfare state, the family world described by Barzini as a closely knit community held together by emotional attachments and material interests, ever ready to form a common front against all outsiders and to take care of its own, could not avoid being effected by all the social changes .[1]

That description accurately mirrored, to a large degree, the main features of the Italian family until the early 1960s. In a nation whose other social institutions are notoriously brittle, the Italian family had indeed long been functioning as the sole unit that, rock-like, withstood all adversities. That picture is becoming a thing of the past.

There is a decline in the number of marriages, an increase in illegitimate births, and a rise in the number of legal separations. Census figures also show that there is a sharp decrease of the "extended family" (i.e. married couple, children and other relatives in the same household). There is an increase of households made up of only one person, of childless couples and those whose children have left the home.

On the one hand, types of family remained little changed. In 1951 nuclear families, composed only of husband, wife and children, formed 55.7 per cent of the total number of Italian families; twenty years later they formed 54.1 per cent; today the percentage has not changed much. In the same period extended families declined slowly from 22.5 per cent to 16.9 per cent of the total, with percentages for the South being much higher. In the last twenty years, however, there has been a considerable increase in "nonfamily" households (only one person), a steady increase, even though more limited than the preceding one, in "married couple" households, a slight decrease in *nuclear* households, and a big decrease in *extended* households. From a rather general point of view, these figures confirm that the structure of the Italian family tends to be moving toward a prevalence of the conjugal or nuclear pattern. Because of industrialization, and the mobility imposed on working individuals, the extended family registered increasing breakups.

In 1971 households comprising five or more members were nearly twice that of one-person households. Between 1971 and 1981 one-person households increased by 5 per cent. Households made up of six or more persons went down from 9.7 to 5.4 per cent of all households. As might be expected, in the North one-person households are now twice as common as large households. In the last two decades there has been a considerable increase in the number of *non-family* households; a lesser increase in "married couple" households, a slight decrease in *nuclear* households; and a large loss of over 10 percentage points in *extended* households.

The main change since the war is that the focus of loyalty has been steadily narrowing from what sociologists call the *extended family* to the *nuclear family*: from the big multi-generation clan to the immediate home cell of parents and children. The trend varies from class to class. In the propertyless lower bourgeoisie the nuclear family has long held more importance than the clan, but now even in rural areas the big patriarchal peasant families have been losing their influence as the young drift away to the town. In the upper bourgeoisie, as property gives way to income, as family managements disappear and sons disperse to new salaried careers in other parts of Italy, the tight network of the big family gathering has become less necessary for the individual's future and security, and also less easy to maintain. Many younger couples are today likely to prefer pleasure travelling, or a weekend cottage shared with a few close friends, to the traditional big family reunions on Sundays and in summer time.

Although the structure of the Italian family has changed in the last two decades, as has changed the interrelation among its members, the family, as the basis of human relations is as strong as it was two thousand years ago. The dynamics of Italian families can easily be compared with those in most Western countries, which have been influenced by a process of progressive nuclearization of family forms over the last couple of decades. Still, in its percentage of extended families, the Italian situation markedly differs from other countries with an equal degree of economic development. For one thing, while economic development has undoubtedly contributed to modify the family unit for a considerable part of the population, it has not caused traditional structures to disappear. Moreover, the social and economic changes have not changed family values. Though clan loyalties towards more distant relatives may be waning, an adult's ties with his own parents and with *their* parents often remain remarkably close. If many younger people are today trying to lead more emotionally independent lives, it is often not without a sense of guilt, or an awareness of the pain it causes their parents who cling to a different family tradition. This may be so in any country; it is especially sharp in Italy.

Family and Familism

It has often been said that the Italian family, especially that belonging to the middle and lower classes has not interacted well in the social milieu. Some sociologists have pointed out that because of the high degree of individualism that characterizes Italians, Italian families do not interact well with the social structures at large, and in fact, some sociologists have argued that the Italian familial institution has been the cause of negative social, economic and political development of the country.

There is certainly some truth in such a charge since excessive individualism and *familism* are compounded by widespread and deeply rooted enmity–sometimes open, often unconscious–toward the state and its institutions.

Strong familism, whether conceived as moral or amoral, also characterizes other societies around the Mediterranean. Domineering patriarchs, clinging matriarchs, and relatives who stick together to defend and further the interests of the family or the clan can be found among Spaniards, Greeks, Turks, and Arabs.

In the case of the Italians, the most frequent reason is attributed to historical circumstances. In his *Prison Notebook* Antonio Gramsci lamented the negative effects of the exclusion of the lower classes in the *passive revolution* that brought about the unification of Italy in 1870 and the failure of the ruling élite to integrate the popular classes into the new state and to establish their own hegemony.[2] The *passive revolution*, by its exclusive nature and repressive tendencies, accentuated the antagonism of the Italian lower classes toward the state and their propensity for autonomous organization; it also made them less open to class ideologies, whether Marxist or anarcho-syndicalist.[3] It should be pointed out, however, that in the Italian lower classes familism did not originate with the unified state, though it may well have been intensified by it. The origins of such attitudes should be sought in the effects of centuries of foreign domination, with the consequent destruction of any *fede pubblica* and the influence of Catholic teaching on the family, with its emphasis on the natural law which determines the pre-eminence of the family in civil society and its separation from the state.[4]

One can say, however, that after unification, in the absence of almost any adequate structures, apart from repressive ones, linking civil society and the state, the mass of Italians concentrated their attention on the single structure in civil society over which they could exercise some control, namely the family. The family became the epicenter of life, the only moral force, so much so that for some observers, like Pasquale Villari, the relationship between individual and community, between family and collectivity, seemed not to exist at all.[5] Luigi Barzini used to say that the true patriotism of the Italians is loyalty to their own families. In a nation whose other social institutions are notoriously untrustworthy, the family has indeed long been functioning as the sole unit that, rocklike, withstands all corrosive elements.

Certainly the Church played a major role in shaping the moral and social core of the Italian family. The weekly magazine *Famiglia Cristiana*, which had its largest circulation in the 1950s and 1960s was used as one of the best media of reaching the Italian family in preaching the sanctity of the Christian family and the primacy of the family in civil society.

The *Enciclopedia Cattolica* (1950) stated that "the precedence of the family over society is above all temporal; the family was the first form of social organization, the first school and first temple." Furthermore, in a hierarchy of values, society was subordinate to the family "since society is a means to assure to the family and through it the individual that which is indispensable for its [family] self-realization."[6] In family-state relations, the emphasis is on the need to protect the family from external control. Again the *Enciclopedia Cattolica* stated: the state must recognize the family as it has been constituted by God." (pp. 994-5) The state's duties were therefore to protect the family and to enable it to "accomplish its mission;" only if the family failed in this task did the state have the right to interfere. Tullio Goffi made a similar point: "the family enjoys a pre-eminence over civil society in an ordering of ends... family duties, founded on piety, love and unity, are of a superior essence, although less defined and distinct, than social duties, which emanate from justice."[7]

In the relationship between family and collectivity, the Christian family thus had many more rights than duties. The family's duties were primarily internal, not external. Such an ideology could be accused of catering to familism, of isolating the family from society, of stressing private rather than public virtues.

If this was the predominant view of family-society relations, it should be stated that Catholic social teaching, as we saw in the preceding chapter, balanced the picture by placing the family in a wider social context. The Catholic family had to be defended against the Communist menace and the threats of modern society. It could only do so if it emerged from its isolation.

The prime mission of the family within the Church was to link with and help other Christian families: communitarian spirit over individualism. Therefore there was a permanent tension in the Catholic view of the family. On the one hand there was the tendency to stress the family's internal values, its primacy over society, the need to protect it from a hostile world. On the other hand, there was the desire to overcome the family's isolation, both with relation to the church and society.

Family and Society

The present structure of the Italian family and its role in society, as in the past, is obviously affected by economic factors. Indeed, there is a definite link between the socioeconomic characteristic of region and the living arrangements that may be found within a single area. In fact, it would be safe to say that the changes are more profound going from the agricultural to the artisan and small-industrial to the industrial areas. In the urban areas, industrially dependent, is more common the permanence of relatively atypical family structure very similar to the pattern of the "modified extended family." Areas of small land ownership and micro artisan and industrial enterprise display the configuration of models of family organization based on the extended (or corporate) family.

There is no question that families have determined the political and economic history of Italy. Countless small or medium-size businesses that have boosted the Italian economy are family enterprises, or started as such. The outstanding case in contemporary Italy is that famous clothing empire founded by Lacuna, Galena, Gilbert and Carlo Benetton. Olivetti, Pirelli, etc. are other family-run businesses that come readily to mind. Family bonds were essential also to the fortunes of the Ferruzzi agrobusiness empire. In 1989 the Agnelli, De Benedetti, and Ferruzzi families controlled 45 percent of all the shares quoted on the Milan stock exchange. Most of Italy's privately owned, large industrial companies have retained some features of a family enterprise. Outside the hefty state sector, Italy has many fewer corporate giants than do the other leading industrial nations; the largest is Fiat, and it is still, in effect, the family holding of the Agnellis of Turin. There have been place and periods when family strategies have acquired an overridingly private dimension and the collective aspect of social life has become secondary. The decline of collective values and the vigorous new emphasis on the material prosperity of the individual family unit have led to a new age of familism: families have become ever more concerned with their own well-being, and less with the collective problems of society as a whole (trend dominant in the 1980's).

Anyone who visits Italy and has occasion to assess the workings of the Italian family and the relationship between family and collectivity will return with a view which is more complex and less one-sided than that presented by Banfield and Altan. The family has both contributed to and worked against collective action; the furtherance of the family can lead both towards greater solidarity and away from it. In other words, attachment and devotion to the family do not necessarily carry the negative social connotation of familism. It is the historical and ideological context in which working-class families operate that to a great extent conditions the degree of asociality and exclusiveness of family values and actions.

The Italian family and the relationship between family and collective action have changed profoundly since the early 1940s. In the early 1940s, when Italy was still predominantly a rural and small town nation, there certainly existed in many parts of the South and the islands those social structures which Banfield found at Chiaramonte: nuclear families, the size of which was largely determined by the agrarian conditions, by the strips of land on which the peasants, by the extensive farming of grains, by the conglomeration of mono-familial dwellings in the agro-towns. In these years Southern and Central Italian families were large and usually multiple and vertical in structure, in the sense of having more than one married couple and more than two generations living under the same roof. Hierarchies within the families were clearly established (in the Center more than the South). The male head of the household had sole control of the family's money and took all responsibility for relations between the family and the outside world. The senior female figure, usually his wife, also exercised considerable power, within the domain of the household and over the other women of the family.

Here too we can find the lack of trust amongst the peasantry, their lack of associationism, their fatalism and despair. It might be expected, given these structures and the extent to which the family was a world unto itself, that Tullio Altan's Albertian family reigned supreme. This was only partly the case, however, for side by side with these attitudes, we also find the greatest mobilizations in terms of land occupations and outbreaks of dissent that the inland areas of the South had ever seen. The southern peasants displayed a strong horizontal solidarity. The habitual distrust and ingrained individualism of the South were eclipsed by those elements which prompted solidarity amongst the peasants.

Indeed, collective consciousness and a strong sense of community did exist in the peasant life of these years. They were based on a complex system of favors and exchanges, and on a social network which was almost exclusively confined to the neighborhood; family and collective action related in a variable and complex way, and certainly not in a simple polar opposition to each other. The core of collective consciousness, the focal point of action was the *paese* (village) itself, with its closed concentrated formation and its *piazza* (square). The dimension of the *vicinato* (neighborhood), of face-to-face relations had fundamental importance; it was the basic element of aggregation. Faced with the uncertainties of work, with the particular harshness of life on the plains (the miles and miles covered on foot or on bicycle, the risk of malaria, the difficult relationship with the landowners), the *paese* was the symbol of peace, of solidarity, of physical rest and recovery, of affections, of friendship. The *paese* offered "civiltà," culture. People used to sit outside their doors, on chairs and stools, chatting away. Allegiances developed between families as well as amongst kinfolk. Even in the agrarian society, where farmers operated in social isolation and the family's binding internal structures would make one expect the degree of contact and cooperation between neighbors to be very limited, the Albertian concept of familism does not reign supreme. Italian literature gives ample testimony of this cooperation and collective work efforts–especially at crucial periods in the agricultural calendar; Giovanni Verga's narrative, for example, provides some classic examples of certain collective practices (salting of anchovies, etc.) in Sicily.

Sharecropping families had, for example, developed a rich network of exchanges and mutual aid. The exchange of labor between families at crucial moments in the agricultural calendar, such as at threshing and harvest times and other farm seasonal work drew families together with a spirit of generosity and strong cooperation.

On a cultural level there was also the important practice of the *veglia*. During the long winter evenings, families would gather in the kitchens of the farmhouses, to play cards and games, to knit and to mend, to tell stories and to listen. Participation in the *veglia* was not segregated family by family, but it involved rotating hospitality and a varied system of visiting. *Carnevale*, which culminated with mardi gras, was the time of maximum community interaction.

One cannot forget the strong Catholic tradition of collective action and solidarity, of mutual aid and cooperative societies which affected the life of every family. We cannot underplay the influence of Catholic ideology and leadership on the relationship between family and collective action, especially in the South and in the Northeast even though Catholic teaching asserted the primacy of the family in civil society and the need to protect it from the interference of the state. On the other hand the Church's strong emphasis on the internal morality of the family–on its indissolubility, on the responsibility of the parents to educate their children in a Christian manner–had its impact. The approach was essentially defensive and inward looking. The Christian family had more rights than duties in a hostile world from which it had to be safeguarded. However, as mentioned in Chapter X, we cannot ignore the important historical experience of Catholic social activism in Italy.

On the political level, the Christian Democrats were concerned with the lack of social activism of Italian families, and at the first congress of the party in April 1946, Guido Gonella, the Party Secretary, made a strong plea to Catholics to emerge from the shell of the family:

> It is an illusion, and the women present should understand this better than the men, to try to defend the family from inside the family. The state with its wars will tear away from you your husband or your brother, and atheist education or the corruption of the streets will steal

the soul of your child. The family is a fortress which cannot be defended from inside the fortress. Certainly we must build up its internal
strength, but we must also issue forth and fight the enemy in open
battle.[8]

Family and collective action combined in a crusading spirit, which was not
to be transformative of social relations, but was to defend the Christian family
from the Marxist and atheist threat.

Sociality was certainly higher in the working class of the urban areas than
in the agrarian South. Italian housing, with long balconies on each floor looking
over the street or inwards onto a communal courtyard facilitated dialogue and
human connection. Even in the working-class quarters on the periphery of the
great cities where the housing usually took the form of flats in tenement blocks,
isolated from the rest of the city, a strong sense of community developed, as did
solidarity between families. They were based on a complex network of favors
and exchanges, on a sociality which was almost exclusively confined to neighborhood, and on the powerful political culture of socialism.[9]

Modernization and the Destruction of Family-Based Communities

Looking at Italy as a whole in the 1940s, there is a danger of idealizing the
relationships that existed between family and collective life at that time. In
reality there was nothing idyllic about rural life or relationship in the South.
Nor was there a linear passage anywhere in Italy from the existence of compact
communities based on mutual aid to the destruction of communities brought on
by modernization.

The next two decades, when Italy underwent a most profound social revolution, with a mass exodus from the rural areas towards the cities, and from the
South to the North (between 1952 and 1962 more than fifteen and half million
Italians changed their place of residence) had a profound effect on the family
and its relation to the collectivity. The mass urbanization which was the product
of individual family strategies (the young who went first used kinship and
sometimes village networks in order to survive the first impact, to find work
and housing; then they brought other members of the family)certainly reshaped
the structure of the traditional family.

As families began to put a new emphasis on home-centered living and
consumption, so the family and especially the woman's role within the family
changed. In the 1960s, more Italian women than ever before became full-time
housewives. Theirs was the responsibility to care for children who were leaving
for school later than ever before. Theirs too, especially in the North, was the
task of looking after the needs of a husband whose day's work in the factory,
with overtime and commuting, often amounted to 12 to 14 hours. The women's

magazines and the television advertisements of the time exalted this new figure of the modern Italian woman.

The material improvement in living conditions also had an impact on leisure time activities which also radically changed. The television set was obviously the most important innovation of these years. At first television was both a socializing phenomenon and an object of political division. People, especially youngsters and adult men, gathered in bars and in political party's section headquarters to watch favorite programs.

Gradually, however, the collective and habitual way of television-viewing disappeared as more and more families bought their own sets, and each family watched television in its own apartment. This startling development obviously increased the tendency towards passive and familial use of leisure time, and decreased drastically other more participatory and collective pastimes.

At the same time, a significant number of people from the Italian popular classes became more mobile. The *FIAT Seicento* and *Cinquecento*, because of their relatively low cost, made it possible for popular classes and *ceti medi* to travel as a family unit, rather than on bus or train with others, or remain in the *vicinato*. Sunday outings by car became a possibility for the first time.

The amount of paid holidays increased slowly but significantly, as did the tendency to travel further. Car and television further encouraged an essentially privatized and familial use of leisure time. All this had an impact on the life in the courtyard and with the extended family. The role of the family unit became even more important than previously. The new urban structures served to isolate families, which were decreasing in size, in small but comfortable living quarters, and provided few spaces for collective gatherings or community life. Women became the principal target of the new consumerism, and the increased emphasis on their service role within the home intensified their isolation. The "economic miracle" increased the atomization of Italian civil society; it linked rising living standards with accentuated individualism, and introduced into Italy a new model of urban social integration.

The Cultural Ferment of 1968 and its Aftermath

The Italian student rebellion of 1967-68, which was seen as a rebellion against all authority and the dominant ideology, was also against the individualist and atomizing values of the "Economic Miracle," against the individualism of the new Italy. The extraordinary flourishing of collective action of these years in the major cities, especially in the industrial North, must also be viewed in this context. During these years, for significant number of people, time at work, but free-time even more so, was filled with meetings, leafletting, mobilizations, demonstrations, discussions. The activities led to new networks of friendship and solidarity, to contacts between intellectuals and workers, to a minor cultural revolution.

How did this ferment of collective action in the new, urban Italy relate to the family? Families were drawn out of their isolation and found a new common purpose. It was noteworthy that women played a greater role than ever before. Collective action and sociality often took priority over family needs.

Conversely, however, the most significant development of these years was that some sections of the collective movement called into question the very structure and bases of the family. The critique of the family took various forms, some of which found widespread support. The need to introduce divorce, to allow the family to be dissolved, won majority support in Italian society, as the outcome of the referendum of 1974 showed.

The attempt by the women's movement to combat patriarchy and change the traditional roles within the Italian family also made significant inroads in changing Italian society. The most radical critics wished to attack the very existence of the nuclear family. Attempts were made to find alternatives to this family unit, and to substitute communal living for family life. Such experiments, though, rarely extended beyond student groups in the major cities.

In central Italy, where sharecropping families started up small family businesses, the 1970s witnessed the extraordinary growth of family capitalism, of decentralized and small-scale industrialization, and family structure and familism remained rather strong.

In the South, in the rural areas, the agro-towns ceased to be the centers of solidarity and collective action. With the great exodus, the class structure was modified irrevocably. No longer was the population divided into the small élite of landowners and the mass of the rural poor and working in a cooperative effort. Although the class structure had become more varied, human relations deteriorated. In whichever direction they went, the potential for collective action in the rural South had been destroyed. Some evidence of collective action could be found in the industrial working class only. However, the dominant trend in the South was an economic growth and development which was chaotic, unstable, precarious, and mainly without respect for any order or civic discipline.[10] In the interstices of this vital but chaotic growth, criminal organizations like the Mafia in Sicily and the Camorra in Naples increased their networks of influence and protection. Society was divided against itself, and each family fended for itself as best it could. Narrow municipal or corporate or criminal rivalries flourished, leaving little possibilities for the sort of solidarities which had existed before the "democratic" chaos controlled by the Christian Democrats. The political class of the South, corrupt and clientelistic, presided contentedly over this spectacular free-for-all.

Notwithstanding all this, today students and parents are very active in school councils, some neighborhood and block associations have sprung up, and new environmental and consumer groups are active. In Sicily churchmen and schoolteachers are taking an active part in the fight against the Mafia. Italy is undoubtedly on the road toward democratic maturity, and its people are becoming increasingly involved in public affairs.

The Divorce Issue

The long debate that accompanied the introduction of divorce into Italian legislation is closely related to the issue of the solidarity of family ties. The fear of jeopardizing the strength of this network of relationships was one of the main reasons for the opposition campaign led by the anti-divorce front.

Although the Christian Democratic Party and the Catholic Church opposed it, divorce was introduced in 1970, when the left-wing parties and the small anti-clerical center groups in Parliament surprisingly mustered enough votes to overcome the opposition. True, the new rules called for a five-year waiting period from the moment a married couple had formally separated. Nevertheless, the old principle that an Italian marriage was indissoluble–save through annulment by state or church court–had been scrapped. The Christian Democrats remained nearly isolated in the Senate and Chamber of Deputies in their defense of the old, rigid legislation, joined only by the neo-Fascists.

Although militant, outraged Roman Catholics collected enough signatures to request a referendum aimed at repealing the divorce statute and the Church hierarchy and the Christian Democrats staged a nationwide anti-divorce crusade, the law was not repealed. The referendum which took place in 1974 (two-thirds of the electorate upheld divorce) dealt a humiliating blow to the Church and the DC. Even many Italians who attended mass every Sunday voted for divorce, proving that they, like Roman Catholics in other countries, were selective in obeying the teachings of their church.

Many couples who had been living apart were at last able to have their collapsed marriage lawfully ended and to remarry. But the large, general rush into divorce that adversaries of the reform had predicted did not occur. In 1987 the legal waiting period between separation and divorce was reduced to three years. By then it was estimated that one out of every fifteen new marriages would end in divorce–a far lower divorce rate than in France, Britain, or certainly the United States, where it is predicted that one out of every two marriages would not last.

Despite almost 60 per cent support for divorce at the referendum in 1974, and the fact that it has been legal since 1970, the Italian divorce rate is the lowest in Europe, apart from Ireland where it is still forbidden by law. Even after they were given legal right to divorce, Italians still were hesitant to dissolve their family unit. In 1981, only 13,000 couples were divorced in Italy. One reason, obviously, is that Italian bureaucracy makes it more complicated. It is also slower: five years–three since 1987–of separation are necessary first, if both partners agree to divorce, and seven if one does not. The influence of Catholic morality on the customs and choices of married life for Italians seems to be considerable. Most importantly, there are economic reasons. The old-fashioned housewife status of a considerable part of the female population, for example, has certainly acted as a check on the divorce rate until recently. The lack of economic independence of the unemployed female, along with the poor protection the law offers to the weaker partner, undoubtedly represents an efficient impediment to the decision to proceed with a request for separation. There are also cultural reasons, and the domestic topography that Italians feel too attached to. They cannot separate from a host of friends, from a part of their own lives. But, most of all, the welfare and advancement of children comes first, as always.

Some Italians seem to need the thrills and stress of adultery. Playwright Luigi Pirandello, Benito Mussolini, the leader of the Italian Communist Party Palmiro Togliatti, film directors Vittorio De Sica and Roberto Rossellini and thousand of nameless citizens had well-publicized extramarital affairs.

Indeed, *adultery* and unfaithfulness have always been major themes in Italian life and art. From Dante, Boccaccio and Machiavelli to many modern writers these themes have provided fertile ground for the imagination of artists. However, despite the fact that the most celebrated works are family tragedies, erotic and adulterous entanglements have mostly been farcical in the eyes of Italians.

Today, even though divorce is legal and fewer marriages are "arranged," infidelity has not diminished. In fact, with more free time and the growth of travel and other leisures, infidelity, especially among the bourgeoisie, has increased.

Despite this behind-the-scenes activity, the majority of Italians have always tended to be exceptionally discreet about their love affairs. Many government Ministers or other public figures have mistresses, but a public man's private life is his own business so long as he is discreet and does not step outside the law.

Notwithstanding all these changes, there exists one of the most absurd paradoxes of the Italian mentality: the obsessive preoccupation that Italian males, especially those in the South, have with a woman's faithfulness, while they themselves are engaging in extra-marital affairs. There is no worse insult to a man than calling him *cornuto* (cuckold). The Italian male seems to want his right to stray from the strict marital path, and knows in his heart and from frequent sociological studies that adultery is not uncommon, but he is obsessed by the fear of being cuckolded, of having his own wife be unfaithful.

Stability and Dissolution

The change in sexual attitudes in the last few years, as has occurred in most industrial countries, has certainly had an impact on family structure. It is important to remember, however, that the Italy of the economic boom was still a society full of taboos about sexual behavior. The restrictive codes of official morality were deeply intertwined especially in the South with codes of honor, and sexual mores were to change more slowly than anything else.

The early 60s did see the first stirrings of a new moral outlook. Timid discussions of pre-marital sex appeared in some women's magazines; one weekly (*L'Espresso*) even published an investigation of infidelity levels amongst Italian wives. However profound changes began to occur in the 70s. For one, the pill was made available everywhere and the whole ferment of the late 60s and early 70s had revolutionized mores. Results can be seen in the population figures and family size today. Population growth is approximately zero, therefore, as low as low as Great Britain and much lower than France. The number of families with several children has rapidly diminished. Italy now has one of the lowest birthrates in Europe, 10.2 per 1,000 population, as against 29.4 per 1,000 half a century ago. By comparison, the 1987 birthrate in the United States was 15.6. Naples today produces proportionately fewer infants than Stockholm. The Italian nation is close to zero population growth and may even begin to shrink after the year 2000. The legalization of abortion and the availability of more reliable contraceptives, including the pill, have certainly had an impact on the population growth. Because many women feared the side effects of the pill, abortions became the most widespread form of birth control—more than 360 abortions per 1,000 live births. Abortions are the second highest within the EC and illegitimate births are therefore low.

Although the South of Italy has changed greatly in the last twenty years, traditional thinking still seems stronger than in the North. Research indicates that established families tend to be less worried about their daughters than those who have only been prosperous since the war. Both might take a daughter's boyfriend along on holiday, but while the first group would accept their being lovers, the second would supervise them closely, and make sure they were never alone together. The stereotypical picture of a grandmother or aunt accompanying the young couple on a walk is a thing of the past even in Southern Italy.

Certainly, the 30 per cent who remain practicing Catholics must be influenced by the Pope's adamant refusal to countenance any variation on the Church's teachings on chastity and contraception. However, here again we are faced by Italian flexibility and spontaneity. The point, probably, is that given the pill and free access to abortion, sexual freedom is no longer a menace to the family structure which itself is the key to Italian thinking.

Italian families are, thus, getting smaller and more nuclear and continue to be cohesive. Even in urban contexts, Italian grandparents remain closely involved in the care of grandchildren; it is still common to see in a public park a child kicking a soccer ball with his *nonno*. Once the older generation is threatened by fragility and immobility, it receives considerable assistance and company, especially from daughters and their families. Nevertheless, some fundamental shifts have occurred in the roles and needs of individuals within the family. There has been an ever-increasing process of "individualization" within the family, of demarcations of activity and consumer rules by age and by sex; women have redefined their roles and responsibilities; youth have increasingly sought their own activities and space at an ever younger age; individual members of the family relate more and more to their peer groups and the outside world.

Old Bonds and New Familism

Notwithstanding the changes, a few characteristics of the traditional family ethos do remain. Curiously, the past few years have even seen a new strengthening of the links that bind the nuclear family, after a tense period of transition. In the late 1960s and early 1970s Italian teenagers shook off the reins of traditional parental authority. This was a blow to the nuclear family. But today, having asserted their right to independence, young people are moving back to closer emotional ties with their parents, on a basis of greater equality than before. So the family today is united less by constraint and convention as in the old days, and more by genuine need and affection. The autonomy of much of northern youth and its partial challenge to the family in the late 60s and early 70s have given way to a new attachment to the family unit. The generational conflict has subsided, now that youth has won its rebellion. Whereas the youth of the 60s rejected the values dictated by its parents, today's adolescents are turning again to the family as a defense and a source of comfort, since they no longer find solid values in the public world. The fears created by rising youth unemployment have increased this homing trend. Grown-up children tend to stay at home well into adult life.

Some of the traditional intra-family links remain untouched by modern changes. Above all, there are the strong mother-son bonds, a characteristic shared with other Mediterranean cultures. The classic *mamma* pampers her boy, keeps telling him he is *bello* and *bravo*. After he is married, she is glad to press her mature boy's shirts, cook his favorite dishes, and discreetly and sympathetically listen to the tales of his erotic conquests and troubles. The self-admiring Latin lover is to some extent a product of such "momism." In the dynamics of Italian family life, father-daughter relations also are close. The new family is geared to the production of income and the meeting of needs through the activity of each of its members.

With women's work increasing notably in the eighties, the family is usually living on two salaries. It also has access, thanks to the reforms of the 1970s, to a far wider range of state services than ever before. Consequently, family savings have risen markedly since 1970, as has the overall standard of living. In their life styles and in their culture, average Italian families have come a long way.

In the Center and Northeast, where small, family-owned businesses are widespread, extended families appear more frequently than in other regions, though obviously not as abundantly nor as numerous as the earlier sharecropping families. In these regions a very strong work ethic, geared to the making of family fortunes, allows self-exploitation and the exploitation of one's relatives at the levels which are no longer accepted elsewhere in Italy. There is thus less leisure time and less mobility here than the working-class families of the North. It is hardly surprising to find that the strong, collectivist sub-culture of these regions has been severely affected by such developments. Political and Catholic associationism have suffered. The ex-Communists, now *P.D.S.*, attract people to their cultural events in decreasing number. The secularization which necessarily accompanied urbanization realized the fears of the Church that with the decline of rural communities there would naturally occur a weakening of the links between the family and the Catholic religion and the family nucleus itself.

In the urban South, the majority of lower-class families are nuclear in structure and have significantly more children than the North or Center. In 1971 the average size of Neapolitan family was 4.7 persons compared to 3.3 in Bologna. These larger families have to survive in a situation of deepening gloom of the labor market. Southern urban families also have to survive in a situation where the services offered by the state are less efficient than the Center or the North. In the southern cities the state pays out a high number of invalidity and 'social' pensions (i.e., poverty pensions) for old people who have never been in regular work.

Family and Money

Despite the recent changes in Italian kinship structures, millions of families throughout the country keep functioning in the traditional way providing warmth, security, moral and economic support, and assistance in crisis. Hundreds of thousands of such self-supportive families have also become successful businesses. Countless small or medium-size businesses that have boosted the Italian economy are family enterprises, or started as such; the outstanding case history is the Benetton family.

There are hundreds of families in Italy who dream that their entrepreneurial ventures may one day take off the way the Benetton's did. Yet as Italian capitalism is maturing, and with fewer brothers, sisters, and children of business clans around or willing to pitch in, outside managers, financiers, and corporate raiders are more likely to get into the act. The decline of the large, close-knit business family is also likely to transform the country's economic landscape.

At the same time, it remains true that most of Italy's privately owned, large industrial companies have retained some features of a family enterprise. Outside the hefty state sector, which now is shrinking, Italy has many fewer corporate giants than do the other leading industrial nations; the largest is FIAT, and it is still in effect the family holding of the Agnellis of Turin. To the Agnellis, Benetton, De Benedettis, Ferruzzis, Gardinis, thousands of other names may be added. On Italy's business-financial scene, it's still largely all in the family.

There is, however, plenty of evidence that family bonds are loosening or even breaking apart. Good times seem less favorable to kinship solidarity than bad ones. Conflicts over inheritance have been very divisive for many families. Scores of ordinary Italian families with sons and daughters estranged from their parents, siblings locked in bitter lawsuits and no longer in speaking terms, and aged widows and widowers abandoned by their children or relegated to old-people's homes with perfunctory visits or telephone calls now and then do exist.[11] Marital and money conflicts bedeviled the descendants of Angelo Rizzoli, who had built a publishing and film empire; of Arnoldo Mondadori, founder of the nation's largest publishing house; and of Gaetano Marzotto, under whom the old family spinning mill at Valdagno northwest of Venice developed into one of Europe's largest textile combines. The Gucci family for years fought messily over control of the Gucci company, which annually sells hundreds of millions of dollars' worth of fine leathergoods throughout the world.

The Problems of an Aging Society

The Italian population not only is decreasing, it is also aging rapidly; life expectancy in Italy has climbed to 79 years for women and 72 for men. By many accounts, however, Italy is not facing up to the aging of its population. At the University of Rome, notwithstanding the rapid decline in birthrate, there are 42 full professors of pediatrics and just one in geriatrics. In all social classes, couples no longer accept so readily that an elderly widowed parent should come to live with them: *nonno* and *nonna*–grandpa and grandma–are now expected to stay in an apartment of their own. It is calculated that about one-quarter of old people in Italy live by themselves. This has caused a good deal of heartache.

In the absence of family-centered care, the state has begun to require the necessity to help the elderly and society is finally accepting that its elderly are no longer solely a family responsibility. In recent years shelters and recreational facilities for the elderly have been opened—a new departure for Italy. However, although public *case di riposo* do exist, they vary greatly in number and quality, depending on the town. In many northern towns there is a well-developed service for old people, including libraries, places for film viewing and general recreation. Unfortunately, private rest homes are out of reach for many people, for their cost is equivalent to a worker's monthly pay. The state of desperation of many elderly has caused a big increase in the suicide rate of people over age 65. To see how serious the problem is, you only have to watch what happens to the elderly during the summer months when many of them are abandoned by their children who leave for vacation. The chronic-disease wards of Italian hospitals fill up every summer with elderly patients whom their relatives park there for several weeks so they can enjoy their vacations.

Municipalities do offer many other kinds of aid and assistance. There are discounts for old people on buses, and at cinemas, and inexpensive lunches are provided. Some municipalities organize mini-vacations to the sea or mountains. These services are more common in the North; the further South one goes, the weaker the central organization and the more the family takes its place. Which solution is preferable is not for us to decide.

An interesting development for old people, mainly in large cities, is the establishment of the *Università della terza età* (The University of the Third Age). Anyone over forty can sign up for courses, whether they have educational qualifications or not. Courses are usually on subjects of local interest and are taught mostly by professors from local universities, who sometimes donate their time.

Whatever the actual effectiveness of the various services, the country is confronted with a new phenomenon which has social dimensions that cannot be easily solved by institutional services. Centuries of family organization make people reluctant to depend on anything less personal. The average Italian still believes that the best social worker is a relative. In general, there remains a deep-seated moral obligation of children to parents, and in this, as in many other situations, the Italian family and its traditions continues at the center of all social intercourse.

Notes

1. Luigi Barzini, *The Italians* (New York: Hamish Hamilton, 1964).

2. A. Gramsci, *Selections from the Prison Notebooks*, edited by Q. Hoare and G. Nowell-Smith (London: Lawrence and Wishart, 1971), pp. 52-120.

3. Paul Ginsborg, *Daniele Manin and the Venetian Revolution of 1848-49* (Cambridge: Cambridge University Press), pp. 371.

4. A. Pagden, "The Destruction of Trust and its Economic Consequences: The Case of 18th Century Naples," in D. Gambetta (ed.), *Trust* (Oxford: Basil Blackwell, 1988).

5. P. Villari, *Le lettere meridionali e altri scritti sulla questione sociale in Italia* (Naples: Guida, 1979; 1st edn. 1885).

6. See the entry "Famiglia," *Enciclopedia Cattolica*, vol. V, Roma, 1950, p. 994.

7. T. Goffi, *Morale familiare* (Brescia, 1962), 264.

8. "La DC per la nuova Costituzione," in *I congressi nazionali della Democrazia Cristiana* (Rome: Arti Grafiche Italiane, 1959).

9. A. Gribaudi, *Mondo operaio, mito operaio* (Turin: Einaudi, 1987).

10. Manlio Rossi-Doria, "Dopo i fatti di Battipaglia," in *Scritti sul Mezzogiorno* (Turin: Einaudi, 1984).

11. Paul Hofmann, *That Fine Italian Hand* (New York: Henry Holt and Co., 1990), p. 116.

XII

Women in a Changing Society

Is Home still the Place for Women?
In a 1954 article, C. Gini and E. Caranti observed that "the existence of a genuine difference of position of the man and woman in marriage and in social life" constituted a fundamental presupposition of the stability of the Italian family.[1] Since then this gap between the roles of men and women has been steadily disappearing. In its transition from a traditional agricultural to a modern industrial society, Italy has also witnessed a significant redefinition of the role of women. Women have made major strides towards fuller emancipation, and legal, professional and sexual equality. The political action of the women's movement, the changes in life-styles caused by economic changes as well as extensive legislative decrees have all favored the acknowledgement and affirmation of the social condition of women and the formal equalization of the sexes. Along with the quantitative growth of the number of women attending school there came a "historically" significant change in the labor supply, especially from the start of the 1970s. It was only at this time that significant changes began to appear, and there are reasons.

The latent *machismo* of a Latin society with Catholic traditions may help to explain these delays. But what is more curious is that Italian women themselves, whose social role in some other ways has always been so strong, did not show much interest in this kind of legal equality or in sharing a man's privileges'at least until recently. Women were little concerned with legal equality, but would rather use their "feminine charms" to win their way. Since then, times have changed; but even today the Italian woman prizes femininity above feminism.

It is also relevant to point out that, socially, women in Italy have rarely been segregated or treated as inferiors. The Italian woman regards herself, and was regarded, as the equal of man—equal, but different. Given an opportunity to play the same role as a man, she often shied away in fear of losing her femininity, and men cheered her for it. Cliché or not, a woman has viewed herself in relation to the family—where her role has been powerful, in every age and in every social class—and to individual men, rather than to other women or the community as a whole. So it is not surprising that the modern "Women's Lib" movement in its more militant form has never been more than marginal in Italy, and usually unpopular. However in the past dozen years a milder and different kind of feminism has taken root among the new generation. Italian girls today expect equality of rights and career prospects, equal personal freedom (sexual and other), and equality in marriage: they no longer expect their husband to make all of the decisions and do none of the chores. They resent, and fight against, *machismo*. But they do not want to become the same as men, and they certainly do not hate or shun men, like some militants. In Italy, men and women alike have a fear and contempt for the bossy, masculine type of woman, and Italian women who emerge as leaders are usually exquisitely feminine people, such as Nilde Jotti, president of the Chamber of Deputies for many years.

Italian women today are emerging from a transitional phase. From the old dependence on a man's world they are moving towards real emancipation. However, the road to full emancipation has been tortuous for the average woman, and differences do remain. Because one can speak more of urbanization than of actual industrialization–given a real exodus from the land to the urban areas, and, a peculiar mix of development and underdevelopment, of tradition and modernity, of economic and geographic dualism–the redefinition brought about by the transition has peculiarities that are typical Italian. The process of cultural unification which has taken place, due largely to the spread of the national education system, the diffusion of mass media and the intense internal and international migrations has reduced differences in behavioral patterns but not eliminated them.

Until the end of the 50s, the role of women in Italian society was generally defined in terms of the institution of the family. Urban women were primarily caretakers of the house and of the home and held a subordinate position to men. The situation was different in the agrarian society which had a more complex family structure. In the South and in the rural and semi-rural areas of the North and the Center, where the extended family was the prevailing feature of the social structure, there wasn't a sharp division between the sphere of production and that of domestic life; women held a very active role in productive activity. As in other countries with a pre-industrialized society, the wife had considerable power due to her productive role in the family economy. In pre-industrial society, familial and work activities overlapped and the family formed the basic economic unit and it was difficult to characterize family structure and domains; families were patriarchal as much as matriarchal. This was the dominant structure in Italy until the end of the 1950s, when Italy ceased to be an agricultural society. "The separation of home and work brought an end to the family economy, and an end to the prevailing family bonds."[2] No longer did the entire family work together, but instead the husband left home early in the morning to go to the factory or office and returned late in the evening. The family ceased to be the basic unit of economic production and social participation. The wife's former productive role in the family economy changed to a subordinate one. Even though she had control over all household duties, she became economically dependent on her husband's earnings; she no longer worked to produce.]

The transition to a modern industrial society brought about a more sharply defined division of labor between the sexes. In Italy, because of contradictions particularly acute–in which the process of industrialization was rapid, uneven and ridden with social conflicts–male roles were more strongly defined in terms of the occupational system and female roles in terms of the family system.

[The subordinate role of woman as homemaker, mother, wife was regulated by laws and encouraged by the Church,]against the position of democratic and liberal view of some prominent intellectuals, civic and political leaders.[3] Mussolini had certainly circumscribed the position of women. Fascism had actively discriminated against women in the matter of right to work by limiting the access to jobs and careers and by mandating separate pay ranges according to sex.[4] Fascism succeeded in promoting sex-role stereotypes that permeated popular mores and behavior, education, and culture in general. In everyday life, for the majority of Italian women–particularly for lower-middle-class women–this meant confinement to menial household chores, made still more deadly by general economic hardship. Under Fascism, the state sought to organize the subordination of women around their central role of devoted spouse and exemplary mother. Women were to be guardians of the hearth and subject to the legitimate authority of the husband; they were regarded as mothers whose duty it was to produce soldiers and workers for the State. The Duce went as far as to state that "War is to man what motherhood is to woman."[5] In those years, the Church was also very direct in forging the social functions of people, especially women. In a 1931 encyclical, "Casti connubi," in unison with the Fascist policy, Pope Pius XI continued to reinforce the traditional role of women as primarily loving wives and caring mothers. The position of the Church did not change with the fall of Fascism and the end of Monarchy. In 1946, Pope Pius XII confirmed the previous position of the Church:

> Every woman is destined to be a mother... For true women, all life's problems are understood in terms of the family... Equality with men, outside the home where she is queen, subjects the woman to the same burdens the man has. The woman who goes to work outside the home...dazzled by the tinsel of a counterfeit luxury, becomes greedy for unworthy pleasure.[6]

The Church's position began to change with the election of pope Giovanni Roncalli. In 1960 John XXIII, declared that women's lives pivoted on "two centers, two nuclei; those of the family and of work." He implied that in a post-masculine society women had to be given the opportunity to harmonize family and work lives.

Notwithstanding the social changes and the "economic boom" of the early 1960s, women did not enter the work force en masse; indeed, the number actually went down. The 6,500,000 women at work in 1959 declined to 5,110,000 by 1972–a unique development in Western nations, where the numbers of women in the work force had been mounting. There are several reasons why industrial employment for women remained relatively low, compared to other well-advanced European countries:

    1. in Italy there has never been a condition of full employment for men searching for a job and, in Italian society, male unemployment is considered a greater evil than female unemployment;

    2. wage differentials between men and women are less marked in Italy than in other Western countries, and employers have therefore little incentive to hire women as their work is not significantly cheaper;

    3. labor legislation for the protection of women workers during pregnancy and in the period following each childbirth is very progressive in Italy, but this very fact produces serious obstacles to the employment of married women. Employers tend to avoid hiring workers who are likely to be absent from work for prolonged periods of time and who show a high rate of absenteeism yet cannot be fired due to the legal protection accorded to motherhood.[7]

Another factor no less important is the fact that the relocation of a considerable part of the population from the backward regions of the south to the industrialized regions of the north radically changed the family's needs, and often profoundly weakened kinship alliances. Consequently, the loss of the traditional functions of care and support supplied by kinship relations was not accompanied by the development of new measures of social policy on behalf of the family and dependent members (the elderly and children). Social ethics had great difficulty in keeping pace with the evolution of customs and ways of living, and the inertia of public policy was justified according to the assumption that urbanized families were able to rely on traditional solidarity to carry out a plurality of tasks they had to perform in the new residential context.

The lack of public facilities for child care such as kindergartens and nursery schools, the fact that full-time schooling is practically non-existent and the demise of the extended family make it extremely difficult for many mothers to have a full-time employment.

However, the official data do not tell the whole story about female employment. Because of the peculiar industrial development and the widespread system of "black labor"—of work not officially registered as such and for which employers evade paying for social security and medical care, and other kinds of benefits—there is a much higher percentage of working women than is indicated by statistics.

In the early years of the new industrial Italy, not only were families restructured—e.g., the extended family came to an end—but the roles of their members were redefined. The role of the husband and father was to be the wage earner while the wife's responsibility involved the "preservation of familial unity in terms of love, personal happiness, and domestic felicity."[8] The wife became the proud *casalinga*, housewife.

For many women, especially those who moved North from the South or to the urban centers from the countryside, the image of the woman in a comfortable and secure setting meant progress in a real positive sense. For the husband, too, to be able to keep a wife at home who was the real "queen" of the house meant real success. To be able to return for vacation to the South or to the rural areas of origin and be able to boast about a "well-kept" wife, meant a profound social improvement for the new urban man. The transfer to the cities gave women greater freedom from traditional family hierarchies and a greater autonomy in a whole number of ways, too. This was especially true for younger women in the North who came from the agrarian society where the extended family was a common structure. However, the new idealized confinement not only intensified their isolation but also acted to enclose them in a purely private dimension and to remove them even more than previously from the political and public life of the nation. The nuclear family, which was seen as the normative family form in modern industrial society, was not the means toward self-realization that women had hoped for. Instead, the family fettered women, trapping them in the private sphere of the household and in the role of housewife.

In the urban society, the *casalinga* was subordinated to man economically and legally. Until the mid-1970s, in Italian civil law husband was defined as the "head of the household." That implied that women had a secondary role in every aspect of Italian society. For instance, before 1969, adultery by women was a crime, with stiffer penalties than rape. The psychology behind this was based on the idea that a man "owned" his wife. Rape was temporary possession of the female body, while adultery was theft not only of the body but also of allegiance, of the whole woman, love, "soul," body, honor and pride. As recently as November 1961, the Constitutional Court defended Article 559 of the penal code which stated that adultery of the woman could be punished with a prison sentence, whereas that of a man was not a criminal offense. The court maintained that this did not contravene the sex equality article of the

Constitution because a woman's adultery is an act of 'different and greater entity' than that of man. The Court changed its mind only in December 1968.

Today, however, the role of women in Italian society and their legal function has changed profoundly. What is also important is that women's attitudes towards men in Italy have been changing even more quickly. Now they demand fulfillment, not just from the simple fact that they exist, but from within the social structure. They demand satisfaction from men; they have discovered eroticism and therefore aspire also to a share of that pleasure.

Women's Movement

The Italian political tradition did not offer much to women. In the marketplace of ideologies there was a version of Catholicism which did offer a role to women, but a subordinate one, that of homemaker and of mother. There was a version of Marxism, which, in spite of the enrichments brought about by thinkers such as Antonio Labriola and Antonio Gramsci was still concerned essentially with the forging of alliances between social classes as organized as specific political parties, not with improving the lot of women.

In the ambience of democratic politics of the immediate post-war Italy, women were not offered simple freedom but a hard choice. Each of the two dominant postwar parties bore a powerful ideology with regard to women, the ideology of Catholicism on the one hand and the ideology of Marxism on the other, both deeply affected by attachment to the traditional Italian gender relations of the countryside. On the one hand, there was an implicit message that the business of Communist women was to work with women, that is, to do "women's work," on the other that Catholic women were to remain in the traditional family structure. Therefore, even for the millions of party members, Communism was an alternative Italy within Italy. The party offered nothing but the abstract utopian hope that, one day, all Italy would be Communist and thus all women equal to each other.

As with so many other things, the place and role of women in society started to change with the student movement which began in Fall 1967. This movement was, among other things, the expression of a social conflict which could not be defined in terms of class, but it was also a movement which at one and at the same time expressed a critique of authority and of accepted forms of organization and behavior while reproducing–within itself–the subordination of women.[9] Thus those radical women who were attracted to the politics of the students' movement perceived fairly early on that there was a marked contradiction between the goals of the movement in general and its patriarchal form of organization. Even though in the first several months women did not play a strong role, (indeed, they experienced considerable ambivalence in their attitude towards the movement), more young women took part in politics than any time since 1945. Although most of them remained subordinate within the movement, unable to express their own needs and desires, there were strong positive elements of new political commitment and an extraordinarily intense sociality. These were important years of fermentation which culminated in the formation of several women's groups which by 1975 constituted a strong national women's movement, a movement that was mostly political rather than intellectual.

While some of the impetus for the women's movement in Italy came from the students protests of the late 60s, it was mainly the outgrowth of small feminist groups which were formed by mostly middle-class women at the beginning of the 1970s in major urban centers. Though certainly a consequence of the many economic, social, and cultural changes that had been transforming Italy, during the seventies the movement took on a life of its own. It became an important interlocutor of political parties, trade unions, and social movements. In the first stage, the movement found its propulsion force mainly in the American women's movement, with its emphasis on separatism and gender consciousness-raising. However, the impact of inflation and the stagnation of economy, due especially to the oil crisis, cannot be underestimated either. Working-class women especially found it increasingly difficult to balance family budgets. Their own potential for contributing to their families' resources through paid work was constantly menaced by the economic crisis. Political action to meet specific social needs became their initial primary demand.

Contrary to the American counterpart movement which was for the most part elitist and engaged in having token women appointed in top visible positions, the Italian movement attracted most of its adherents from the middle and lower classes and worked to develop a collective consciousness. Italian women became involved in social struggles on an unprecedented scale. The battles for housing, for improved services in the neighborhoods among others, saw women emerge from the private sphere and take a leading role in collective action. By this we do not mean in any way that they were not interested in gender issues. They were certainly interested in dealing with their experience in a men's world (patriarchal, fraternal, etc.) that was hostile to them. They did pool together their experience to analyze their own sexuality and women's oppression by men and to formulate demands which were less for parity than for women's rights in an autonomous sphere of their own. They wanted a loose and non-authoritarian form of organization of all form of institutions. However, for the most part, women worked with man in having pieces of legislature that affected the life of women in the private sphere and in the social and global environment.

Different groups in the Italian women's movement raised different demands and issues. *Lotta Femminista* ("Women's Struggle") raised the slogan of "wages for housework;" the issue, which touched all classes, was meant to equalize the household environment, provide healthier context for decisions on procreation and sexuality and improve relationships between men and women, which the group attributed to women's economic dependence on men. The *UDI, Unione delle Donne Italiane*, the traditional movement of Communist women, put more emphasis on the intervention of the state to relieve women's oppression, while *Rivolta Femminile* denounced marriage and the family as the site of male domination. One of the most influential groups was the *MLD*, the *Movimento della Liberazione delle Donne Italiane* (Movement for the Liberalization of Italian Women). *MLD* combined demands for equality–the elimination of gender discrimination in the schools, of sexual discrimination at work, etc.–with those which would increase women's autonomy–the right to control their own bodies through free contraception and the liberalization of abortion. In 1975 the *MLD*, with the support of the small Radical Party organized the collection of signatures for a referendum on the abortion question. Five hundred thousand signatures were needed; 800,000 were collected. Women's mobilization on this issue was able to transform it from an important civil-rights question into a wide-ranging discussion on women's position in Italian society. The concept of adultery as a criminal offense was abolished, legal separation could be obtained when the marriage had broken down and no longer, as used to be the case, only when one of the two parties was "guilty." Children born out of wedlock were given the same rights as "legitimate" children. Moreover, it also dealt in a more egalitarian manner with economic and patrimonial relationships inside the marriage bond. In 1977 a law was passed against sexual discrimination. In 1978, against strong *D.C.* opposition, a law legalizing abortion, was passed by the Italian Parliament and the attempt to reverse it with another referendum was clearly defeated with a majority of 67.9 per cent.

Pressures from the women's movement were also a determinant in bringing women legally on a par with men. In 1971, women obtained equal rights in the matter of acting as guardian in the case of separation or divorce. In Spring 1975, a long-awaited reform of the family law was approved. The most important principle of the new law was that which established parity between the two partners in marriage. Previous insistence on the supremacy of the male head of household, and of the right of the husband to control his wife's behavior and activity, was abandoned definitively. The new laws also stipulated that the housewife share equally in family property, thus acknowledging the contribution represented by the domestic work. In 1977, a law was passed giving them equality at work, including equality of pay, and retirement rights at sixty. Also a wife now has personal ownership of any property she has brought to the marriage, while those working in the civil service can get a pension after fifteen years if they have one child.

Working life has been regulated by sweeping pieces of legislation. Legislation hinged on the idea that women's basic rights–the right to work and have economic independence–should not be infringed because of childbearing. Starting in the 1960s the Italian parliament responded to the protection of motherhood with very progressive laws. Maternity leave lasts five months (two before giving birth and three after) at 100 per cent salary for employees and 80 per cent for self-employed and professionals; a further six months unpaid leave is available, with the right to return to the same job afterwards. The Constitutional Court has issued a ruling that in the absence of the mother, due to death, disease, or other serious cause, the father may make use of the leave after childbirth, thereby guaranteeing child care. The laws also provide for optional leaves in the event that the child is sick or handicapped.

The concept of the "social value of motherhood" also fueled a drive for kindergartens and day-care centers. In 1968, kindergartens (for children age three to six) came to be part of the educational system in many towns and cities; the system has expanded remarkably over the past years, in spite of much criticism of the schedules, which often do not meet working women's needs.

To accommodate the new role of men and women in the family, the pension system has also been changed so that a pension plan can be transferred not just from a husband to his widow but from a wife to her widower. The most important instrument of change was Bill 903 of 1977 which eliminated all discrimination in hiring practices, promotions, salaries, and social security.

The first major demonstration of the women's movement, some 20,000 strong, took place in Rome on 6 December 1975. Throughout the following years the women's movement developed rapidly. Women had become the center of political controversy. Another good indication of changes is provided by the 1976 general elections, for here, for the first time, every political party felt the need, in its campaign, to address itself specifically to the female electorate, to include many women in its lists of candidates to Parliament; and, finally, to manage to have them elected with an unprecedented number of votes. Women had become social actors and, probably, a social force in their own right.

There were also some structural preconditions behind the women's movement such as an increase in female education which would make women more competitive with men in a number of occupations and a decrease in the birth-rate which meant that women were anchored to domestic chores for a shorter period of time.[10]

As the women's movement gained momentum, the two leading parties increasingly cultivated women's support. Although the *P.C.I.* had always had a smaller proportion of women members than the *D.C.*, it certainly did more to promote the advancement of the women in their party than did the *D.C.* In the Chamber of Deputies that was elected in 1983 19.9 per cent of *P.C.I.* deputies were women (38 out of 198) against 2.6 per cent for the *D.C.* (6 out of 255) and 1.4 per cent (1 out of 73) for the *P.S.I.* The total of women corresponded to 7.9 per cent of all deputies'more than twice those in the British House of Commons or the American Congress. The highest office in Italian politics ever held by a woman was held by Nilde Jotti, a communist leader, when she became President of the Chamber of Deputies in 1979 and held the position until 1992.

About twenty-five years or so have elapsed since the birth of the new feminism in Italy. There is no doubt that it has scored some remarkable successes both in the domain of ideas and in the institutional field. Nevertheless, it too, is in crisis. On the one hand modern feminism criticizes institutions (parties, government, religious institutions, etc.), yet at the same time it accepts the fact that the legal changes which are necessary require the intervention of these institutions.

The women's movement of today has come to the understanding that it needs the cooperation of men on the political level to create enough mass support for change, to bring women's issues from the fringe to the forefront. This generation of young women generally welcomes men into the movement. Feminists do not speak anymore in terms of "us" vs. "them" but of cooperation and of natural and social relationships. They recognize that men are basic to women's life as women are basic to men's, and young women have been able to create a discussion about men's stake in the women's movement and reasons for which they should contribute to social and political change. Italian men have understood that the solution of women's issues directly benefit men too.

Moreover, the number of grassroots groups has grown larger. Especially women's networks in various sectors of professional life. The same is true of women's cultural centers, resources and support centers, which have opened in various larger and middle-size towns, with the purpose of providing counselling on matters of sexual violence, battering, harassment, etc. or advising women on issues of professional and work discrimination.

Women's participation in political life has had a determining effect on the Italian democracy. Since they were given the right to vote in 1946, women have always participated in elections in numbers that exceed 80 per cent. Nevertheless, there are still not enough women holding public office. In the administrative elections in 1990, 8.5 per cent of the candidates elected were women; in the political elections in 1992, the figure rose to 10.2 per cent.

Although these figures appear very low, they are not when viewed in comparison to other countries.

It is in the participation in social life through volunteer associations that the number of women becomes predominant. Women volunteers are not rejecting traditional values but trying to use them to change society and the condition of women from outside the political system.

Women's biggest social advancement has been registered in education. In 1945 Italy was third from the bottom in the ranking of European countries in the number of illiterates, and women represented the highest percentage of those illiterates. Today more women receive high school diplomas than men, and there are as many women as men in the universities, even if the percentages vary from department to department, with the highest concentration of women in the humanities. This has had a positive impact on the work market.

Code of Honor

A radical change in achieving equality with men is the way women are treated in cases dealing with sexual issues.

Today police investigators and magistrates are showing greater respect for victims of sexual violence than they did only a few years ago, even though rapists often still receive lenient sentences, which may be even further reduced on appeal. In the past a man facing assault charges got away scot-free if his victim was unwed and he then married her in what was known as a "reparative marriage." A legal reform in 1981 abolished that semi-barbarous institution. Another archaic usage –elopement to force reluctant parents to give their consent to an undesired marriage–still survives in the Deep South.

What survives too, mainly in the South, is violence caused by outrage over real or presumed sexual looseness: fathers or brothers chastising the seducers of girls, husbands killing their wayward wives and their lovers, betrayed wives taking revenge on their rivals. Italian courts have long conceded extenuating circumstances to perpetrators of violence presumed to have acted to defend their own or their family's reputation. (The judicial recognition of the "crime of Honor" lingers on.)

Between 1979 and 1980, the criminal code dealing with rape, sexual violence, extenuating circumstances by reasons of "honor" came under scrutiny. An all encompassing and radical reform bill was introduced in Parliament thanks to the action promoted by women groups. The cases of the extenuating circumstances on account of "honor" were repealed in 1981 and so, too, "crime of passion" vanished from the criminal code.

As late as the 1960s, the old codes of this Catholic society remained in force; all evidence still suggested that Italian unmarried girls as a whole, especially in the South and in the provinces, were still among the most virginal in Europe. Virginity in unmarried women is still highly prized by many Italians despite the changes in sexual mores. When a nationwide sample of 1,000 people of both sexes was polled in 1987, 57.1 percent were found to attribute prime importance to female virginity before marriage. Predictably, the strongest response against premarital sex for women came from the South.

However, following the lead of the Nordic countries, sexual freedom finally began to spread. Parents became readier to allow their daughters to go out with boys; young people got more leisure and money for going off together. At the beginning, the new freedom was welcomed with mixed feelings: on one hand they welcomed the growing climate of frankness between the sexes, on the other, they felt uncomfortable without any form of convention.

Nevertheless, in the 70s there was a major shift in values due to several factors: foreign influence, the freeing of legal controls of contraception, the steady decline in the role of the Church. The majority of teenagers are now promiscuous for a while. Sex in this phase is rarely linked with love; it is simply a means of communication and self-discovery. For most teenagers, virginity is no longer considered a virtue. It should be pointed out that, once again, the liberalization is far less evident in small towns or rural areas than in large urban centers. Some social classes, too, remain more strict than others. Working-class families tend to retain a more stringent sense of morality, a tighter watch over their daughters, than the middle classes. But overall, the fathers cannot expect to bring to the altar a virgin daughter, and the groom, after having slept with so many girls, cannot expect to marry a virgin girl.

Until the early 60s birth-control was almost as taboo in public discussion as during the Fascist period. Hypocritically, on the pretext that they limited syphilis, male condoms had always been freely on sale in drugstores. Abortion was legal only when the mother's life was in danger, and most doctors interpreted this with a religious literalness. Consequently, death from clumsy self-abortion ran into several thousands per year. Certainly, rich and informed women would avoid these problems by visits to private doctors in Switzerland or England. But millions of working wives, faced with the horrors of raising a large family under Italian housing conditions, came to regard sex and their husband's desires with panic. Reform had been blocked mainly by Catholic opinion, but the 1960s saw a steady change of heart among fervent Catholics, including the clergy. The campaign of a few pioneers forced a breach in the curtain of social prejudice and brought the whole issue into the open. The prejudices waned first in the middle classes, while working-class wives remained reticent far longer. It seems there was a political element here, since official Communist policy for many years was to oppose birth control as a capitalist trick to reduce the numbers of the proletariat. But since the early '70s the *P.C.I.* swung in favor of contraception, as of abortion, and this paved the way for a steady change in working-class attitudes.

As with birth-control, the Government for years was afraid of legalizing abortion for various political reasons. Not only was the opposition from the Church and traditional Catholics far stronger in this case, but there was a clear hostile majority among the pro-Government parties in Parliament. The law gives women, married or single, the right to claim an abortion within the first 12 weeks of pregnancy; after this, termination can take place only if there is medical evidence that there is grave risk to the health of mother or child, verified by two specialists. There are some other restrictions: minors (under eighteen) must obtain parental consent; a woman must first be interviewed by a psychiatrist to establish that the abortion is desirable. Abortion is not free; it is covered within the social security which reimburse a percentage of the cost. So today, very few women are going abroad or resorting to the back-street hacks; the situation is certainly helped by the continuing spread of contraception. However, problems do exist, due partly to a shortage of hospital facilities and especially to the fact that many doctors, nurses and hospital directors are refusing to cooperate. Practicing Catholics have the right to invoke a conscience clause.

The belated legalization of contraception, and then of abortion, has been a major factor behind women's great leap forward in the past decades. Psychologically and practically, it has liberated them from so much. It lies at the basis of their new pre-marital sexual freedom, and inside marriage it has helped them to order their lives as they would wish. But these advances are still contested by traditional Catholics.

Despite the new sexual freedom and equality, traces of the old Latin mentality persist, at least among the over-thirty crowd. Even today, a woman must not be too brash or assertive, she must use guile to achieve her sexual ends, or she will not be found attractive, and what she treasures above all is male appreciation of her femininity. This she is given abundantly. The Italian male's demonstrative pleasure in female company gives to relations between the sexes a certain romantic tenderness and intimacy not always equalled in countries with an older tradition of emancipation. In spite of his egotism, and partly to flatter his own vanity and sexual power, the Italian man is more sensitively concerned than most males to see that his woman, too, is fulfilled.

All these changes have also had an impact on the political behavior of women. Education and work opportunities have freed many women from the pervasive electoral influence of the pulpit. This is especially notable in the South and in the Northeast, traditionally Catholic regions where the *D.C.* enjoyed until very recent years its most impressive bedrock strength. In fact, in these regions, electoral shifts away from the Christian Democrats could not have occurred, or would not have been as strong, were it not for some radical changes in the voting patterns of women.

Women in the Work Force

As a result of the progress women made, there has been an increased complexity of women's roles in society and their relation to it. Because her role is not defined exclusively or mostly by family but instead by work, it is important to see women in the job market.

Their entry into the world of work occurred at a rate which was much lower than that of other Western countries. Although women were given the chance to obtain the same education as a male, as we have seen, there are many reasons why in Italy women have not been competitive with men in the labor market.

The fact that Italian legislation does protect the institution of motherhood to a very high degree, makes young married women less attractive in the job market. The Italians have made it a criminal offense for a woman to work during the two months before the birth of a child or in the three months after, and there is no reason for women to work during this time because by law they are entitled to full pay. Afterwards, they are entitled to flexible working hours to facilitate their nursing responsibilities and needs. Although maternity leave plans do vary from company to company and from the public to the private sector, Italy is the most progressive country in the world when it comes to statutory rights to work-leave for birth and marriage.

However, the issue is much more complex. Female employment decreased by 1.1 million units between 1959 and 1967 as women were replaced by young male migrant workers from the South. This did not take place through the deliberate firing of women workers, but by taking advantage of their high turnover in the labor market (due mainly to pregnancy and child-rearing). Female labor was eliminated from agriculture because of the general shrinkage of employment in that field due to the sudden wide use of machinery. It was edged out from industry because of the competition from migrant male labor. The proletarianization of the rural labor force thus followed the pattern of employment in industry: a preponderance of male labor. Furthermore, the crisis in the textile industry, a traditionally large employer of female labor, accelerated this tendency. The rise in the standard of living facilitated their being kept out of the labor market. The wages earned by male workers increased and this maintained and reinforced the division of labor between male breadwinner and female homemaker. It should be added that Italy was the only industrialized country in Europe to exhibit the dual feature of growing industrialization and a decrease in female employment. One could speculate as to the political reasons behind the inadequate support for women in the work force. Could it be that the government feared that rapid entry of female labor into production would further disrupt the foundation of the family (already profoundly modified by industrialization and emigration) thus generating social pressure difficult to control? In other European countries female employment was on the increase throughout this period thanks to the growing introduction of part-time labor; but part-time labor was resisted by the Italian trade-union movement.

When the "miracle" was over, women began to return to the labor force, but they tended, on the whole, to take jobs in the so-called 'hidden economy' of casual labor and small family firms. Women workers can stay at home and look after their children, and at the same time contribute to the family income. But there are many factors which have influenced the entrance of women in the job market. It seems that women between the ages of forty-seven and fifty-seven (born between 1936 and 1946) who had their adolescence during the emergence of the culture of consumption and the availability of washing machines, refrigerators, cars and televisions, moved into the labor force in large numbers in the mid-seventies, after they had raised their children.[11] Women now aged about thirty-five to forty-five (born 1947-57), who experienced the political turmoil and changes of the late sixties and early seventies and faced gender debate and changes (including the legalization of abortion and contraception) at the onset of adulthood, while dealing with the consequences of their first adult choices—marriage, childbearing, and holding or giving up a job—were the first to enter the labor force in great numbers and to remain in it after marrying and having children. Women in the youngest group (born between 1962-68), who entered adulthood in the middle eighties, seem to have a different social identification than older women because they have greater equality with men and have benefitted from the gains that the preceding generations obtained. However, these women no longer have a sense of collective identification and goals as previous generations had. Thus, older feminists complain that communication with those under thirty is difficult or non-existent.

A survey taken in the mid 1980s showed that 22.5 per cent of Italian women had full time jobs, 5.8 per cent had casual employment and 71.8 per cent did not work. However, it is difficult to have exact figures in this area because many Italian women carry on industrial production in their living rooms ranging from knitting and sewing clothes to being mechanics and making electronic components. It is estimated that women make up 70 per cent of the unofficial labor market.

If we examine women's employment in various categories of the service sector we find that, without exception, they tend to be concentrated in the lower-paid jobs, although there has been a marked improvement in the last decade. The increase of women's entrance in the civil service occupations occurred concurrently with a lowering in the prestige in such occupations. It has been found that women, unlike men, are attracted to civil service jobs not because of status but because of the security of tenure of work and welfare benefits as well as the formal criterion of "equality of opportunity." Women's presence in the labor force increased steadily from the mid-seventies onward, from 27.3 per cent in 1972 to 35.7 per cent in 1986. Their activity rate (the proportion of women in the labor force measured against all women) went from 21.3 per cent in 1972 to 28.9 per cent in 1986. And their specific occupation rate (the proportion of those holding a job measured against all women of working age) went from 31 per cent in 1972 to 38 per cent in 1986. More than 80 per cent of the increase in the number of workers, both male and female, in the period is thought to be due to the increase in women's labor force participation. Women make up 66 per cent of the education work force: 79.4 per cent of elementary school teachers, 63.7 per cent of middle-school teachers, 49 per cent of high-school and 21 per cent of university professors are women. The health profession also has a strong presence of women; 22 per cent of doctors and over 65 per cent of nurses are women.

Unquestionably, women now in their mid-twenties entering the job market experience a greater equality than their mothers, legally and in daily practices and behavior, although these experiences vary according to social contexts. They enter the job market with the same expectations as males; they want to work throughout their adult lives without leaving their jobs to get married or have children. In addition, the mothers of these young women support their daughters' plans to find a job and keep it throughout the years of raising a family. Work for women is increasingly viewed as valuable for reasons of personal autonomy, as family insurance in a time of insecure employment, and as personal insurance, perhaps against the hazard of divorce.

The less a job offers them rewards, the more likely it is that young women will perceive marriage and motherhood as the only place to find a sense of self-worth. Certainly, women's lifestyle and desire depend also on the level of education achieved and the desire to prove themselves. Indeed, education was a key factor in changing the role of women in society. Studies have shown that a woman's education is consistently and strongly related to gender-role attitudes.[12] Formal education is a means of social mobility and the right to an equal education has made women more competitive with men. Education has empowered the process of change in women's roles in Italy, but this process has met with definite constraints. Women must confront the problem of the outside labor market while trying to assure that the family organization functions adequately.

The New Complex Role of Women

Younger women have more education, enjoy equal social status to men and full emancipation. At the same time, women's life styles and life strategies have become explicitly more diversified, as resources and options have opened up. Childlessness, celibacy, divorce, and remarriage increasingly are legitimate options. At the same time, the social competence women show (and are expected to have) in dealing with social institutions on behalf of themselves and their families is significantly changing the public/private boundaries, creating new resources for social relations and self-definitions and perceptions. It should be clear that class differences matter a great deal in the analysis of women's changing roles in Italy.[13]

Many young women still think that marrying someone they love and are loved by, and having one or two children is the most valuable option they can choose. More often this type is found where there is no rooted tradition of women's work. An increasing number of young women however, do not focus on marriage and motherhood as an important goal in their near future. Rather, they see having a family as a potential burden for their career and as a hindrance to having a "full life," in terms of interests and social relations. Although they do not reject the possibility of a family, they put it off into a still indefinite future.

Moreover, the decline of the extended family and the lack of support from grandparents to rear children has put an additional burden on women. The growth of the Welfare State did not compensate for the service that the extended family was providing. "The services of the Welfare State are available only if there is an individual who is prepared to engage in the necessary bureaucratic practices needed to obtain these services." (Sassoon, 103) This job falls in the laps of the women—who must also compensate where public services fail. Moreover, the extension of the consumer society and the constant and dramatic decrease in the self-sufficiency of the household (compare a peasant family with an urban family which must purchase virtually everything it needs) adds on another task for women: the purchase of private services. Regardless of their occupation, employed women spent on average 2 1/2 to 3 hours more per day on housework than employed men.

By entering the male working world, women gained freedom of movement in society; but they also brought to their lives a burden: the splitting of their roles and identity. Many young wives have found it a great strain, both physically and psychologically, to combine a career with running a home, especially in the North where the tempo is so fast and standards so exacting: office hours are long, bosses are demanding, and a husband will expect everything just perfect when he wants to entertain. By entering professions or jobs–teaching, caring services, etc.–that somehow required the same behavior and values of the activities performed at home, the internal conflict is lessened but they still need to readjust and redefine their role and the roles of other family members. Nevertheless, what is appropriate for a woman is less and less dictated by tradition and more and more by the career and highly educated woman.

To sum up, women work before they have children, then they abandon their work in order to look after their children, then they often return to work, when they must function as the agents of the Welfare State within the family, as the agents of the consumption sector of the economy within the family (purchaser of private services), and they must also compensate for the deficiencies of the Welfare State. Furthermore, they must also fulfil their natural role of procreators and traditional role of homemakers. They are citizens of two worlds: they have full-time responsibilities in both, family and work. Not only do they assume two roles, they also belong to two complex social systems that are interrelated, yet separate; and they have full-time responsibilities in each. Working women generally have a different experience from working men, because the latter do not have full responsibility for the everyday maintenance of the family and, therefore, are not penalized by society for their reduced participation in it. As Sassoon indicated, compared to women's life, the life of the man is a rather simple one: "work, leisure and sleep."(104)

In the process of female emancipation, married women have found it especially difficult also because the man had found the adjustment hardest because of his *machismo*. Traditionally, in this Latin society, women have exerted their greatest power within the family or in relation to one man, or to individual men, rather than to the community. Pleasing a man had the reward of remaining queen of the house. For Italian men, notoriously egotists, have exploited their advantage both emotionally and in practical ways, down to refusing to help with the chores because it is thought unmanly.

This has been the general pattern, but in the past twenty years Italian women, mainly younger ones with a college education, have rebelled against it. These are the generations influenced by British and American societies via the media. Today, if her man behaves with thoughtlessly arrogant *machismo*, a woman will simply walk out on him. She expects the same degree of sexual freedom as a man; and, conversely, the same degree of fidelity from a man. Inside marriage, she demands equality of decision-making, and equal control over shared finances; and she insists that her own leisure interests, her own cultural or other needs, be taken as seriously as her husband's. Younger men generally adapt easily because the egalitarian experience of their student days is carried on into marriage.

Notes

1. C. Gini and E. Caranti, "The family in Italy," *Marriage and Family Living*, 1954, p. 354.

2. E. Lupri (ed.), *The Changing Position of Women and Society: A Cross-National Comparison* (The Netherlands: Leiden-E. J. Brill, 1983), p. 5.

3. Already during the Risorgimento, in the pursuit of a just unification of the country, Giuseppe Mazzini was proclaiming the parity of women: "Cancel in your minds every idea of superiority over women. You have none whatsoever." D. Meyer, *Sex and Power'The Rise of Women in America, Russia, Sweden and Italy* (Connecticut: Wesleyan University Press, 1987) 141.

4. The Fascist legacy in matters of pay differential between men and women ranged in 1945 between 30 and 50 per cent in the manufacturing as well as in services. In the textile industry, where women made up 75 per cent of the workforce, they were paid from 20 to 40 per cent less than men for the same work.

5.As reported in M. Clark, *Modern Italy 1871-1982* (New York: Longman, 1984), 276.

6. G. Ascoli, "L'UDI tra emancipazione e liberazione (1943-1964)," in *Problemi del Socialismo,* Oct.-Dec. 1976, p. 119.

7. A. Cavalli, "The Changing Role of the Women : The Case of Italy," in E. Lupri, ed., *The Changing Position of Women in Family and Society* (The Netherlands: Brill-Laiden, 1983), 183.

8. E. Lupri, ed., *The Changing Position of Women and Society: A Cross-National Comparison*, p. 4.

9. G. Filippini, "Movimenti femminili, femminismo," in *Istituto Gramsci, La crisi della società italiana e gli orientamenti delle nuove generazioni* (Rome: Edizioni Riuniti, 1978), 110.

10. F. Alberoni, "Movimenti e istituzioni nell'Italia tra il 1960 e il 1971," in Luigi Graziano and Sidney Tarrow (Eds.) *La crisi Italiana* (Turin: Einaudi, 1979), vol I, p. 263.

11. In a very informative study, Chiara Saraceno gives persuasive evidence on women's shift in working pattern in the last twenty years: "Changes in Life-Course Patterns and Behavior of Three Cohorts of Italian Women," *Signs: Journal of Women in Culture and Society*, 1991, vol. 16, pp. 502-521.

12. K. J. Diecplt and A. C. Acock, "The Long-Term Effects of Family Structure on Gender-Role Attitudes," *Journal of Marriage and the Family*, 50 (August 1988) 711.

13. See Alessandro Cavalli, pp. 186-189.

XIII

A More Open Society

A New Affluence

Overall, during the last fifty years Italy has become more industrial, more educated, more urban and more secular. All of these changes have struck at the very heart and soul of the country. There have been profound alterations in well-established ideas about compulsory public education, marriage, procreation, abortion, divorce, exposure to the views and life-styles of others, separation of Church and state, the relative responsibilities of spouses and their children, the nature of work and leisure, in short, in almost every aspect of Italian life. But perhaps the most influential change has been the new affluence which has come to Italy.

The post-war rise in prosperity has touched practically everyone, even though in some social areas, the increases have been somewhat fictitious, due only to a generous policy of awarding old age and disability pensions. Albeit unevenly, living standards have risen faster in Italy than in most other West European countries. The upper-middle class in particular today lives better than in Britain and the United States mainly because it rarely inflicts on itself the same burden of high private school tuition bills. Many families can thus afford expensive clothing, frequent dining out and two long vacations each year. Surveys indicate that Italians have improved their traveling habits; indeed, in the last twenty years the number of Italians going on vacation has doubled from 28 per cent in 1969 to 56 per cent in 1991. Taking two vacations a year and going abroad is the popular trend: 17.3 per cent have chosen to go abroad in 1991 versus 15.3 per cent in 1988. Among those who travel 43 per cent have taken two vacations, while 21 per cent have taken three or more vacations. In this as in so much else about Italy, the percentage of those going on vacation is still much higher in the North than in the South–64 per cent versus only 41 per cent.

The Italians are less insular than they used to be; they have become more aware of other peoples and curious about how they live. Many of them have become less ready to spend long weeks at the Italian seashore or in a country villa; instead they go to Spain, Greece, the Balkans, France and Eastern Europe. America especially is now popular, at least when the currency exchange was favorable. Among the middle and upper classes, the trend for some years has been towards more unusual, varied and active kinds of vacation: a growing minority of people may opt for an archaeological dig in Mexico or even a safari in Kenya.

In the urbanized Italian society, the middle classes have become the dominant social sector of Italian population. It is a population, however, that cannot be viewed as a very composite stratum because it includes people coming from many sectors of employment and of the economy.

There has, of course, always been a strong middle class, never a real aristocracy. Since the days of the mercantile city-states of the twelfth century—the Florence of the Medici excluded nobles from the government of the city—until 1922 when a definitive "Debrett's" of the Italian nobility was drawn up, middle-class was *the* social class. And even after 1922, aristocracy was a vague term which included people so diverse that they had little in common.

The affluence has been particularly strong in the new middle-class which has arisen and whose influence has been growing fast. Economic expansion, especially of the new tertiary services, has elevated from the ranks of the lower bourgeoisie a new group that lacks inherited property but has achieved significant affluence: sales and advertising executives, skilled technicians, together with shopkeepers, artisans and small industrialists who have modernized and moved with the times. This is an assertive status-seeking world of new social mobility, that is immensely in love with American material values. Elsewhere in the middle classes the rise of prosperity has been more uneven. The less enterprising artisans and small traders, outclassed by the new consumer economy, are sliding into decline. The public servants—postal workers, clerks, primary teachers—have seen their wages rise less rapidly than in the private sector. Their ranks have now been infiltrated by the sons and daughters of the peasantry and the working class—young people who prefer soft jobs as clerks or typists to the drudgery of farm or factory.

In all these changes, class divisions have been fading, even though *class-consciousness* is still very much alive, especially in the South. In fact, it is another paradox of Italian life that the Italians are far more class-conscious than the Americans and French, but are less class-divided. It is a psychological more than an economical division. In fact, except between families and groupings, there are few social barriers in Italy. Snobbishness exists, but playing a role is more important than any innate sense of superiority. The boss of a firm will probably treat the employees in an authoritative way because he is in charge. however when he is outside his firm that power is no longer present. There is no equivalent at the high school level of the British fee-paying public schools or American private prep schools, or of Oxford, Cambridge, Harvard, Yale, or the many other prestigious colleges to separate people socially. There is no upper-class in a permanent, innate sense.

The gap between the extremes of wealth and poverty has been reduced unlike in the United States, however, there is not the same social mobility and therefore the same freedom of opportunity. Certainly there is more mobility than before the war, and children of all classes now mix in the same state schools till age fourteen; but there is little sense of a classless meritocracy where a worker's gifted son can rub shoulders with a doctor's or a university professor's. The causes of this division lie deep in Italian history and character. Class patterns are certainly changing, more through the economic merging of different classes than a blurring of the outward distinctions between them. Under modern conditions their interests and habits have drawn closer. A skilled worker may own the same kind of car as a member of the bourgeoisie, and off duty he may dress much the same way; the new working generation has given up its old class "uniform" and is dressing like the middle class, so it becomes harder to tell them apart. A lot certainly has to do with the *bella figura, the facade* that everyone wants to present to the outside world.

Bureaucracy: Twenty-first Century Baroque

If there is one "class" that all Italians could agree to despise it is the bureaucratic class, *la burocrazia*. There persists a general consensus that public officials do not work and are not to be trusted. In Italy, the idea that any official organization is there to serve the citizen is not only unfamiliar, it is laughable. Most civil servants are neither "civil" nor "servants." It is a known fact that people join the bureaucracy not out of love for a certain kind of work or out of a calling for public service, but mainly because they want stable employment, a secure job and very little hard work. After all, most government and municipal offices only open from 8 a.m. till 2 p.m.; there isn't another organization in the universe with such schedule! Anyone who goes to an Italian consulate abroad can easily get a good taste of what happens in Italy! Government employees think in terms of rights not obligations.

This sprawling bureaucratic maze conceals all sorts of illegal or quasi-legal activities on both small and large scale. It is impossible to get anything accomplished rapidly. In a request for a drivers license or a permit to use public space, a citizen may easily be tempted to pay for speed, or to create a network of mutual favors. On a larger scale we need only look at the scandals uncovered in 1992-93 that revealed wholesale kickback abuses, *tangenti*, in every sort of government control. The increase of scandals to the level of shameful obscenity has finally turned the public opinion against dishonesty in the public services and magistrates are conducting a campaign of clean up by jailing hundreds of public officials, including major political personalities in the "clean hands" (*mani pulite*) campaign.

There is a complete mistrust of the public towards the bureaucrats. The mask of anonymous authority stands between them. No attempt has ever been made in Italy to personalize the employees' relations with the public, for example, by putting name-cards on desks and guichets as in the United States.

Some change is taking place slowly in certain areas. The telephone service in particular has made a real effort to improve its relations with the public, and operators are now far more polite and helpful. Overall, however, the situation is still deplorable and Italians dread those occasions when they must deal with governmental offices.

Unfortunately for those who need to be "served" and must pay for the "service," the total number of bureaucrats is very high. Almost four fifths are from the South, and it is ironic that the heirs of the conquered Bourbon state now administer united Italy.

Italians spend their lives devising ingenious rules and then finding equally cunning ways of evading them. Thus they are able to cut corners and circumvent some of the bureaucratic absurdities. That is, everyone, including officials, accepts the fact that red tape can be tacitly ignored from time to time, especially when it is done between pals.

One basic problem in the bureaucratic system is the Italian concept of authority as something absolute. Consequently, there is much less delegation of power than in Britain or America. There is less sense of team responsibility: the head of an office or department will tend to concentrate the key work in his own hands rather than sharing the load. This extends even to relations between a boss and his secretary, for Italian managers tend to make inadequate use of their secretaries. The reluctance to delegate is one more aspect of the Italian centralist tradition, which operates just as much within a firm or other small unit as on the wider level of the government. And it has some unfortunate effects. It tends to create a gulf, more noticeable than in most countries, between the dynamic few at the top and the frustrated or time-serving many at more junior levels.

In the private sector, however, the efficiency of individuals and groups is remarkable. For example, the attitude and performance of the labor "class" is relatively high now; there has been a considerable improvement since the 1970s. The industrial transformation may have had an effect on working ethics and workers' behavior. Today, the number of employees in industry has declined. The balance between those working in large factories and those in small ones has tipped significantly in favor of the latter. Because of the upsurge of small-firms, family-owned businesses and the underground economy, it is difficult to assess change, but there has been a significant change in the number and the make-up of the working class.

One of Italy's most significant achievements in postwar is its expansion of social insurance coverage to include the entire population; but that has also been the major cause of the financial disequilibrium. In 1982, 13 percent of the GDP was spent for pensions, that is equivalent to one-quarter of the total public expenditure. The major problem is certainly the high numbers of those who receive aid; in the South, especially, pensions are a form of welfare assistance. Another serious problem is certainly the low contribution to the pension plan by employer and employee and the concomitant heavy subsidy by the state. Moreover, the Italian pension system is the most generous in the EC in terms of age. While in most countries men retire at age 65 and women at 60 if they do not follow the same age limit as men, in Italy, as in Japan, men are eligible for retirement at 60 and women at 55. However, Japanese pensions are calculated on the earnings average of one's entire career, whereas in Italy the average is based on the last five years of employment. Because of low birth rates and an increase of the elderly population, Italy, like France and Great Britain, is reviewing its pension system. The OCSE (the Organization for Cooperation and Economical Development) has anticipated that Italy may, in the near future, end up spending more than one third of its national product for social security expenses, if no changes are made. This growth in increased social benefit will, of course, cause a further increase in the bureaucratic machinery.

On the positive side, one result of the vastly improved health care system has been an improvement in longevity and average height. In addition to eating better and being better housed, the Italians live longer and have become taller. A 1991 survey conducted by ISTAT, Central Institute of Statistics, revealed that the Italian life span has increased: men's average life expectancy is 73.2 years while women's is 79.7. Italy is preceded in this category only by Japan, Sweden and Switzerland. Better diet, living conditions and health care not only have improved longevity, they have also disproved the common stereotype that Mediterraneans are genetically short. The average Italian height is now 173.67 centimeters; an increase of five centimeters since the 1930s.

La Bella Figura

All of those improvements in personal health and individual well-being are important, for Italians have always been concerned about appearances. From the way they prepare their food to the way they dress, there is always an attempt at style and beauty.

To most foreigners, Italian "style" often means extraordinary elegance and dignity. Italians lavish much attention to presenting a good appearance, and compliments in that regard are an ordinary practice. In fact, compliments are an essential part of a mutual admiration society. This partly explains the success of Italian men with Northern women, and the disappointment which Italian women feel when they go to Northern Europe where compliments tend to be regarded either as insincere or as a way of playing on vanity.

This *bella figura*–putting on a beautiful facade–and the slavery to fashion, can be irritating. But of course it is the surface of personal living. Much of the attitude to fashion and *bella figura* comes originally from village life where

everything is personal, you know everyone, and the way you appear and behave is important. That attitude was brought to the cities; today, only a small
percentage of the people living in the city were born there, but, notwithstanding
the profound changes, it is impossible to suddenly eradicate the previous two-
thousand-years attitudes.

An interesting indication of their sense of proportion and their concern for
la bella figura is that Italians rarely get drunk. They seem to know that alcohol,
after all, does not generate exuberance, but rather it deadens the senses and
makes people sloppy. Even at soccer celebrations most fans do not fall prey to
the excesses of alcohol–contrary to what occurs in many parts of Europe. Italians drink alcoholic beverages mainly at dinner time to complement a meal or
at a *caffè* to enjoy a conversation with a friend.

Italy's new post-war affluence, as in other countries, brought great changes
in spending and leisure habits. Italians are eating far more meat than before the
war; it was served only once a week on Sunday, whereas today it's daily common food. They have also been adopting American spending habits. Cars,
televisions, summer vacations by the sea and other new 'privileges' have been
altering their lives. Relatively Italians still place more emphasis on enjoyment,
but their former reluctance to spend their money on useful possessions has
waned sharply. During the boom years, the Italians steadily increased the share
of their budget that went on their homes, not only on rent and mortgages but on
comfort and equipment too.

With the growth of individual housing and the middle-class vogue for
buying and restoring crumbling villas, castles or old farm houses for weekend
retreats, skilled hand work has also become a major pastime. For example, in
the outskirts of many towns, one sees big new garden center supermarkets
attracting a new generation of gardening enthusiasts. Even a respectable doctor
no longer considers it undignified to be seen by his neighbors doing work
around the house.

Urbanization

The Italian concept of *la bella figura* was put to a stern test when the country attempted to respond to the need for more and better housing for everyone.
In the post-war decades of growth and modernization, the main urban emphasis
went, rightly to solving Italy's terrible housing shortage, a legacy of many
years of neglect. New high-rise buildings were erected often with little regard
for aesthetics or amenities. But after the high-rise boom in suburbia of the 70s,
which unfortunately, spoiled the old charm of Italian cities, the accent today is
on much-needed improvements to 'quality of life'–more parks, fountains,
traffic-free streets, rehabilitation of poorer districts and so on. There was also
a shift in priorities, as an affluent society began to react against the negative

aspects of too rapid urbanization. Italians demanded that their new individual prosperity be matched by better public amenities and by steps to make city life more tolerable. Since the late '70s many town councils have shifted their emphasis from building monolithic housing projects to developments that paid more attention to ecological or aesthetic considerations. However, because of their *socialità* and love for nature, Italians always built housing that made for easy human relations–houses giving onto squares, balconies etc. The new environmental trend took many forms and often was due to local or private, rather than state, initiative. Throughout the country there are new open-air or heated public swimming pools, well-equipped leisure and sports centers, advisory clinics, new homes for old people, renovated *palazzi* and castles, new museums–and campaigns against noise and litter abound. The urban revolution has steadily molded new life-styles and new social attitudes. The many millions who moved from the farms or from slum districts to the new dwellings had to adapt, some times painfully, to very different needs and patterns of modern suburbia. Many people reacted by a scared retreat into privacy, others by trying to form new clubs and associations–for sport, culture, civic and so on.

Slowly a new style of local community life is emerging in Italy, more informal and less institutional than that of the old urban bourgeoisie society but less warm and less relaxed than that of the old village or agrarian world. Among the cities' zestful, nervous crowded terrace-*caffé*, smart shop-windows and frenzied *piazze*, these new citizens had to get used to a new tempo. The congested narrow streets with their more aggressive and angry drivers are not easily acceptable to the newcomers. Even italophiles who spend a month or two in an Italian city, finding it fascinating and exciting, find it difficult to adopt to the strains that cities such as Rome, Naples, Milan present.

Italy has solved the housing shortage, but at a price. In the mid-1950s only about 10 per cent of all Italian homes had a bath or shower and only about 30 per cent had flushing lavatories. The Italians used to live in overcrowded and often squalid conditions, but cheaply. Since then homes have been built for over half the population, and every town is ringed with modern blocks of flats–a common enough sight in the Western World. In many parts of the country, the new housing complexes built around cities, called *borgate* around Rome, were usually poorly planned. There are no meeting places, apart from the occasional café, which is, however, reserved for men in the evenings, and very few cinemas, which show only films of the lowest quality. There is a striking shortage of parks, hospitals and cultural services, schools, libraries, theaters, concerts halls, cinemas, and sport centers, relative to what is available just a few miles away.

Another feature is a distorted pattern of consumption. As in the fast-urbanizing capitalist countries, a burgeoning consumer goods sector goes hand in hand with inadequate social spending (for houses, roads, sanitation, hospitals, social services, etc.). It is characteristic of all capitalist societies in the course of their development that economic activity and the population it supports become polarized spatially. Wealth and people become concentrated in core regions occupying a relatively small part of the territory and the rest remains underdeveloped. According to recent statistics, 60 per cent of the Italians own their own homes, and many have also purchased vacation homes as well.

Today, housing is far more plentiful and very comfortable, but prices have sky-rocketed. The average share of family income devoted to rents or mortgage, plus basic charges, has risen since the war from the incredibly low figure of 3.4 per cent to over 25 per cent. But the burden is unevenly shared. State housing policy has made repeated U-turns since the war, and its complex bureaucratic system of controls and subsidies has relieved some injustices but created others.

Nevertheless, now that the Italians are well-housed, they are freer to pick and choose the kind of homes they really want, and this has led to some striking changes. In the first thirty years of the post-war period, new high-rise blockstyle housing was constructed as this was the quickest and cheapest way of solving the shortage. Later, there was a shift towards buying rather than renting and an emphasis on single dwellings. In fact, in all classes there is a steady trend towards the buying rather than renting of new property. This satisfies the Italian's property-owning instincts and it provides developers with quicker returns. The Italians have become quite "house-proud," and no longer do they readily reject home comfort in favor of food, holidays or other pleasures. Their expectations have risen; they no longer tolerate the old overcrowding, and they want larger and better-built apartments or houses.

The housing urge has also expressed itself in the increased construction of second homes, and Italy is supposed to have more of these than any country in Europe. Some are ancient family houses deserted by emigrants to the city who, once they were earning well, returned to modernize their house and turn it into a summer resort.

Foreigners are amazed by the type of first and/or second housing that even the Italian with modest income is able to afford. One possible explanation is that in many cases the houses are an inheritance. As for the new housing, money comes through parents' sacrifice and personal *arrangiarsi*; with a peasant background, Italians have maintained the habit of saving frugally for something they really want. However, the enthusiasm for second homes has tended to deaden some small towns. Moreover, many of the old houses are being bought by foreigners; parts of Tuscany have been referred to as Chiantishire because so many British own property there. But these foreigners or the rich Italians occupy them only for a few weeks a year, with the result that villages are losing their identity.

Speculation over land and property has for many years been a major cause of the soaring rents and house prices. However, the tempo of new building has now slackened considerably since the main needs have been met and the birth-rate has been declining. On the other hand, the new trend in modernizing old buildings instead of demolishing them has been strong. Especially for historic city centers, Italy has turned towards a policy of rehabilitation; regulations for rehabilitation of old housing in *centri storici* are very strict and detailed. The restoration of old housing is seen as the best socially human way to preserve Italy's architectural heritage and re-animate city centers. Any visitor is bound to be impressed by the way Italy cares for its "historical centers." And so today there are two trends, going in opposite directions. On the one hand, more people want to move back to city-center living, when good housing is available; on the other hand, more people are wanting their own individual houses, amid greenery in the outskirts or at least within commuter range. Both groups reject the sad high-rise apartments of the expansion years.

Italians tend to buy instead of lease because living in dwellings for a short time is incompatible with the Italian idea of *domus* which evokes solidity and permanence. And if you have a house, you do not normally sell it to buy a better one as you get more prosperous with age. You keep it for your children, who were brought up in it, and add to it if you can when you need more room.

Decadence or Renewal of *Gastronomia*

Italians also like to spend their new wealth on eating. They spend as much as 38.8 per cent of income on food, of which only about 5 per cent goes for restaurant meals. Traditional Italian good eating has undergone many changes in the past decades and has come under various conflicting and complex pressures, pushing it simultaneously towards decline and recovery, and a foreign visitor may at first be baffled by what he sees, hears and tastes. *Fast-food* places serving hot-dog and hamburgers or pizza abound all over Italy. These are crowded, cheerful places, popular with youngsters in the evening and office-workers at lunch-time, and they compare favorably with their American equivalents. The *McDonalds* in Rome is the most successful of the chain worldwide! Certainly, the social change has affected eating habits. A modern nation in a hurry no longer has time or concern for serious daily cooking and eating: both at home and away from it, routine meals have become more simple, slapdash and utilitarian.

Yet, the Italians' gastronomic zeal is not dying; Italians are increasingly channelling it towards the once- or twice-a-week occasion with friends, or ritual at home. There is a national style of cooking and an assortment of different regional styles which overflows into neighboring provinces. Pasta is certainly the common denominator of most cooking from one end of the peninsula to the other. And pasta comes with hundreds of names for hundreds of types: *spaghetti, tagliatelle, rigatoni, lasagne, orecchiette, ravioli, cannelloni, tortellini, linguine,* are only the more obvious. Depending on the locale you may be offered *strangozzo, trenette, strozzaprete* or dozens of other varieties. And then you may choose among the hundreds of rich flavoring and sauces that may be used: *all'arrabbiata, puttanesca, bolognese, carbonara, pesto, napoletana,* to name just a few.

Home cooking habits are not as consistent as just a couple of decades ago. Television, cars, foreign vacations, better housing and other possessions all developed new rival claims on the average family's budget and interests–and especially on the wife's time. In the middle classes, far fewer wives now have servants than before the war, more have jobs, and life is more hectic. Some younger wives do not want to be a "slave" in the kitchen.

The Italian housewife still has a far wider variety of fresh foods to choose from than in most parts of Britain, Germany and even France. But after a long period of resistance her opposition to the idea of frozen foods is now thawing out. Even today, the Italians eat less than half as much frozen produce as the British and the Americans, but the consumption figures are increasing each year, and frozen-food freezers in supermarkets have been lengthening. The main difference is that while in the USA the best-selling frozen foods are ordinary items, the Italians prefer much more complex and expensive deep-frozen pre-cooked dishes.

Other changes may be inevitable. It seems that Italians are starting to move over to the light-meal habit for at least one of their main meals of the day. It should be possible for the light snack and true gastronomy to coexist, each for its own occasion. Italy has long been a nation of over-eaters where too much stress has been set on the convention that a meal must contain three or four full courses–*a tavola non s'invecchia* (at the table one doesn't grow old), the saying goes. Fortunately, being the masters of the now-fashionable Mediterranean diet, Italians are on the average less obese than Americans. Nevertheless, with the nervous speeding-up of life, today far more care is being given to dieting.

Consequently, as in America and Britain, sales of cook-books have soared, in Italy another reason is that after the war many middle-class urban mothers ceased handing on their culinary lore to their children, who are now having to learn it for themselves.

We have mentioned that Italians find it disgraceful to get drunk, but this does not mean that good food goes unaccompanied by good wine. Italians have not made a religion of their wine-drinking as perhaps the French have done, but an appropriate *vino* is an integral part of a good meal. There is an expression:

"un pranzo senza vino è come un giorno senza sole," which translates as a meal without wine is like a day without sunshine. Today Italy produces and exports more wine than any other country, yet there is a suspicion that they keep the best for themselves. From cold, dry whites like frascati, soave, pinot grigio and verdicchio, to smooth, hearty reds like chianti, brunello, amarone, bardolino and barolo, there is a vino to accompany any dish. To whet the appetite, there are dozens of *apperitivi*, and after the meal one might try a *digestivo*. Italian cordials are world famous–anisette, sambuca, amaretto, galliano, strega, just to name a few–although two fingers of *grappa* might be a more usual way for an Italian to end a good meal.

Sexual Behavior

Whether it is enjoying a good meal with friends or just greeting someone on the street, Italians are personal, and often difficult for the American or Northern European visitor to accept is the naturalness with which Italians touch each other. Usually it is simply an extension of the physical warmth and affection of the family. The way men embrace each other without self-consciousness can also be surprising to an Anglo-Saxon. The fact that the "Northerners" recoil from touching or embracing each other is possibly due to excessive consciousness of sex. Certainly the fact that they are less demonstrative within their families could mean that for them touching is associated more with sex and less with warmth and spontaneous friendliness.

Despite strictures by the Vatican and the clergy, Italians have always had a reputation for sexual permissiveness, and foreign artists and writers, such as Goethe, Stendhal, Byron, Schopenhauer, and Tolstoy learned much about the country from their Italian loves and praised the passionate nature of its women. The Italian lover, a movie cliché since Rudolph Valentino, is still an unadvertised asset of the Italian tourist business. "Summertime" in which Katherine Hepburn falls in love with the dashing Rossano Brazzi on her first visit to Venice perhaps epitomize this romantic vision of Italy.

In fact so much about Italy is part of this image: the gondolas, the songs, the wine, the sunlight, the Ferraris, *la dolce vita*. And the magic and romantic associations of names: Capri, Sorrento, Positano, Venice, Verona, the Trevi Fountain, the lakes. A number of women visitors to Italy seem to look forward to instant masculine attention and feed the notion that a lot of foreign women are coming to Italy in search of erotic adventures. Unquestionably, what is known as *caccia alle straniere* is also a pastime of young Italians to prove their virility and seductiveness.

The most striking change in sexual behavior, certainly happened with women. Today, the Italian woman expects the same degree of sexual freedom as a man; and, conversely, the same degree of fidelity from a man. She no longer accepts that his peccadillos are more forgivable than her own. The sexual attitudes and behavior of Italian girls have also been changing dramatically, though the new permissiveness is still very recent, more so than in most countries. As late as the 1960s, all the evidence was still suggesting that Italian unmarried girls as a whole, especially in the provinces, were still among the most virginal in Europe. Well into the 1960s the old code of this Catholic society remained in force, at least on the surface. According to a survey in 1960 more than half of Italian mothers still thought a girl should not be allowed out with a boy till she was nineteen, and many still acted on that belief. And less than one-third of girls said they approved of pre-marital sex even between fiancés, while about 70 per cent of married women under thirty claimed to have been a virgin on their wedding night.

However, following the lead of the Nordic countries, sexual freedom began to spread. Parents became readier to allow their daughters to go out with their boyfriends; young people got more leisure and money for going off together. In some student circles, relations had become very free by the mid 60s. The 1970s saw a further change, essentially among the very young and in parental attitudes toward them. This came from foreign influences, from the freeing of legal controls on contraception, from the steady decline in the role of the Church. Today at school teenage girls treat boys as sex objects in a free market, just as boys treat girls. However, lately there has been a swing away from promiscuity, mainly due to the spread of AIDS. In general, sexual freedom in Italy has now reached the same level as in France, Britain, Germany or Sweden—and that, for this so-called Catholic country, is quite a transformation. It would be wrong, however, to infer from the teenage revolution that every adult woman has become *leggera* overnight. Most of those in their mid-twenties or older are still *serie* and will not give themselves except for love.

La Gioventù: Footloose but more Sincere

Naturally these changes in social behavior have had their effect on Italy's youth, *gioventù*. They have their own consumer markets for music, clothes and cars; their own world of rock groups and other singing idols. All enjoy far more freedom from parents than cloistered Italian youth had twenty years ago, and far more sexual license too.

Today's *gioventù* is not rebellious and is not fired with revolutionary ideals for trying to change society, like the seething youth of the late 1960s. Tolerant and reflective, they seem curiously passive. And rarely do they show much sense of public initiative.

It used not to be so. Many of the most important changes in post-war Italy were due to a new generation rising against the standards of its elders. The post-war climate was very different from today's: more austere, but also more open and adventurous. The upheavals of wartime had broken down some of the barriers that previously kept youth in its place, and an idealistic new wave was gradually able to make inroads into the fossilized hierarchy. It is remarkable how youthful many of the post-war pioneers were at the outset: former Prime Minister Andreotti was in his early 20s, President of the Republic Scalfaro was in his early 30s. Today these and other pace-setters are established old figures, some of them still in key positions, corrupted and without vision; but the new generation, born into an age of greater affluence but also of greater skepticism, has seldom shown the same innovating spirit. The spirit that animated neo-realist artists which so accurately captured those years of ferment, was replaced by a spirit of desolation which was foretold in the prophetic *La Dolce Vita*. Later Italian youth, it seems, became too much attached the world of *Dallas* and *Falcon Crest* which were just as popular in Italy as in the U.S..

In the 1960s, a new generation, sipping its Coca-Cola and listening to pop music and singing American rock'n'roll was born. Quickly, the Italian pop was born. At first the movement was highly derivative. Not only did the stars borrow American tunes, several of them found it smart to adopt Anglo-Saxon names as well. Open-air concerts attracted tens of thousands of teenagers which showed the high sense of solidarity of the new generation. There was a tone of revolt in all this, but the revolution was purely one of music and rhythm, not morals and standards.

The situation changed from the end of 60s on. Italian youth today is something of an enigma, and one that many adults find disquieting. Through the 50s and '60s it remained very much under parental influence, leaving a dominant impression of docile reticence. Then from the end of the 60s, giving vent to the frustrations that had lain beneath the surface, youth became almost an independent political and cultural force. This was the golden age of faith in ideologies and the belief that the new generation could after all change society. Youth burst into action. But when the dust had settled, and society had not been changed very much, it soon became clear that the 67-69 crisis had not turned all Italian youth into revolutionaries.

However, those years were not without their permanent legacy, notably in the way they modified the relations between Italian youth and its elders. The old barriers of authority were broken, and this was true as much within families as in schools and universities. But, almost twenty-five years later, what use has been made of this freedom by the ensuing generation? Well, most of today's youngsters were born after those years of *contestazione*. For most of them those years of high ideals are history, and are seen with skepticism and passivity. Recently, whenever the youngsters have engaged in demonstrations, they have done so more in opposition to change, rather than as a constructive demand for change. They are much closer to their parents' interests and attitudes: rejection of ideologies and formal organizations, concern with private pleasures, and "feathering the nest." The new Italian concern with an ethos of personal fulfillment, and with hedonism, is even stronger among the young than with older people. It is easy to lament this apparent shift towards egotism and rejection of ideals of wider community service. They cling to their own trusted circle of family and friends and reject any wider allegiance.

One feature common to most young people in the past decade, even the more conformist ones, is that leisure and privacy have been replacing work as the essential paths to self-fulfillment. The young attitude to a job or career is frequently utilitarian; work is seen as a means of ensuring the quality of their leisure lives; and few of them share the passionate work ethic that drove their elders to build the modern prosperous Italy. The country should, certainly, be concerned about the decline of the old dedicated work ethic. It seems, however, that there have been signs of a new swing of the pendulum among some very young people. Although very often individualistic and self-centered, they are more ambitious and are prepared to work harder. They have drive and initiative, but they do not challenge the system or seek to change it for the good of society as a whole; in fact, usually they would rather run their own business than work for a large organization or institution.

Idealism over a united Europe has also waned recently, for young people as much as their elders have grown cynical about the EC as an institution. Yet in a more general sense they still feel "European", more so than the French, and much more so than the insular British. They have less sense of frontiers than the older generation. These young people not only are not racist, they take pride in showing solidarity with new immigrants, mostly of color, and also feel a strong concern towards the Third World.

Overall, however, *la gioventù* has won a new freedom from parents and teachers, but it has also lost its sure moral leadership. It cannot trust the values of an adult world that is corrupt and no longer offers certainties, so in the search for its own values it retreats into a shell.

XIV

Conclusion:
A Country in Search of Equilibrium

"Not I" Says the Culprit

Throughout this book I demonstrated that Italy is alive, well and thriving; that the Italian democratic system ultimately is one of the most stable in the world, despite its political map; the Italian society is as lively as ever, paradoxically because problems very often are not solved frontally and Italians have an innate ability to "manage" in all kinds of situations.

We have agreed with Robert N. Putnam, that one of Italy's major problem is the low sense of civic community; indeed, Italy's problems are the more serious in the least civic regions, for they lack the horizontal bonds of collective reciprocity that work more efficiently in the civic regions. In the absence of solidarity and self-discipline, there is an horizontally fractured community which produces daily justification for feelings of exploitation, dependency, frustration and, consequently, cynicism and alienation:

In the less civic regions nearly everyone expects everyone else to violate the rules, if you expect everyone else to cheat. (The Italian term for such behavior is *fesso*, which also means "cuckolded.") So you cheat, too, and in the end everyone's dolorous, cynical expectations are confirmed.[1]

Therefore, while in most regions in the North citizens are engaged by public issues instead by personalistic or patron-client politics and value solidarity, civic engagement, and cooperation, in the less civic regions of the South life is marked by hierarchy and exploitation, not by share-and-sharealike.

However, there is a cynical attitude toward government that is equally strong in both South and North and which is charged with both heartfelt hate and unconscious civic irresponsibility. To have an idea of what we mean, let's take a look at how the Italians deal with the many "crisis," real and fictitious, which afflict the country. The average Italian is accustomed to associate with a crisis any problem that he encounters in his daily activities. Very often minor or accidental problems are equated to national or regional or local crisis. In such a labyrinth, real crisis cannot be disentangled from imagined ones and the country appears to be constantly at the brink of chaos.

The average Italian faults the ***classe politica*** and *classe dirigente* for such a nightmarish atmosphere. In fact, the political and the ruling classes are the culprit for anything that goes wrong. Here, too, it is difficult to identify what is real or who these classes really are. They are like an accordion; they can be expanded or contracted, depending on the nature of the crisis, who "sees" it, whether one is talking about a city or province or the whole nation, and so on.

The *classe politica* is "they", those people, those incompetents and mischief-makers. Certainly not "we" or "I" or any close friend. It is not even uncommon to hear a "prominente," a member of Italy's ruling class excoriate the *classe politica* as if he or she were in no way responsible for the political, fiscal, social *crisi* of the country. There is much unintended irony and self-deception in all of this. One may argue that the Italian situation is nothing uncommon, that everyone likes to blame a scapegoat at one time or another, that we all tend to look elsewhere for the cause of those aspects of society, and of our own lives within it, that we find unpalatable.

But Italy does appear different, not only in the frequency of hostile references or attacks to the *classe politica*, but also in the vehemence with which each condemnation is expressed. The criticism is so ritualized, so well integrated into the citizens' role, so much part of Italian play-acting that it is difficult to tell how much of it is deeply felt. Moreover, what is important is the fact that there is no persuasive evidence that these hostile attitudes have negative or corrosive consequences on the Italian democracy; on the contrary, it seems that Italian democracy thrives on hostile criticism. Criticism calls for constant reassessment of situations, conditions and prominent individuals.

Notwithstanding the self criticism, that at times is picked up also by foreign press, in less than three decades, Italy has become an advanced industrial country, where the number of persons who work in agriculture has been drastically reduced, and where, as in many other democracies, the so-called tertiary employment sector is in rapid expansion. Modern, well-off Italy got where it is because of the ideas, imagination, and hard work of its people. The progress arrived not by chance or "miracle" but because, the *classe politica* concocted political and economic formulas that the people accepted and, when applied, worked. The *classe politica* has demonstrated how primary political rights and democratic processes can be used to improve the material and the moral condition of the citizens. The Italians created a capitalism which is a peculiar phenomenon and which does not fit any "ideal type" or rigid preconceived framework. It is rational, of course, and at the same time highly traditional, and while following universal rules it has never abandoned its firm original family base. It is a mixture, a cocktail of different attitudes and contradictory value-orientations. Being called "dynastic capitalism", it is recognized as a masterpiece of adaptation of traditional "virtues" and traits to modern functional requisites. For Italian capitalism the conventional concept of "profit" is too narrow just like the current concept of "productivity" is too one-sided. Productivity and profit are not conceived only in terms of an individual productive unit. They are measured and assessed in terms of social stability and satisfactory performance of the system as a whole.

It would be wrong to overlook the social dimensions of Italian capitalism. It is less efficient, but has less "conspicuous waste," it allows for more individual self-expression and permits more conviviality. That is not necessarily bad; human beings desire and probably crave change but they also want and need stability. They might desire competition to vent their aggressiveness, but they also need cooperation, security, and the feeling of working together toward a reasonable goal.

In its leap into industrial prosperity, Italy has escaped the "flatness," the existential monotony that characterizes other industrial countries. In such societies, life is dynamic, but it tends to be tedious and tasteless; things and people become gradually homogenized and interchangeable. Things are still different in Italy. The tempo of life can be irritatingly slow, especially in the south. Italians still prefer to do things "leisurely." There seems always to be time for everything. Time is not regarded in Italy as a scarce raw material. One may find hurry and confusion at times, especially in a *piazza* or at a social function, but it is not a purposeful hurry.

Thus, people are usually late for their appointments. In Rome to be a half an hour late for *un appuntamento* is not considered serious. It is commonly accepted. South of Rome, arriving on time may be regarded as an almost offensive behavior. Punctuality on the part of one person is viewed as a lack of trust toward others and a clear symptom of petty-mindedness. In some respects Italians' attitudes to leisure still differ from the Anglo-Saxons', notably the way they like their free time divided up; that is, since the war they have shown a preference for longer annual vacations rather than shorter daily working hours. The Italians are those in Europe to take the longest vacations. Today, the strains of daily city life incite many people to take off for the country on the weekend, and most likely they will go neither to a hotel nor to relative's but to their own country cottage or villa, *la seconda casa*. Italians can boast about holding the first place among Europeans in owning a second house. The race to the countryside has to be tied with the new trends of ecological back-to-nature and the either hedonistic or spiritual search for privacy. If weekends are now more important, lunches are less so. The leisurely two-hour family lunch, weekdays included, is one Italian tradition that is in decline due to suburban commuting and economic change. This has habitually been the main meal of the day, with children coming home from school and husbands from work—and so it still is, in many small town and rural areas. But the cities have seen big changes.

The Art of *Arrangiarsi*
The Italians have a way to "manage" their lives and their institutions in manner to surprise even the most open minded political science experts or the most informed sociologists. The area of politics is very revealing in this regard.

Italy has one of the most active and participating electorates. The picture is very positive indeed if one assesses the strength of its democracy on the basis of public participation in the election process. Even the high percentage of votes for the communists was something positive because the strong opposition to government provided a high level of check and balance in the democratic process. Contrary to the general American belief that a vote for the Communist Party by Catholics was a sign of political pathology, the Italian vote was highly calibrated to maintain a democratic system from falling under the control of groups with extreme ideologies. Now that the heat and the smoke of the Cold War have settled, it is easy to assess the political behavior of the Italians in those years. The fall of Communism has brought about a shift of political adherence from the Communists but also from the Christian Democrats–their traditional political enemies–to other political forces, creating a new political landscape which brings an end to *immobilismo*.

The political behavior cannot be understood by the American mind which prefers everything in black and white. Matter-of-factness which is usually and somewhat pompously referred to as "scientific habit of mind" has not trickled down to permeate mass mentality. Facts per se have no value; there is only interpretation of facts in Italian life. Everything is debatable. The activities in any Italian *caffè* reflects such Italian behavior. Pirandello and his relativistic view of life is the product of a general Italian conception of existence. The Italian mind is still poetic, anthropomorphic and unpredictable. This is why when the American tourists, who are fond of empirical details and ask questions such as "how tall is the Colosseum" or "how wide is Piazza S. Pietro," the average Italian looks up surprised and a little amused at such questioning.

Foreigners are amazed by such a way of thinking and behavior. The question is always, why? Centuries of foreign domination have, according to Eduardo De Filippo, a post-war Italian actor and playwright, created a mind that subconsciously represses truth. In a hostile environment, truth was a luxury that few people could afford; invention at the individual level, a keen sense of life as a permanent theater, a profound and irreducible diversity, a living challenge to the rules of logic became the normal behavior. Regardless how tough a situation may be, Italians have learned to face life always with dignity and elegance. Needless to say, the end result of such efforts is the supreme value given to *bella figura. Bella figura*, which may mean roughly giving a good impression, is more than simple make-shift or bombastic rhetoric. It has to do with an aesthetic ideal and at the same time with a question of survival.

Italians want it to be known that they are present; the fact that Italians are noisy and Italy is a noisy country can be traced to this particular attitude. Noise could be nervewracking and, in terms of efficiency, time-consuming, but Italians seem to like noise. They regard it as a therapy against solitude. Noise is life, message, exchange, presence, *socialità*. And being sociable has remained a major Italian trait. With the advent of *progresso*, many social manifestations have not changed or become part of a rational notion of society, that is, of a functional society. In a functional society every major activity is planned toward a definite goal and is to be accounted and evaluated in terms of costs-benefits analysis. In industrialized Italy, ceremonies are still done for purely ceremonial purpose because people still have a love for ceremony.

Measuring Success

Today Italy presents a confusing picture, for society appears to have evolved in certain respects but not in others. Personal attitudes and life-styles have evolved rather more than the formal or official structures that dominate public life. These still tend to be impeded by strong obstructions' the survival of many out-of-date laws, regulations and routine practices; the "stratified society" with its strong vested interests right across the board. Society is still too corporatist and compartmentalized, with each body protecting itself from its rivals.

Moreover, Italian society is still segmented and individualistic because loyalties are usually restricted to small groups held together by strong personal ties. The family is the most important of these but it is followed closely by the patron-client relationship, which is very strong and is by no means restricted to the South. Italians join associations with fellow-members of their own trade or social group, but it is done more for mutual self-defense than out of altruistic sentiment or civic duty.

This book has also attempted to trace the positive changes in attitudes and human relations—the greater freedom for women and young people, the rise of social informality, the freer climate in education and in working life, and a small sign of a new cooperative spirit of self-help. All this might have led, one would suppose, to a waning of the old Italian traits built around mutual mistrust, and to the rise of a less divided and therefore more civic-minded society. And in some ways it has. But there are some failures. Some can be found in any capitalist society; some are merely part of the wider human condition—other nations too, including Britain and the USA, have their own full share of vested interests, corruption, clumsy bureaucrats.

Italians have now modernized their country, or most of it, and have managed to adjust successfully without losing their essential Italianness. Anyone who travels around Italy today, will find a country that is very modern, but in its own way, a blend of the new and the traditional, the native and the imported. Of course a highway or a skyscraper is much the same in any land, but the Italians add stylish innovative touches of their own. Inevitably the new

Italy has lost some of its old quaint picturesqueness, yet the Italians today show a flair for giving a phoenix-like rebirth to the picturesque.

The Italians are showing less success at re-inventing the novel, the play or the great painting. For some years now, Italian creative culture has remained at a low ebb. Intellectual life is dazzle and frenzy more than substance; the theater turns to brilliant gimmicks; and Italy still awaits the arrival of outstanding new talent among novelists, playwrights, painters, even film-makers. But is this vacuum any deeper in Italy than elsewhere in Western Europe? The Italian cultural staleness is part of the staleness of the West in this age of technology and mass media. This is a time that favors individual creativity less than it does the disseminating of culture to new audiences; and here Italy is full of an impressive activity, notably in the world of museums.

It seems that in today's anxious world, the Italians have been turning in search of security, of personal fulfillments, of what can loosely be termed 'quality of life'. This could lead them as individuals to become more passive and self-absorbed, more anti-social in a civic sense. Certainly there has been a new stress on personal initiative, ambition, and material success, especially among young people. This is certainly not a sign of passivity, but it is somewhat egotistical rather than civic-oriented.

The issue is whether the Italians can harness their abundant energies to work together for new social goals; or whether their old individualism will lead them down new entrepreneurial paths; or whether as individuals they will relapse into the shuttered, mistrustful isolation that is one strong facet of their nature.

The Ills of Prosperity

In the last few decades, Italians have gone through experiences that have a strong American flavor. In the early 1960s, most Italians believed that prosperity would create the ultimate good society. As in the USA of the 1950s and 1960s, in the Italy of the 1960s and 1970s there was a general, fervent belief in the power of prosperity. Soon after the economic recovery, the Italians increasingly became accustomed to believing that they were entitled to a great deal: more opportunities, job security, better housing, better education, earlier retirement, rising living standards, a clean environment, and more. While family income grew rapidly, the quality of life improved in countless ways. In the process, their expensive notion of entitlement grew increasingly unrealistic.

When the fiscal and political crisis swept the country at the beginning of the 90s, Italians felt a need to reassess their wants, needs and moral attitudes. They started to answer some very basic questions: is upward mobility a birthright? Can the state continue to provide the high level of social and public assistance? Is prosperity going to continue? It seems that they started to learn from what the Americans had painfully learned, that prosperity can never satisfy all our expectations. Prosperity is not quite the social stabilizer that we thought to be. Faith in prosperity is an infatuation, and like all infatuations, one is seduced by its pleasures and blinded to its shortcomings. Economic growth–the creation of new industries and technologies–can be disruptive: it may spawn excesses, overinvestment, speculations, too much borrowing and recession. Moreover, not only are some social problems beyond prosperity's power to cure, some social ills are the creation of prosperity.

Some Italians have been questioning the worth of such progress. In a book published in 1989, entitled *Non siamo più povera gente* (We Are No Longer Poor People), Cesare Marchi lamented the cost of economic success. It was the follow-up to another book of his, *Quando eravamo povera gente* (When We Were Poor People), in which he had called to mind the Italy of poverty while underlining the solid moral values of that society.[2] Is Marchi's lamentation symptomatic of a real situation or is it part of the general Italian behavior to be critical of everything?

However, most Italians still remain prey to the economy's euphoric expansions and dispiriting declines; they should realize that prosperity cannot be created at will and that is the most important term in the equation of the high achievements of a country. They must finally realize that even great amounts of prosperity won't solve all their social problems and that prosperity could bring moral decay. In fact, the prospect of the harmonious society is disfigured by huge blemishes–high unemployment, tension between south and north, staggering budget deficits, an uncontrollable mafia, unprecedented corruption among public officials and the breakdown of moral values—which cannot continue to be overlooked.

As the country moves towards the twenty-first century, past progress has to be redimensioned. The sophisticated constitution has to be attuned to new political realities; the responsibilities of the state to the citizens and those of the citizens to the state have to be revalued. The "Italian behavior" while keeping its valuable traits has to start to conform to that of a united Europe and of a shrinking world. With its unique cultural patrimony, artistic tradition and creative strength–from Dante to Michelangelo, Giotto to Botticelli, Vivaldi to Verdi, Machiavelli to Gramsci, Volta to Fermi–it is unlikely that she will fail to contribute greatly to a Europe which may well be on the threshold of a radical new era. Italians have always known how to pair technical expertise with artistic genius, a tradition dating back at least as far as the Renaissance, when painters were also sculptors, architects, scientists, and men of letters. Italian design–the "made in Italy" trademark–has contributed to this tradition of uniting beauty and usefulness. The real challenge to Italy for the next century is how she is going to weld her two cultures, the Western European and the Mediterranean.

How can we conclude and generalize about a people, which in our own time has produced types as different as Mussolini and Pope John XXIII? Ever since they began to emerge as a nation the Italians presented contrasting facets. Which is more typical of the national genius, Dante on his austere quest for truth and perfection or Boccaccio bubbling over with laughter at the human scene? Saint Francis with his love for nature and human kind or Machiavelli with his cynicism and "scientific art?" Which is the real Italy, the country that rose to a major economic power without natural resources, or the nation of economic and fiscal irresponsibility? Both exist, both are real, and as things go, they are probably both eternal.

No other people over so long a history have shown a greater knack for survival and adaptability than the Italians in a manner that is full of paradoxes. The national art of "arrangement"–dodging taxes, double-dealing, working only as hard as one must–is counteracted by Italian inventive genius, gusto for life, fierce individuality, deep family bound as well as animosity, and a marvelously hedonistic sophistication. The Italians are highly resilient, resourceful and practical people, and will keep a balance between work and leisure. Perhaps more than any other nation in Europe, the Italians bring a vast heritage of wisdom, taste and humanism to the difficult task of preserving the best of the past in order to marry it with the future. They will do it by preserving a *gusto* for life.

Notes

1. Robert N. Putnam, *Making Democracy Work*, p. 111.

2. Cesare Marchi, *Non siamo più povera gente* (Milano: Rizzoli, 1989) and *Quando eravamo povera gente* (Milano: Rizzoli, 1989).

Bibliography

General

Barzini, Giuseppe. *The Italians: A Full-Lenght Featuring Their Manners and Morals.* New York: Atheneum, 1964.

Chubb, Judith. *Patronage, Power and Poverty in Southern Italy.* Cambridge: Cambridge UP, 1982

Ginsborg, Paul. *A History of Contemporary Italy: Society and Politics 1943-1988.* New York: Penguin Books, 1990.

Gramsci, Antonio. *Selections from the Prison Notebooks,* edited by Q. Hoare and Nowell-Smith. London: Lawrence and Wishart, 1971.

Gribaudi, A. *Mondo operaio, mito operaio.* Turin: Einaudi, 1987.

Haycraft, John. *Italian Labyrinth: Italy in the 1980s.* London: Secker & Warburg, 1985.

Mammarella, Giuseppe. *Italy After Fascism: A Political History.*Notre Dame: Notre Dame UP, 1966.

Murray, William. *The Last Italian: Portrait of a People.* New York: Prentice Hall Press, 1991.

Rusconi, Gian Enrico and Scamuzzi, Sergio. *Italy Today: An Eccentric Society.* London: Sage, 1981.

Sassoon, Donald. *Contemporary Italy: Politics, Economy & Society Since 1945.* New York: Longman Inc., 1986.

Politics

Di Palma, Giuseppe. *Surviirng Without Governing: The Italian Parties in Parliament.* Berkeley: University of California Press, 1977.

Gozzini, Giovanni and Anderlini, Luigi, eds. *I partiti e lo stato.* Bari: De Donato, 1982.

Guidorossi, Giovanna. *Gli italiani e la politica.* Milan: Franco Angeli, 1984.

Kogan, Norman. *A Political History of Italy: The Postwar Years.* New York: Praeger Special Studies, 1983.

La Palombara, Joseph. *Democracy Italian Style.* New Haven: Yale University Press, 1987.

Pasquino, Gianfranco. *The End of Post-War Politics in Italy.* Boulder: Westview Press, 1993.

Spotts, Frederic and Wieser, Theodor. *Italy: A Difficult Democracy.* New York, Cambridge, 1986.

Treu, Tiziano, ed. *L'uso politico dello statuto dei lavoratori.* Bologna: Il Mulino, 1975.

Vacca, Giuseppe. *Quale democrazia?* Bari: De Donato, 1977.

Wollemborg, Leo J. *Stars, Stripes, and Italian Tricolor.* New York: Praeger, 1990.

Economy And Industry

Amato, Giuliano. *Economia, politica e istituzioni in Italia.* Bologna: Il Mulino, 1976.

D'Antonio, Mariano. *Sviluppo e crisi del capitalismo italiano 1951-1972.* Bari: De Donato, 1973.

Lange, P. and Tarrow, S., eds. *Italy in Transition: Conflict and Consensus.* London: Frank Cass, 1980.

Lash, Scott and Urry, John. *The End of Organized Capitalism.* Cambridge: Polity, 1987.

Lazerson, Mark H. "Organizational Growth of Small Firms: An Outcome of Markets and Hierarchies?," *American Sociological Review,* 53 (June 1988).

Mershon, Carol. *The Micropolitics of Union Action: Industrial Conflict in Italian Factories,* Ph.D. diss., Yale University,1986.

Nannetti, Raffaella Y. *Growth and Territorial Policies: The Italian Model of Social Capitalism.* New York: Pinter, 1988.

Nannetti, Raffaella Y. and Robert Leonardi, eds., *The Regions and European Integration: The Case of Emilia-Romagna.* New York: Pinter, 1990.

Trentin, Bruno. *Da sfruttati a produttori.* Bari: De Donato, 1977.

Valli, Vittorio. *L'economia e la politica economica italiana.* Milan: Etas Libri, 1979.

Villari, L., ed. *Il capitalismo italiano del Novecento.* Bari: Laterza, 1975.

Society

Altan, Carlo Tullio. *L'altra Italia.* Milan: Feltrinelli, 1985.

Balbo, L. *Stato di famiglia.* Milan: 1976.

Arlacchi, Pino. *Mafia Business.* New York: Verso, 1987.

Ascoli, U. and Catanzaro, R. *La società italiana degli anni ottanta.* Bari: 1987.

Banfield, Edward. *The Moral Basis of a Backward Society.* Glencoe, Ill.: The Free Press, 1958.

Baranski, Zygmunt G. and Vinall, Shirley W., eds. *Women and Italy: Essays on Gender, Culture and History.* New York: St. Martin's Press, 1991.

Birnbaum, Lucia Chiavola. *Liberazione della donna: A Cultural History of the Contemporary Italian Women's Movement.* Middletown: Wesleyan UP, 1985.

Caldwell, Lesley. *Italian Family Matters.* London: Macmillan, 1991.

CENSIS. *Italy Today: Social Picture and Trends, 1985.* Milan: Franco Angeli, 1986.

Ceolin, Carlo, ed. *Università, cultura, terrorismo.* Milan: Franco Angeli, 1984.

Labini, Paolo Sylos. *Le classi sociali negli anni '80.* Bari: Laterza, 1986.

Della Porta, Donatella, ed. *Terrorismi in Italia.* Bologna: Il Mulino, 1984.

Fraser, R. *1968: A Student Generation in Revolt.* New York: Pantheon Books, 1988.

Hofmann, Paul. *That Fine Italian Hand.* New York: Henry Holt & Co., 1990.

Kertzer, David. *Sacrificed for Honor.* Boston: Beacon Press, 1993.

Lupri, E. ed. *The Changing Position of Women and Society: A Cross-National Comparison.* The Netherlands: Leiden-E. J. Brill, 1983.

Meyer, Donald. *Sex and Power: The Rise of Women in America, Russia, Sweden, and Italy.* Middletown: Wesleyan UP, 1987: 119-156, 445-491.

Pantaleone, Michele. *The Mafia and Politics.* London: Chatto and Windus, 1966.

Pivato, S. *Movimento operaio e istruzione popolare nell'Italia liberale.* Milan: Franco Angeli, 1986.

Parks, Tim. *Italian Neighbors.* New York: Grove Weidenfield, 1992.

Watson, James. *The Mafia and Clientelism: Roads to Rome in Post-War Calabria.* New York: Routledge, 1986.

Zuccotti, Susan. *The Italians and the Holocaust.* New York: Basic, 1987.

Arts, Intellectuals, Culture

Baranski, Zygmunt G. and Lumley, Robert. *Culture and Conflict in Postwar Italy.* London: The Macmillan Press LTD, 1990.

Bondanella, Peter. *Italian Cinema From Neorealism to thePresent.* New York: Frederick Ungar, 1983.

De Mauro, Tullio. *Storia linguistica dell'Italia unita.* Bari: Laterza, 1976.

Forgacs, David. *Italian Culture in the Industrial Era 1880-1980.* Manchester: Manchester UP, 1990.

Grossi, Giorgio. *Rappresentanza e rappresentazione. Percorsi di analisi dell'interazione tra mass media e sistema politico in Italia.* Milan: Franco Angeli, 1985.

Inglehart, Ronald. *Culture Shift in Advanced Industrial Society.* Princeton: Princeton UP, 1990.

Jewell, Keala. *The Poiesis of History: Experimenting with Genre in Postwar Italy.* Ithaca: Cornell U.P., 1992.

Lanaro, Silvio. *L'Italia nuova. Identità e sviluppo 1861-1988.* Turin: Einaudi, 1988.

Mancini, Paolo. *Videopolitics: Telegiornali in Italia e in USA.* Turin: ERI, 1985.

Marletti, Carlo. *Media e politica.* Milan: Franco Agnelli, 1984.

Mauri, Stefano. *Il libro in Italia. Geografia, produzione, consumo.* Milan: Hoepli, 1987.

Michalczyk, John J. *The Italian Political Filmmakers.* Cranbury: Associated University Press, Inc., 1986.

Mondello, Elisabetta. *Gli anni delle riviste: Le riviste letterarie dal 1945 agli anni ottanta.* Lecce: Edizioni Milella, 1985.

Pansa, Gianpaolo. *Comprati e venduti: I giornali e il potere negli anni '70.* Milan: Bompiani, 1978.

_____. *Carte false.* Milan: Rizzoli, 1986.

Pasolini, Pier Paolo. *Scritti corsari.* Milan: Garzanti, 1975.

_____. *Letture luterane.* Turin: Einaudi, 1977.

Pinto, Francesco. *Intellettuali e tv negli anni '50.* Rome: Savelli, 1977.

Porter, William E. *The Italian Journalist.* Ann Arbor: University of Michigan Press, 1983.

Vacca, Giuseppe. *L'informazione negli anni ottanta.* Rome: Riuniti, 1984.

Index

Abbas, Abu, 60
abortion, 208-210
Abruzzi, 79, 93, 113
Achille Lauro (hijacking), 60
ACLI (Association of Italian Christian Workers), 175
Afghanistan, 62
Africa, 3, 146
AGIP (Azienda Gas Idrocarburi Petroli), 101
Agnelli, Giovanni, 133,158
Agnelli family, 107, 186
agriculture, 91-96; agrarian reform, 10, 93; agricultural reconstruction, 93-96; sharecropping, 188
Albania, 89, 144, 146
Alighieri, Dante, 2, 193
Alitalia, 101
Allies: invasion of the South, 7; occupation of Italy, 7; and the Resistance, 7; liberation of Italy, 7-8
Alps, 3
Altan, Carlo-Tullio, 187
Alto Adige, 68, 120
Amato, Giuliano, 26, 65,118
Amendola, Giorgio, 57
American cultural presence, 77-86
American mass-media, 76
American media, 73-74
American (see also United States of America)
Andreotti, Giulio, 34-35, 57, 60,172; and the move towards the centre-left, 39; flirting with Communists, 40-41
Apennine, 2, 93
Argentina, 136, 139
Armistice between Italy and Allies (September 8, 1943), 7
Arnall, Ellis, 78
Asia, 3, 146
Australia, 139

Badoglio, Marshal Pietro, 6

Banfield, Edward, 187
Bank of Italy, also Central Bank of Italy (Banca d'Italia), 50, 116
Barzini, Luigi, 183, 185
Belgium, 139
bella figura, 1, 14, 221-222
Benetton family, 112
Berlinguer, Enrico, 31, 51; historic compromise, 40-42
Berlusconi, Silvio, 46, 158
Berto, Giuseppe, 79
"black" economy or underground economy, 112-114
Boccaccio, Giovanni, 2, 193
Bologna University, 157
Bonomi, Carlo, 108
Bonomi, Ivanoe, 18
Borsellino, Paolo, 64
Bossi, Umberto, 47
Boston, 2
Bourbons, 5
Brazil, 131
Breda, 101
Brindisi, 6
Brusati, Franco, 143
Buonarroti, Michelangelo, 2
bureaucracy, 219-221

Calabria, 3, 61, 64, 93, 139
Calabria University, 157
Califano, Joseph, 41
California, 2
Calvi, Roberto, 60, 179
Camorra, 61, 64, 65
Campania, 65, 93
Canada, 139
Caputo, David, 45
car industry, 1, 109, 111
Caranti, E., 199
Carter, Jimmy (also Carter Administration), 11, 40-41, 71
Casaroli, Cardinal Agostino, 178
Cassa per il Mezzogiorno (Funds